MAXWELL'S GHOST:
An Epilogue to Gavin Maxwell's Camusfearna

MAXWELL'S GHOST:

An Epilogue to Gavin Maxwell's Camusfearna

by

RICHARD FRERE

with decorations by
Robin McEwan

Birlinn

This edition published in 1999 by
Birlinn Limited
Unit 8
Canongate Venture
5 New Street
Edinburgh EH8 8BH

Originally published by Victor Gollancz Ltd, London, 1976

Subsequently published by Balnain Books, Nairn, 1994

ISBN 1 84158 003 1

British Library Cataloguing-in-Publication Data
A Catalogue record of this book is available from the
British Library

Printed and bound in Finland by Werner Soderström

CONTENTS

ABOUT A YEAR after the last events described herein, and while the book itself was no more than a twinkle in my mind's eye, I called in to a country pub on the road to Camusfearna. The day was bright and the sun strong: I wore sun-glasses which I had been often told increased the impression of a certain resemblance.

In answer to my tap upon the bar counter there emerged from the wings the wife of the proprietor—known by custom to my late employer and to me—who gazing at me with a combination of joy and disbelief said breathlessly: "Major Maxwell, is it yourself? It is indeed a wonderful thing to see you. I was told that you had died."

Before I could explain her mistake a young stalker, filled to the brim with whisky and the sense of importance that goes with it, wobbled to his feet and pronounced: "That's no' Maxwell, though it looks like him. Maxwell's dead, right enough. Yon's his ghost!"

PROLOGUE

"THAT'S GAVIN MAXWELL," remarked my friend, and to him: "Gavin, this is Richard Frere, of whom I told you."

Whatever had been said of me had obviously made no impression, for the man thus addressed turned to greet me without enthusiasm or interest. He wore the darkest of dark glasses which completely hid any critical change in his expression, but his general mien and the flat tone of his voice suggested clearly that the making of new acquaintances was not one of his delights. "How do you do?" he said briefly, and prepared to move away. My friend made a brave attempt to keep the conversation alive; he had promised me this introduction and wished to give the event full value. As he did so I idly studied the author of the much commended *Ring of Bright Water*.

He was of middle height and held himself strictly; the handshake he had given me grudgingly had yet been firm. The uneclipsed part of his face was pleasing, the chin strong but not aggressive, the mouth sensitive with but a hint of weakness; the skin of his cheeks and the broad forehead were much less weathered than one would have supposed in a man who divided his time between arid Africa and the salt-slinging wind and rain of our own west coast. His face was indeed remarkably unlined for a man who was nearly fifty, and his hair was thick and without a trace of grey.

His manner was abrupt and uneasy, offhand in a random way, and consequently touched the edge of rudeness. I felt that here was a man who liked to prepare himself for meetings; chance encounters held no charm for him. Soon he made it clear that he wished to talk no more and stalked away in a kind of outrage, like the offended ghost of Hamlet's father, to take shelter behind his spectacles in a quiet corner of the bar.

At this time I knew very little about him. My wife Joan had met him once before—at Glenelg, where our friend lived. The friend had a fair amount to say about him and much of it was a condensed and modified version of the wild rumours that build up around anyone who is unusual or eccentric in a thinly-populated countryside. It was said that he drank like a fish, spent money like water, tipped massively with some condescension, drove his powerful car with fury and to the public danger, and, it was added with a snigger, was always surrounded by young boys. Few of the local rustics had much good to say of him except to his face, for with many notable exceptions they are an envious race who distrust what they cannot comprehend and are disapproving of success. Years before, as I had read in *Harpoon at a Venture*, his shark fishing venture had failed; I warrant they liked him better then. The West Highlander has a high regard for disaster, which he ascribes to a mark of recognition from his sombre God, a special token of interest if not actually of love.

None of this was any particular concern of mine in the spring of 1962, and within a few days I had almost forgotten the churlish seeming author and had little reason to expect that I would ever come across him again; but Fate has a capricious way with her and Chance—if not always a fine thing—has often something unexpected to offer.

Yet it is indeed unlikely that we should ever have known Gavin Maxwell had it not been for Jimmy Watt and Terry Nutkins, his two young assistants. They were lusty and jubilant young men, of Viking stature and Nordic good looks, and were then at an age when everything at Camusfearna (lower Sandaig, formerly a lighthouse keeper's cottage, four miles south of Glenelg, as most of Maxwell's readers had worked out) was seen in boyhood's visionary gleam as a rough playground spiced with adventure and endeavour. My wife had met them at the friend's house in Glenelg and invited them to call in on their trips to Inverness. Soon we began to look forward to the visits of the two cheerful boys and to hearing their light-hearted accounts of life at "The Bay of the Alders", which is the translation of the name which Maxwell had given it in his book. Both it seemed were doing just what they wanted to do, and joy in perfection is contagious.

Very soon we found ourselves at Camusfearna.

Jimmy and Terry called for us one October evening, and took us there in the big safari Land Rover which Maxwell used on his African journeys. The 60-mile trip itself had an adventurous quality about it. I knew the road through Glenshiel to Skye very well, but I had never crossed the Mam Ratagan pass to Glenelg before. Allocated a seat in the back of the Land Rover, which only had a rear window, I watched the lights in the scattered houses around Loch Duich grow small and twinkly as the powerful vehicle wound its way up the steep zigzags to the 900-foot summit of the pass. Then, more like an express train in the days of steam than a motor vehicle, we began to gain speed on the long descent, first winding as had been the climb, then down an undulating slope to Glenelg village. Here we stopped at the pub, a rather squalid but atmospheric place. Jimmy Watt, a good raconteur of the bizarre, pointed out to us, as we sipped our drinks, a round indentation in the plasterboard at one end of the drinking chamber. This, he said, was made by the impact of a man's head, at the height of a jolly revelry. They must be sturdy folk, I thought, to do such things.

Suitably refreshed we left this place and climbed back into the Land Rover. Our route now took us up a steep hill—on which was impractically sited a cattle grid constructed of revolving tubes—and round a series of S bends overhanging steep drops into the sea. I had only just recovered from the jarring metallic clatter caused by the passage of the Land Rover over the grid when Jimmy Watt, who was a confident and I hoped competent driver, left the road and apparently took to the heather. Looking back, in the vehicle's rear lights, I could see a pitching and tossing foreground of ruts and boulders and could hear, from time to time, the gurgle and swish of mud beneath our wheels. Suddenly we plunged into a river and, as I saw a rush of water passing the window, I hastily tried to recall to mind the bleak advice which concerns the escape from a sunken vehicle. Wait until the car has quite filled up, I seemed to remember, before attempting to open the door. Sadly I had not forgotten the fact that due to some fault in the locking device it was not possible, at present, to open the rear door from the inside, which put me at some disadvantage. Thus gloomily debating my fate I had not noticed that the Land Rover had come through the river and was now once again on dry land.

We went on, rocking from side to side. About half a mile on, the almost level ground had the comparative quality of a motorway after a country lane. Then we began to wallow in peaty ground. The engine roared and the Land Rover struggled to go forward, sliding sideways in the process. When it had finally overcome this new setback we went forward quite reasonably for a short way and then stopped at a gate. Jimmy got out to open it. I had a few words with my wife. As he returned to his seat Jimmy gave the back door of the Land Rover a playful slap and shouted to me: "Hold on tightly, won't you? It's rather rough down the hill." I could hear him chuckling as he started the engine.

We nosed down a steep glade between young trees. Here the track was rutted to the depth of about two feet and every now and again the ruts were traversed by ribs of bare rock. The Land Rover jerked from side to side, jarring and clanking horribly. It grew even rougher, then steeper, and I could see that we were edging our way down a sloping ledge which was apparently cut across the side of a cliff. The most precipitous part came at the end. We flattened out and there was another gate to be opened.

They let me out. I saw that we were in a flat sea meadow. A faint moon illuminated the outline of two houses. One lay darkly beneath the cliff down which we had come. The other, a few hundred yards across the meadow, was a small blaze of light. A thin mist lay across the meadow to the height of a man's waist and the coarse reeds that grew here and there were grey and stiff with the beginnings of a frost. Somewhere, not far away to the north, a waterfall rumbled within the hillside down which we had come, and the sea, more sensed than seen in the prevailing half-gloom, overlaid its sound with the rhythmic rush and grate of rollers. Walking over to the head of the dunes I saw that a high tide had left a short sandy beach. To the south the bank which contained the meadow ran in close to the sea and became precipitous. The other house—not Sandaig (which I imagined must belong to a friend of Maxwell, of whom I had heard)—was there, its back right up against the slope. Across the Sound of Sleat scattered lights shone on Skye, and the lighthouse at Isle

Ornsay winked intermittently at its neighbour which stood on the largest of the Sandaig islands.

It was a rather splendid scene. I might have lingered but for my curiosity to see inside the house of Camusfearna.

It was then nearing the end of a transition. Originally it had been built—for the keeper of the light—to the solid, unimaginative pattern of the traditional Scottish croft house. Two and a half rooms below, two upstairs, a landing and a porch; the parlour, the "best room", the tiny kitchen at the back, two bedrooms over, the main and the guest; that is what it had been, and how it was when *Ring of Bright Water* was written—but now it had undergone a change. With the success of his book and the large amount of money that became available Maxwell had sensibly sacrificed the more spartan aspects of life in favour of a working sophistication. In that process there had been equal gain and loss; there was less peace, less solitude, but much more uncommitted time to enjoy what was left. Inside the house powerful electric heaters now dispelled the west-coast damp, deep freezes anticipated meals for weeks ahead, there were telephones galore, gallons of hot water, a bath, books on every subject under the sun, even a cinema show was held from time to time in the adjoining cottage. "All mod. cons.", as the estate men say; but one could overlook its commonplace connotations in nights of wind and rain after a walk down the storm-tossed path. And although the inside of the house was cosy it was not prissy; much of its furnishings were still made up of raw materials gathered from the beach. Fish baskets hung from hooks in the rafters and fish boxes formed the supports of the red hessian-covered seat that ran round one side of the living-room. On the heavy sandstone lintel above the large open fireplace the scholarly Raef Payne—Maxwell's friend, who had the other croft across the meadow—had carved a Latin inscription which read: "*Non Fatuum Huc Persecutus Ignem*" (It is no Will of the Wisp that I have followed here). Above the mantelshelf there was a fine model yacht. All sorts of things were in that room, even an expert exponent of Kim's Game could have made no more than a modest showing here, and I suspected that many of them were the gleanings of Maxwell's worldwide travels.

The wooden wings, recent additions to the house, which had been added to give bathroom and lavatory facilities and an extra room, were shoddy. They only existed on sufferance. The owner of the estate had given Maxwell tenancy of the house on a "grace and favour" basis and it was understood that if he were to terminate his interest the additions would be removed. They formed an L in reverse pattern and sprang from the southern gable of the house. They were built of light-timber framing. Weatherboard on the outside did little to repulse the rain and spray, and these trivial additions shamed the solid, old house.

The otters, Teko and Edal, had separate enclosures formed by high wooden fences around the house. In happier days they had lived *en famille* with the humans, sharing their beds and board, but quite recently, it seemed, they had tired of this anthropomorphic arrangement and had reverted to savagery. There had been painful injury and bloodshed, but only the unfortunate Terry Nutkins had received permanent mutilation. He had lost some finger joints to the otter Edal's sudden pique. After this it had been clear to all that the old order must change, and for some time the otters had been confined to zoo conditions—a sadly altered state of affairs than that which had been the popular, heart-warming theme of Maxwell's famous book. It seemed that their owner was having to pay dearly for the fame and fortune which these alien creatures had brought him, for not only were they totally unreliable with humans but they were permanently at odds with each other, and could never be left together.

When, on the morning after our arrival, I was introduced to them I found it impossible, as did the poet in a wider context, to say: "What jolly fun." They looked slimy and sinister. I suppose it is a matter of what one is used to, but I could not envisage feeling for them what one does for a dog. With tempers so unpredictable, and jaws so strong—I saw them crunch a sizeable fish in half with one bite—it was not surprising that even those who knew them approached with the utmost caution. I was amazed that Terry who presumably knew them better than anybody (except Maxwell) could bring himself to look with equanimity upon the creature whose ferret-like ferocity had robbed him of his fingers. Maxwell, I was told, still had rapport with them. For myself, not being immediately attracted, I saw no reason to get to know them, and indeed in all the years of my association with Maxwell I never did. I don't think I touched either of them more than half a dozen times; yet I am aware that in this aversion my feeling was purely personal, for I grew to know many gentle, kindly people who thought the world of these creatures.

Despite the absence of physical contact, much of the day-to-day life of Sandaig revolved around Teko and Edal. Eels, travelling live from London in special containers, had to be brought down the track, sometimes on foot. The supply of running water to their swimming pools, ducted by alkathene pipe from the waterfall, had to be kept running, and disruption by spate or blockage by leaves and débris was a common occurrence. The high wooden fences were often in need of repair, especially after a strong wind. The creatures themselves were—or appeared to be—sometimes unwell, and, in the absence of their owner, no chances were taken with them. The "local" vet—a dedicated and long-suffering man who lived between 20 and 50 miles away in Skye—the variation in distance depended on what ferry was running at the time—was often summoned to attend some mysterious condition or other. That his ministrations were always successful speaks highly for a man in general practice, as it were, who took time to understand and treat the unusual with such skill.

The guests' day at Sandaig—at least in the absence of their host—was euphoric. It began when Terry Nutkins—self-appointed tea maker in the establishment—woke one with a hearty "Good morning" and a steaming mug. Breakfast, being somewhat late, was usually entitled "brunch", and was a lingering meal over which the boys discussed the day's work. If the day were good people would then go down to the beach and, at low tide, cross to the Sandaig islands. There were lots of places to explore. In the late evening a baronial meal was cooked, at which every qualified person helped, much whisky was consumed and the conversation sparkled.

We spent several weekends at Sandaig during the autumn of 1962. It pleased me, but it fascinated my wife. Looking back in honesty I am aware that I was slightly jealous of her obvious enjoyment of the two boys' cheerful company, and during our visits there I would make solitary expeditions along the sea coast or into the mountains behind the house. Quite apart from this trivial pique (or used as an excuse to justify it) was my feeling that it was not quite honest to enjoy the hospitality of someone about whom one had reservations. I had not been greatly impressed with Maxwell at our first and only meeting (probably because he was so obviously unimpressed with me), and what I had heard from various people had served to strengthen my unease. On the other hand Jimmy and Terry seemed to hold him in affection and respect.

To absorb random opinion in this way is unlike me; whatever else I am, I pride myself on being liberal of mind. So I must conclude that my aversion was due, at least in part, to my jealousy at the man's great success in a field which I had always wished to enter. I began to sense that in some ways we might be very much alike; and I wondered sourly where he had gone right. Certainly I should not have been deterred by turgid tales about his character emanating from poverty-stricken little minds, for I have always held that art has nothing to do with morality and if his *Ring of Bright Water* was even half as excellent as it was said to be Maxwell might have been murderer, cheat and liar; and good luck to him as far as I was concerned.

No, it was quite simple. I was soured by jealousy of his author's situation which was so suitable to the kind of life I liked, it irked me to see my wife's pleasure in it, and for these reasons I was not at ease in his house. So, brunch over, I would put on my walking boots and stride away towards the cliffs above the lonely shore, chewing the cud of personal inadequacy with a kind of truculent relish.

Towards the end of that year, Terry left. A woman had arrived at Sandaig, one of the many who had been enchanted by the Maxwell way of life as outlined in his book, and she came to confirm her dreams. Whether she did or not I do not know, but when she left Terry went with her. There was nothing culpable in that, but we learned that Maxwell had become very angry indeed over it; Terry's defection disturbed the settled pattern of his life, and he claimed to have a guardian's authority over his young assistant. This seemed reasonable enough, but in some ways I am an incurable romantic, and so was able to add to my list of prejudices the postulation that my host was an arid Victorian moralist.

In May we kept a solitary Jimmy Watt company and I, to my disgust and perverse satisfaction, contracted a strange, lingering fever which I was quick to blame on the primitive plumbing. Within a few days of our returning home I was able to offer this possibility to Maxwell himself who called upon us on his way north. How different he now seemed from the forbidding character I fleetingly remembered or from the sinister recluse of many a wild report. Only Jimmy's warm description seemed to fit the man who was so charming, erudite and glittering with sophisticated wit. While he caught and held our attention and made us laugh at his accounts of things seen and heard in North Africa and Majorca, he was careful to show an intelligent interest in our more homely and mundane recitals; surely the mark of true charm and good manners. Reading between his words we sensed another facet of his character—that of the modest humanitarian. He had used a basic medical knowledge to relieve quite a lot of suffering in the many remote places to which he had travelled.

When this amiable meeting had gone on for a few hours, and Maxwell seemed relaxed and at ease in our company, as we were in his, I felt it was time to mention, though not directly, my misgivings at spending so much time at Sandaig in its owner's frequent absences. "We seem to spend more time at Sandaig than you do," I remarked. "I hope you don't mind." "Of course not," he replied. "Any friends of Jimmy are more than welcome there—or of mine," he added quickly; "and now that Terry has seen fit to leave us . . ." but he seemed unwilling to pursue the theme of Terry's defection, and left it at that. I sensed that in a way he was glad that we should keep Jimmy company from time to time. He was obviously very fond of the boy. Their relationship was more that of father and son than employer and servant, and the light-hearted badinage they exchanged suggested a strong mutual understanding.

In due course he took his leave of us with many expressions of good will and as his powerful Mercedes roadster turned out of our drive and shot away to the west I remarked to Joan: "Well, what a good fellow he has turned out to be. I hope we shall see more of him."

I

A FORTNIGHT OF MY TIME

IN 1961 GAVIN MAXWELL bought two lighthouse cottages. The Northern Lighthouse Board had converted their equipment to automatic operation so the services of resident keepers were no longer required. One of the cottages, perched on a semi-tidal rock, was near Isle Ornsay, a small village on the peninsula of Sleat in Skye. The other, on a true island, was close to Kyleakin. He had two reasons for buying these isolated properties. He wanted a home, alternative to Sandaig, should it become necessary for him to leave there. He also wanted an investment that would bring him extra money. His idea was to renovate his purchases and, using their splendid wild situations and his well-known name as joint inducements, let them to the public at enormous rents.

In April of the following year he asked my wife, Joan, if she would prepare the cottages for this purpose. She was delighted, and agreed to undertake the whole conversion. To start with I shared her enthusiasm, but when I knew more of the background of the project doubts crept in. We both knew that Maxwell had been having an expensive time, but he confided to Joan that his accountants were holding him on a very tight rein. Therefore he could offer her no fee for her present services, and he said that this was a great sadness to him and an embarrassment, but he warmly assured her that when the time came to work on the second house things would be quite different. The signs behind this forecast of good weather seemed to have been interpreted hopefully rather than logically, and this I recognized, without applause, for I have spent most of my own life with Mr Micawber's philosophy. What one sees in oneself one does not necessarily want to see in others, and I distrusted

Maxwell's prognosis of his present illness and sensed that his means were on a terminal decline. Joan, on the other hand, was enchanted at the prospect of applying her creative energies to such a challenging proposition; she was ready to accept his optimism and postpone all doubts until later. This explained her attitude, but I was still surprised at Maxwell's belief— apparently shared by Joan—that substantial results could be obtained on the tiny working budget he had mentioned to her. How, in particular, did they propose to meet the cost of labour? I remarked that while designers might do the thing for the kudos, tradesmen usually work for more immediate advantage. I might have known what was coming for, not for the first time, she suggested that *I* might like to do it.

Now I must tell of the circumstances that made good sense of such a remark. No honest person who knows me could say that I have made a material success of my life. Where money matters are concerned I have what mariners call a "negative buoyancy"; I tend, in brief, to sink. I have never had a conventional profession, or wished for one, for I work badly under supervision and dislike routine. Also I have *no* business acumen, none at all, to the extent that it has been said that any man who employed me in an executive capacity would face early ruin. When other eyes sharpen at the sight of a bargain mine become dull at the certain prospect of disadvantage, and I have always been reasonably convinced that such talents as I possess have no market value whatsoever. In my youth I ventured such small sums as I had available in minor businesses; each struggled, failed and died away, without even a decent liquidation to send it, wake-like, into oblivion. Of late years my body and soul, and those of my dependent family, have loosely adhered by the gossamer cord of a small income from a family trust. Before the onset of this felicitous state, I pursued a variety of occupations which pleased me so much in their pursuit that I overlooked the fact that their object was to make me money. So, as the world counts success, I was not at any time successful, but in these random years I acquired a manual capability at many things and a degree of artisan's skill in a number of trades. Therefore my services were an obvious choice in the present ploy. For not only am I efficient at making and building but I count such activity as my greatest

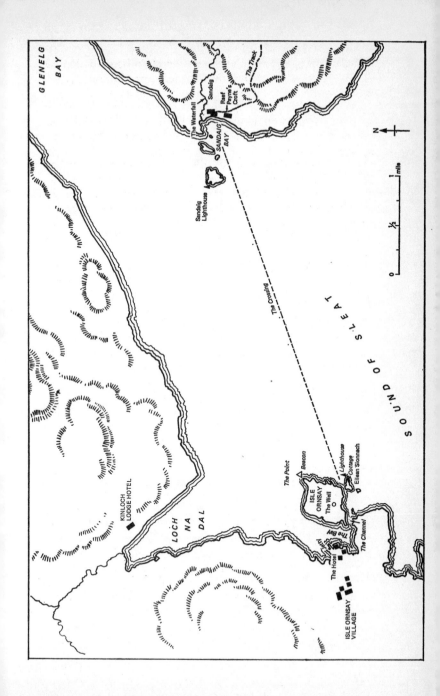

pleasure and satisfaction. It had been safely assumed that my skill and labour would be free and my sole remuneration a miserly expense account.

Yet as I grew used to the idea my interest grew, for apart from my weakness for the work I have always loved the Isle of Skye where I spent my boyhood climbing mountains. I still had misgivings about Maxwell. I did think it was important that Joan should receive more than token recognition at the end of the second conversion—in which I supposed I would be included—for my private means are too small to have much resilience, and any departure from cautious living results in a rapid slide into debt. Twenty years earlier I might have embraced the idea without question but even my hedonistic approach to living has been modified by some painful situations. I was quick to recognize in Maxwell's improvident outlook much more than a little of my own, and his casual—or unthinking—attitude to the time when the Piper should receive his dues rang a familiar bell within me. I thought his spirit was willing, but his fleshpots weak.

With my own record behind me, and with me still, I could not carp at my wife's happiness and enthusiasm with these destructive doubts, so I merely grunted neutrally when she assured me that Gavin was sincere in his intention, adding: "But leave me out; it's bound to involve us in some expense", although I never for a moment expected that my denial would satisfy her. It did not. "I have no time for such a hare-brain scheme," I went on, with the growing pomposity that accompanies weakening purpose. She brushed this aside without comment and went on to say that all she wanted me to do was to make an archway in a wall and paint a few rooms. "About a fortnight of your valuable time," she added. I smiled, ready to submit. "The whole idea is ridiculous, but I suppose I can give it a try. Will Maxwell pay my petrol? I won't go, otherwise. All right, then, if that's all that has to be done; it won't take long. When do we start?"

And so we both went to look at Isle Ornsay cottage. Gavin was unable to come but he sent his general factotum, Alan MacDiarmid, to show us the place. Alan was often at Sandaig and I knew him as a tough, fair-minded chap who loved his own countryside, and, as I came to know later, just the man to have with one in a storm at sea.

We came to Isle Ornsay village on a dull grey May morning with a cold east wind. I was not taken with the place. It comprised a few scattered houses, a small hotel, a boarded-up shop, the shell of a ruined mansion—it had a progressively backward look which I found depressing. Now little more than a ghost-town, it had once been the centre of a busy fishing industry. The public bar—which ought, one feels, to be the centre of a village—was a wooden shed attached to— but not part of—the hotel, a blatant expression of the Calvinism which is still quite strong in that part of the country. With the tide far out the foreshore was a sweep of almost level sand, for the bay was shallow; near to the land it was poisoned with all manner of household débris, from the immortal plastic bottle to the transient cardboard box and many other things best left unmentioned, while the colour of the mud which oozed down shallow channels to the beach suggested that sewage treatment was not taken too seriously.

A few sheep grazed on the low green hills around the bay. Few humans were to be seen. To the right of the semi-tidal Ornsay Island the tower of the lighthouse stood upon its lonely rock. In front of it one end of the cottage was visible, a white-washed structure whose two gables were joined like Siamese twins. It looked interesting, but I felt depressed. My mood was at fault. It was as poisonous as the débris in the bay. I was having second thoughts about the whole thing, and I wondered in what moment of madness I had contracted to spend even a fortnight in this place. This was not Skye of the Cuillins, but an alien and somehow sinister shore.

The extremely low tide—which I was surprised to learn was called a spring, though having nothing to do with that season— enabled us to walk straight across the part of the bay which separated us from Ornsay Island. The sand was firm, yellow-grey and ridged and filled with the casts of tiny worms. We clambered over some slippery rock and crossed the side of Ornsay Island by the suspicion of a path. Then there was a sandy bar which sub-divided the lighthouse rock from the main island. Beyond this a steepening slope led up to the cottage, passing a garden whose sturdy stone walls made nonsense of the wilderness within. Now we saw that the building was perched upon small cliffs and all around it the gulls shouted hoarsely and wheeled about at our approach. Below us the restless Atlantic swell sluiced through deep crevices and boomed in rocky holes, and over our heads the east wind sang. I thought, this is better; always I have loved wild places where men have not set their hands.

And across the Sound of Sleat a change was taking place. Over the sea the sky was still grey and the water reflected its mood, but on the great furrowed hills of Knoydart and behind the black ditch of Loch Hourn the mists were twisting and dissolving in a sudden hot May sun, and the colours were beginning to shine. I am, I hope, no more dull of soul than the next man and I could not pass by this royal pageant without a quickening of the pulse. My moods are transient; small things set me off. Suddenly I was quite restored to excellent humour.

Alan opened the cottage door. We went in. The interior was pitch black and smelt of the grave. This was not surprising, for the windows and other openings were hermetically sealed by tightly fitting steel sheets. This arrangement had kept all marauders at bay, except the damp to which it had given safe lodging. When we had unbolted some of the sheets, the unaccustomed light of day revealed an unpleasant picture. The damp was widespread, the walls were black and streaming; mushrooms would have grown well there. In fact small fungus growth could be seen dotted around the skirting boards. The woodwork was painted a practical brown. The house was of unusual design; the two structures, each with its own long pitched roof, were joined by a common wall in the middle. The object of the deep gully thus formed was to increase the catchment of rain water which from it, and from the gutters round the whole, ran into two large slate tanks at either end of the house. This had been the original source of drinking water, but Alan pointed out that more recently a gravitational supply had been introduced, its origin being a well on a high point of Ornsay Island. Although the basic division of the house was the thick central wall, the accommodation was separated by a slim brick partition at right angles to it. There were two doors in the side of the building that faced to the north. Originally two families had lived there, the lighthouse-keeper's and his assistant's, and each had been provided with two bedrooms and a kitchen. In addition, in recognition of his seniority, the keeper had a small sitting-room. In the corners of each kitchen there were tiny inner chambers. One contained a chipped and discoloured sink; the other, a lavatory unit. This arrangement must have presupposed a friendly relationship between the occupants of the divided house.

Joan's plan—heartily supported by Maxwell—was to join the two compartments by setting an open archway in the brick partition. This part of the plan would not take long to effect, but to decorate these dripping walls was another thing altogether. It would take weeks of drying wind—and how often are the winds of this coast dry?—to dispel the accumulated damp, and until this happened any attempt at painting would be a waste of time. Furthermore, normal amenities in the house were almost entirely lacking and, as it stood, even when freshened up with paint, none but the least fastidious tenant could be expected to offer more than a pound or two a week for rent—a sum in no way related to that which the landlord had in mind. This, however, was another story whose implications—as far as I knew—did not concern me.

On my return home I wrote to Maxwell with a list of the materials I should require to do the work. He replied with an excess of charm, thanking us both in advance for our time and trouble, and remarked how fortunate he was to have gained such support—with which I privately agreed. He insisted that I should stay at Sandaig for at least the first few days and travel each morning to the island. I welcomed this suggestion. Despite occasional meetings, I still knew next to nothing about him; and my curiosity was on the increase. As a preparation to our further association I borrowed *Ring of Bright Water* and read it. The book enchanted me; there was a warmth in it that flowed through my veins like whisky. It did not seem to me like the work of a worldly, sophisticated man, as I knew him to be, but like that of an incredibly literate child. It seemed that he had not lost sight of that "visionary gleam" which in most of us fades with the passing of the years. Colour, form and detail, all were there, as seen in childhood's candid, uncritical glance. I read of his life with otters with some interest, but unusual pets do not have much appeal for me; I felt a sadness at his loss of Mij, but I had met the two current otters, Teko and Edal, and found it impossible to believe that they could be as endearing as dogs. We had come to Sandaig, of course, when their integration with the household was over; their random attacks on humans had made zoo conditions necessary. No doubt, in the early days, they may have been very captivating.

To me, the glory of *Ring of Bright Water* rested in Maxwell's wonderful description of his own countryside, and in unerring use of simple prose. His rare vision of Nature became instantly fused in my mind with that of the English naturalist Richard Jefferies. I felt that there was a strong literary kinship between these two men, diverse as they were in every other way—the small Wiltshire farmer's son who showed neither promise nor ability on leaving school, and the much-travelled, well-read and widely-educated son of an ancient Border family. It so happened that Jefferies had been my youthful passion, and had subsequently exercised the strongest influence on my thinking. To find so much of Jefferies' essence in Maxwell pre-set my approach to that man and set a pattern in our future relationship.

When I first read *The Story of My Heart* I had a great wish to go to Liddington Hill in Wiltshire where Jefferies wrote his pagan hymn. I had an opportunity to do so during the last war. There in the sunshine and the soft south wind I had lain in a kind of trance, trying to open my mind to the reception of whatever thoughts my master had left there. It had been beautiful, unforgettable but not enlightening; no thoughts came. The monstrous, unseen presence of the war was stronger than any lingering impression that might have lain dormant in the grass or hovered gently in the air around the hill. Overhead the larks sang, the scents of the summer maturity were strong, down below a distant dog barked, the cornfields were swept and creased by the gusting wind—just as they had been for Jefferies; but Jefferies was gone, dead and buried long ago, his thoughts blown willy-nilly about the wold, or only existing in a book now out of print.

Therefore I was greatly excited upon reading *Ring of Bright Water* to find so much in it to remind me of Jefferies, and I looked forward to talking to its author. So, in the five evenings I spent with him at Sandaig, I tried to investigate Maxwell's mind, a presumptuous task if ever there was one, and doomed to total failure. The part of him that held the storehouse of these delicious, evocative descriptions was not on public view.

Yet though nothing of the writer was revealed, I did begin to learn something of the man, but here, too, dark veils of inhibition and conscious suppression hid many aspects of his character. At this time he was slowly recovering from the results of a motor accident; apparently slight, the injuries had all but crippled him. From no more than a bruise grave complications had come, and the new condition demanded major surgery. Nor had that been the end of his ill fortune, for although the sympathectomy—designed to restore circulation to his foot—had been successful, a hospital infection had followed. Now, five months later, walking any distance was still a misery to him. Such a bad state of affairs was underlined by a doubt that he would ever fully recover the use of his leg. Occasionally neurotic—as might be expected—for the most part he bore both the condition and the prospect with gloomy stoicism. I found him to be a great schemer and given to quick enthusiasm over extravagant projects, but basically he was not a believer in good luck and counted success in anything as a bonus gained against the odds. In later years he would often say to me quite seriously: "Richard, things are going *too* well for us. I don't trust this situation. Someone up there is getting more and more angry, and will strike." Oddly, he usually did, occasionally aided by my friend who was not without a strong sense of the dramatic.

He was a thoughtful host, well versed in hospitality which he gave more freely than his time. He was then in the middle of a creative spell and I gained the impression that writing did not come easily to him. He disciplined himself to attend his study for this purpose and seemed relieved when his stint was over. Jimmy Watt had told me that domestic problems had retarded the production of his latest book, *The Rocks Remain*, and that Gavin was now making up for lost time. He said he did not like writing; this, having regard to his excellence, I found hard to believe. But he *had* to write. His small kingdom of Sandaig was demanding of money and in order to maintain it his publishers and agent called for a completed book each year.

He was usually calm and collected and he wore an air of urbanity. But he had a quick temper. Small, avoidable stupidities on the part of his staff, or careless oversights, would produce a flash of anger, but major mishaps he took in his stride. Then there were few words of reproach, but "less said, soonest mended" only applied when there was really a great deal that might have been said. He would often grind the bone of small contention into tiny fragments. Those whom he thought fools he did not suffer gladly, and having a spike of vindictiveness in his nature he was glad to see them suffer, if they could be brought to it. His sense of humour was dry, concise and fine, but sometimes repetitive; then he would take a funny tale and squeeze all the fun out of it. Those things he knew, he knew well; he had the capacity for infinite research and a powerful memory. Of those of which he had a layman's knowledge he would affect a total ignorance, and throw up his hands in mock alarm. In the field of learning he had modesty, and none of it was false.

He was fiercely possessive of both objects and people, and seemed to believe that money can buy loyalty and friendship as it does goods and chattels. This cynicism suggested to me that he had been betrayed more than once. He gifted munificently, but because his gifting was more often studied than spontaneous it gave the unfortunate impression of a "tip"— more to ensure services to come than out of gratitude for those done. He demanded absolute loyalty from both friends and employees; and it was cramping. It produced an attitude of slyness in those of whom he was fond, for if they accepted his dominance they could no longer call their souls their own.

He was a steady drinker. When he worked, or when he talked, a well-watered glass of whisky was always at hand. He would often begin early in the day. He was an experienced drinker who had studied his limitations carefully and knew how far he could go. When his mood was buoyant, nothing showed; his wit was as sharp, his mind as clear. But in depression he did not care and perversely used the spirit to foster his distress, so that before an evening was done he might invite argument or quarrel. In fact he used alcohol in a practical fashion, adapting his intake to his needs. One example I remember was when he had been invited to meet a woman he had not seen for many years. In a wayside pub, near her home, he ordered two doubles for each of us, with the remark:

"It's 25 years ago, Richard. She will have changed; so will I. I think two doubles should suffice for this situation." Despite his social standing, his success, his confident manner, he was still, at heart, a rather shy man.

After my first few busy days at Isle Ornsay, evenings at Sandaig were pleasant. It would be easier to remember the Sandaig as it was then if anything at all remained of it now, but after the disastrous fire of 1968 and the razing of the ruins in the following year nothing stands proud of the dunes except the great stone we placed above Gavin's ashes. Were it possible to superimpose time upon space and refabricate the vanished house, that stone would stand in front of Maxwell's desk, right in the middle of his study. It would be material company for the mystic boulder that confronted a fusion of sky and sea in Michael Ayrton's creation that hung above the fireplace there. This was the work that had attracted Maxwell's interest, for it seemed to express a theme he used in the title of his book *The Rocks Remain*, a theme concerning the power of rock both to save and to destroy. The words of the title he took from an old Scottish folksong which ends with the line "Pass away like visions vain", and it is this line which holds some significance for me. Few things have passed away so completely as the Camusfearna of *Ring of Bright Water*; it remains only in Maxwell's written word, and in the hearts of those to whom it gave delight.

Apart from Jimmy Watt and Maxwell there was a third person in the house during the April of that year. Maxwell had recently taken under his wing a young English lad named Brewster to whom he had given a lift while driving in the south. Brewster had turned out to be a runaway, fleeing from both home and probation officer. Having heard his story Maxwell had taken a liking to the boy, accepted responsibility for him and installed him at Sandaig in the role of general help.

For me he rather spoilt the atmosphere of the place. Maxwell was a good host and in his absences Jimmy Watt deputized perfectly; but Brewster, bewildered and knowing, obsequious and aggressive, by turns, was at best an embarrassment. I assumed that this was Maxwell experimenting to see whether a transition to an "outward bound" situation would heal whatever scars he detected on his protégé's character. Personally I could not see very much true harm in the boy. He was very young and the misdemeanour for which he had been indicted was no more than a prank that had got out of hand. True, he did not appeal to me, we had nothing in common, and he showed signs of a growing amorality which I felt must be firmly suppressed. Maxwell, on the other hand, did not appear to believe in an excess of discipline. It surprised me to see how he went out of his way to treat Brewster without condescension; he would sometimes even refer to him as though he were the son of a social equal whom he was employing as a favour to the father. I suspected that this meant nothing to the defiant Brewster to whom a modified form of jungle law had probably been accepted since childhood, and the look of happy incredulity that blossomed on his face at such times spoke of his awareness of being "on to a good thing". Like all young people he was ready to take advantage. He had carefully assessed the limits to which he might go in offering impudence to his employer and these exercises in brinkmanship never failed to embarrass me. I found it most displeasing to listen to this callow youth abusing a man of such good standing— and with apparent immunity—but Maxwell made it clear that he would appreciate a neutral attitude in me. "We must not gang up on him," he said, "for he will feel persecuted; he is not in his environment and that makes him deeply vulnerable."

I thought this attitude lacked punch, and I told him so. I contended that Brewster was like a child or a young animal with a random approach to good and evil. To allow him undisputed expression of his ill nature was as foolish as turning a friendly back on the dog who has just jumped on the table and eaten your breakfast. Maxwell did not agree. I could not shake him in his belief that kindness and sympathy would make a paragon of the small-time delinquent.

More than once I asked him why he continued to employ Brewster, but he gave no direct answer to the question, merely remarking that since I was ignorant of the boy's background I was not in a position to pass judgement upon him. During one late whisky drinking evening he went so far as to say: "His character is your fault and mine!" Being unclear by virtue of the spirits I took him literally, and denied all responsibility. He went on: "Of our unheeding society, then."

Drink had sharpened my wish to debate into a need for argument: "Thousands from homes like his are leading citizens. And much more credit is due to them than to people like us, if they do well. They haven't reached their positions through being mollycoddled. You can't sharpen intentions on a blunt file. Brewster needs to be taken firmly in hand."

Nothing either could say convinced the other so we relapsed in quiet drinking. But I could not keep quiet for long. I resumed: "But you *can't* like him!"

"Oh, but I do. Have you ever watched him when he isn't surly or resentful? His face is soft like a young girl's beneath those curls he's so ridiculously proud of, and then his expression is gentle. There's a bloom and freshness about him which, despite all his faults, makes him attractive."

I said: "I can see nothing like that in the young man!"

"I can, Richard," he said heavily, out of the depths of some private darkness. "That is exactly how I see him. But I suppose that I shouldn't even expect you to agree."

By the fifth day of my stay it was apparent to me that I would never finish the work I had taken on at Isle Ornsay unless I stayed on the island. Every stage of my journey there provided an occasion for delay—the walk from Camusfearna to my car, the drive to Kylerhea ferry and subsequently on to Ornsay village behind slow-moving tourist traffic that was daily increasing, the wait at the ferry itself, and finally the need to adjust the time of my arrival and departure from the island with the tides. On my return, unless I left the cottage in good time there was a likelihood that I might miss the Kylerhea ferry's last boat—at 8 p.m.—and thus be faced with the 40-mile drive round by Kyle of Lochalsh and the possibility of a further wait at that ferry. When I told him about it Jimmy Watt, who was in charge of these things, said: "What you want is a boat, and I have the very thing for you. I'll bring it over in the Land Rover tomorrow. Unfortunately, I have to go to Armadale for Gavin so I can't wait, but I'll leave it on the foreshore on the Skye side of the channel."

I asked him what sort of a boat it was, and explained that I had absolutely no experience of the sea. As a small boy my father had given me a punt to row about in on our Norfolk duckpond; I had even managed to fall out of that and it now seemed poor preparation for the Atlantic ocean. Also, despite the fact that I can swim, I have a deep-seated irrational fear of curling waves, finding a nameless horror in the dark caves below their breaking crests. "What sort of a boat is it, Jimmy?" I repeated, my first question having produced a delighted grin. He admitted that it was not large but substantial enough for the short crossing for which it would be required, but seemed unwilling to go into details of its dimensions. This I found alarming, for a boat would have to be quite substantial to give me any confidence at all, and I said so, but he only remarked that at least I could swim while neither he nor Gavin could swim a stroke. Then he relapsed into a jovial silence, only repeating in answer to my suspicious glance that something seaworthy would be left near Ornsay village by next evening. It was called a pram; the unfortunate connotations of childhood did nothing to reassure me.

The access to the rock on which Isle Ornsay lighthouse stands is complicated. At high tide the rock is separated from Ornsay Island and the latter from Skye by two fairly narrow channels. At low water the whole area is dry. The larger tidal inlet—that between Ornsay Island and Skye—fills first, the other about half an hour later. The access is dry for several hours each day but the time that this period starts varies with the tide. If you have no boat the problem is obvious; if you have a boat—and providing you like them, and are not afraid of the sea—there is no problem. Then you can go either through the two inlets—a kind of skulking approach, albeit a safe one—or round the north side of Ornsay Island which can be quite an adventure. At this stage in my marine education I had absolutely no desire to do either.

The next morning I walked round the rocky path on the west side of the bay, filled with curiosity and misgiving in about equal proportion. The tide was rushing in avariciously and Ornsay bay was filling up. I reasoned that I should have to drag the boat across to the other side of the inlet in order to effect my escape in the evening. I anticipated a panic-stricken dash across alien water. I hoped that it was not going to be too heavy to drag over the soggy mud and sand now: I needn't have worried.

The object that lay behind a small rock had the rigidity of a leaf and less substance than a paper hat: it was about seven feet long, not broad and may have weighed as much as 40 lb. It didn't look to me as though it would float at all, even empty; it was like a tiny shell, everything about it was just too small and frail. Its oars were about four feet long and slender as the arms of an undernourished child. A seat made of thin plywood and the remains of a single buoyancy tank completed its meagre furnishings; a length of string wound through a small ring tied it more than adequately to a rock. It wouldn't have been at home on the Serpentine, far less here on the margin of one of the world's greatest oceans. It was made of fibreglass of which I had an ignorant mistrust, and was soon to bear me on a sea of which I had an innate horror; I was most unhappy about the whole thing. It gave me no comfort to find that I could swing it easily up on my shoulder and walk across the inlet without feeling its weight. I laid it cautiously down on a dry, soft patch of grass, having first examined the surface carefully for sharp stones that might damage the paper-thin hull.

The day's work programme was frequently punctuated by glances at the weather. As the day wore on the wind increased in strength and a heavy sea began to pound the rocks to the south-east. The main inlet was now filled with restlessly moving water and I was on a true island for the first time, with only a toy boat to restore me to safety. It did occur to me—and this is a measure of my inexperience and timidness—that I might wait for the tide to go out even though this would mean a long drive home. It was an escape clause in my contract with the pram. But how could a man of my age be such a coward? I sternly banished the thought.

An hour later I hoisted the frail thing on my shoulder and took it to the edge of the inlet. Small waves were bubbling and bursting between the contending wind and tide. I laid it in the water with great care and climbed in. My seafaring days had begun.

It took a few seconds to reach the other side and as soon as the little boat displaced water all my fears vanished. They were exchanged for a mounting exhilaration. The pram bobbed about like a cork, but it had a cork's buoyancy; adhering lightly to the water it could be easily rowed and accurately steered. In no time at all I had gained complete confidence in it and instead of leaving it on the other side of the inlet as I had intended I rowed round the edge of Ornsay bay and landed a few yards from my car.

By the end of the week I knew that I must leave Camusfearna. Despite my mastery of the pram all the other time-wasting factors in my daily journeys still existed. I told Gavin that I must go, and I had a feeling that he regretted my decision. Jimmy had manifold duties around the place which Brewster did little to lighten, and the boy had now taken to sulky departure to his room as soon as the evening meal was over. I understood from Jimmy that Gavin had had no option but to rebuke him sternly for a notable piece of rudeness in front of two of the author's oldest friends. Gavin, it appeared, had asked the recumbent Brewster if he would be good enough to select a certain book from the library as he wished to refer to it to settle an argument. The boy had slouched into the adjoining room and ten minutes later had neither reappeared nor given a reason for his delay. Gavin called out to ask what he was doing and the reply took the form of a rhetorical question— "What the —— hell do you think I'm doing?"—delivered in a loud and truculent voice. The missing term was the adjectival form of a short, unlovely word that gains in popularity day by day. It was not so popular then and neither Gavin's friend nor his friend's wife were prepared to stomach it: both left their chairs in instant outrage and made for the door, assuring their embarrassed host that they would darken it no more until he had drastically revised his taste in employees.

This was more than Gavin could stand, for they were both *very* old friends. In stone-cold soberness he gave Brewster a massive dressing down and sent him helter-skelter to his room. It was at about this time that I arrived back from Isle Ornsay. The emotional stresses of the afternoon had set Gavin off and he soon became very drunk indeed: the usual change in his character took place. The sharp edge of his very appropriate anger blunted into maudlin remorse at the fact that he had lost his temper with the unfortunate delinquent, and that this lapse could well have destroyed the small progress he had made with the boy. This meant nothing to me in terms of common sense, so I said nothing, nor could I answer him when he asked if I thought he should go to the boy's room to reason with him. Finally, after fidgeting for some time and trying to justify his weakness he left us and went to the boy. His room was overhead: we heard the mumble of their voices going on and on. Then Gavin came downstairs and went straight to his own room, and we saw no more of him that night.

I asked Jimmy, "Why doesn't he send Brewster away?"; and because Jimmy looked upon Gavin as a father and would not speak badly of him, I hoped my question could be answered in such a way as to produce neither silence nor embarrassment. Jimmy looked at me brightly and said at once: "Send him away? Well, he can't really, at least not easily. You see, he's on probation and Gavin's taken responsibility for his behaviour and welfare. And he's very fond of Brewster really and sure he'll make something of him. I must admit that I'm not quite so sure——" At this I nodded in silent agreement. Jimmy thought for a moment and then went on: "Apart from the legal thing, there's a much stronger reason why he won't give up Brewster as a bad job. Gavin's assured him that he'll let him have this job and give him a decent background and all that, and no matter how beastly Brewster is to him he won't go back on it. If Brewster wants to leave that will be a different thing, but Gavin is the loyalest person there is, and if he says he'll help someone he'll go on helping to the bitter end."

The next morning Gavin saw me off to Isle Ornsay. He was quite himself again, and very thoughtfully insisted that I should take with me a quantity of provisions from Camusfearna's ample stocks, including two bottles of whisky. He also suggested that Jimmy Watt, who was free for the day, should go along and help me to install myself on the island.

The tide was high so we were able to go to and from the cottage through the channel, but the pram's carrying capacity was minuscule and it was a slow process. Afternoon slipped almost unnoticed into evening and Jimmy Watt prepared to leave for home. He asked me what time it was and when I told him remarked in alarm: "That was the time about an hour ago. Your watch must have stopped. I'll have to 'phone Gavin. I don't want to drive round by Kyle and I'm sure it's too late for the other ferry. Perhaps he'll say that I can stay the night on the island."

He went into the village telephone booth and spoke for some time. When he came out he looked relieved: "Gavin says it will be all right, but he wants me back first thing. He wasn't very keen at first. Doesn't want to be on his own with Brewster after last night's do. However, this is going to be fun."

I welcomed his company. I am an imaginative person, and I knew that my first night alone in the cottage would be restless and uneasy: apart from anything else it was at that stage a depressing place, and it was only now Jimmy had decided to join me that I realized how little I had looked forward to the solitary prospect.

It became an uproarious evening. We found that there were gaps in our household planning. We had no plates, knives or forks and only one pan, but we had a quantity of magical whisky which touched off infinite capacities for invention. We made what we needed and before long we had a weird-looking but effective selection of eating equipment. Gavin had given us a small Calor gas ring on which we set our meal to cook, and while this was happening I showed Jimmy round the house. The arch now rested upon its wooden cast and it seemed a good time to take away the latter and thus reveal the graceful sweep of Joan's design. It looked just as I wanted it. The house had been open to the four winds of heaven for a week and the walls had dried to a surprising extent. Another week's work, at this rate, should complete the decoration, I thought, but surely that would not be the end of it?

As the night went on Jimmy Watt's humour became grotesque. In my absence he found a paintbrush and spent the time skilfully sketching in a skeleton in white paint on the outside of my bedroom door, an effigy which never failed to strike terror into my heart right up to the day when, weeks later, I painted it out for ever.

After a rather basic meal we wandered round the island in the soft May twilight, examined the inside of the lighthouse tower (the key to which I had found, rather oddly, concealed in the sewer) and set out to investigate a hitherto unopened room in the cottage. It had a door without a key and its two windows were covered by the usual steel sheets. We unscrewed one of these and eased the unlatched window down to make a narrow entrance. Jimmy chose to be first inside. After much grunting he vanished into the gloom, was briefly silent and then shouted: "It's a BATH!" Bemused by my spirituous condition and this strange comment I demanded further information, but he said no more until he had unfastened the door from the inside and invited me to see for myself. It was indeed a bath, of large and graceful proportions, covered by a well-made wooden lid. It was in the middle of the floor. There were no pipes anywhere. Jimmy began to chuckle madly: "You wait until Gavin hears about this. He'll want Joan to design a bathroom around it. And do you know what that will mean? You'll be here for the rest of your life."

There is many a true word spoken in jest.

We lit a fire of driftwood in the cast-iron Victorian grate in the sitting-room and laid our bedding down beside it. The flames crackled and sprang greenly from the salty wood, casting sharp shadows on the walls of the empty room. I was filled with whisky and my wits soon lost grip of consciousness, but later I awoke with a dry throat and pounding heart. All around me were new sounds, some known and understood, some as odd and mysterious as the dark shadowed island outside. I could hear the soft rush of water as the sea thrust and withdrew its questing tongues in the craggy cavities at the rock's root. Above me, somewhere in the roof, the wind was agitating a plank as a dog worries a bone, with determined incessant rhythm, and to its soporific beat I fell into a sound sleep.

Jimmy went back to Sandaig the next morning, and after a day of brisk activity I spent my first night alone upon Eilean Sionnach—the Island of the Foxes—as the rock is called. How different it was from the previous one. The Skye weather had changed, and in violent contrast to the soft summer night which had so lately embraced it the lighthouse rock now cringed before a pitiless onslaught of rain-laden wind. The dark came early despite the time of year; soon I lit my Tilley lamp to move about the house and my great shadow, cast upon walls and roof, mocked me as I went. I gazed with suspicion into dark corners and jumped at each unfamiliar sound. I cursed Watt in all the languages I know for his skilfully executed symbol of death which so aptly focused my ridiculous

fears, for each time I walked down the corridor to my room
the bony brute would appear to leave its wall and march
with mincing menace towards me. The house was filled with
weird, amorphous shapes and pulsed with strange noises: it
groaned, and grated and whistled, and the roof rustled as
though filled with an army of rats.

As I grew to know it better I realized that there was no
sight or sound in that remote cottage that could not be
explained, but the process of finding out played havoc with
my imagination. Only after each unusual noise had been
traced to its origin was I at peace with it, and there were
many to choose from: the chief offender was the wind whose
invisible force and capricious approach were the main makers
of mystery, but the sea also had a hundred riddles to contribute.
The heavy, muted thud of a ship's diesel engine sounded like
the beating of a human heart locked in the sand and seawrack
below my feet. One night there was no wind at all, no movement in the sea, a dead, black silence punctuated by the white
flash of sound that was a seabird's squawk, or the watery
entry of a seal. My ears sang for hours with compulsive,
nervous listening.

By the end of a week I had come to terms with my fears: I
had also done a lot of work. It was time to tell Gavin and
Joan how things were going, and I rowed my little pram
through a calm channel to the public telephone in the village.
I imagined that these two people would have been closely in
touch with one another, and I had a strong suspicion that the
scope of the work at the lighthouse cottage was by now hypo-
thetically extended. On this issue Gavin hedged to such an
extent that my suspicions were confirmed: he added that
Joan was coming over to Sandaig that very day to discuss
furnishings and it would be nice if I would join them. It struck
me that much more than furnishing would have to be discussed, and that Joan's practical yet artistic nature would give
her no rest until a high standard of renovation was reached
and many more amenities installed. I knew that by now she
would be fully involved, and that having no patience with
the mediocre and a strong taste in excellence she would soon
bully and badger Maxwell into the acceptance of an overall
design for his cottage of which he had not even dreamed. I
wondered how he would reconcile such an ambitious yet

rational programme with his self-admitted state of present poverty. I need not have worried. Maxwell was an extremist, unversed in the art of compromise, seldom prepared to modify an approved plan which he would prefer to kill rather than mutilate. And Joan, in her design, was much the same. If she could not achieve the results on which her heart was set she would want no results at all. I should have known that when they really got together to discuss the renovations at Isle Ornsay a picture would emerge that owed little of its grandeur to the original modest sketch. I suspected that once seated on the horse of his sudden fancy, Maxwell would ruthlessly ride down his faint-hearted counsellors and leave them to address their warnings to the dust.

So, on that May morning, we sat in the Sandaig living-room, and talked all about it. Joan soon convinced Gavin—or more accurately, made him admit—that much more would have to be done to the cottage before he could attract any worthwhile tenants. After that point had been made, ideas proliferated with a wild abandon. Fitted cupboards, hanging wardrobes, tiled floors, a great open fireplace, a modern cooker, were all part of the plan and—as Jimmy Watt had predicted—a bathroom of some luxury, with its attendant plumbing, centred around that mysterious bath about which nobody, including the former owners, knew anything at all. They discussed things which meant little to me—I was born without a taste for antiquity although of late years a process of osmosis from Joan has resulted in a sharpening of my perception—but I was able to see that Gavin favoured a period which contained much that Joan did not like. He fancied the cluttered elegance of Victoriana, while she had as much of the spartan austerity of the first Elizabeth about her.

I was soon asked if I would extend the period of my service, to which I agreed. Now that I had acquired a modest mastery of the sea and banished my night fears, I was beginning to enjoy the whole thing in my quiet way. I love isolation, and being alone: all human contact bothers me to some degree. I had found the right place to pursue my hobby, and providing I was given clear instructions I was sure that I could give substance to their dreams.

Gavin greeted my acquiescence with amazed gratitude. He did not know what to make of it. Why should I work for nothing?

I explained that I liked challenges, and he stored up this piece of information and adroitly used it at intervals during the years that followed to prod my natural indolence into a show of activity. He told us both that better days would bring us the recognition we deserved.

2

DRUNK IN CHARGE OF A PRAM

———————

IT WAS A week or more before we had collected from Inverness the wide variety of items that our new programme needed. They were all assembled at my house in Drumnadrochit, and when everything was ready we asked Jimmy Watt to drive it to Isle Ornsay village in the big Land Rover.

We were allowed to store the materials in the old shop near the jetty; from there I could load them, piece by piece, into the pram. One fine June morning I was cautiously lowering a number of boxes into the tiny boat when a man approached me and introduced himself. He was the former lighthouse keeper at Eilean Sionnach and he still kept an eye on the correct functioning of the apparatus.

He came to the point at once: "Good God," he said, "surely you're not going out in yon wee thing?"

It was true that the pram did look rather unequal to its task, and a few weeks earlier I would never have set foot in it. In the stern a large bag of plaster was tightly jammed between four tins of distemper, a bag of nails wedged below my seat, while in the bow a heavy box of plumbing joints was suspended from the mooring ring.

"You'll not be going round the island with that?" pursued the lighthouse keeper in alarm.

"Oh, no," I said, "I'm waiting for the tide so that I can go through the channel."

"Ach, it's not safe at all," he answered, disapprovingly, "and ye can have my boat for the asking, and go round to your lighthouse—never mind the tide—any time you have a mind to." He added flatly: "Ye'll not be knowing much about the sea?" I shook my head. I hadn't thought it had shown to such an extent.

"But I couldn't take your boat," I said, "it might be

damaged, or even lost. It would be on my conscience—"

He interrupted, with an expressive gesture which embraced the village and all its Christian souls: "You get in a rough sea in yon"—pointing at the pram in disgust—"and you'll be on all our consciences."

My new-born confidence died at that moment, and I deferred to his huge knowledge and experience. After all, he had probably known this coast for twenty years: I had only completed my third week, albeit without drowning or even serious incident; but plainly I still had much to learn.

"I'll borrow your boat," I said, "and thank you kindly."

"And you'll be the wiser man for that," he replied, only slightly mollified. "There's my boat"—pointing to a sturdy wooden dinghy in her early adolescence—"take her when you wish, but for God's sake see that she's tied well up the beach at nights. There's a puckle tide around here."

He nodded briefly and turned his steps to the wooden hovel which served as a bar. Decency and gratitude made me follow him. Over our drams he told me many a story of the sinister Sound of Sleat. He dwelt with some relish over the tale of an Englishman who on a night of wind and storm had rowed out to his anchored yacht. He had never reached it and had not been seen again. His boat was found weeks later, holed and battered, on the Skye shore.

"What kind of boat was that?" I asked, half in interest and half because I had an idea it was expected of me.

"I was just hoping you'd be asking that," he replied, lingering lovingly over the punch-line of his story, "for it was a wee pram, just like your own. Ach, I was thinking for a while that it was the same boat."

I shuddered suitably.

The lighthouse keeper's kindly—and certainly trusting—gesture quite transformed my life. Using an outboard motor, which Jimmy had provided, the fifteen-foot dinghy gave me complete confidence. Its greatest advantage was that I could approach Eilean Sionnach at any state of the tide by going round Ornsay Island and had no need to wait for the Atlantic to fill the narrow, reedy channel. The seas that washed the island's northern shore could be unruly in certain conditions and even the sturdy dinghy pitched and tossed as it motored out of Ornsay bay to receive in one concerted blow the east wind streaming out of Loch Hourn at violent odds with the withdrawing tide. At these times the waves came at you from all directions, short, steep and deeply green, the spume gusting from their crests as one blows the froth from a pint of beer. But the solid, seaworthy boat laughed at their petulance and made the journey round the point a fresh, clean and exhilarating experience, and not one to be dreaded and feared.

Inside the house I was pleased with my work. The prize bath had been moved to what had been the assistant's kitchen, I had forced a water tank into the loft and with most of the rooms painted the house was beginning to look quite attractive. In about the middle of June, Joan came over to Isle Ornsay. At Drumnadrochit she had been busily assembling a large load of furnishings which would be taken over to the west by lorry when the time was ripe. On her arrival at the island she remarked that things seemed to be going well, and we had a general discussion which included a few new ideas. It seemed appropriate that Gavin's opinion should be sought, and I suggested that since the weather was dead calm we might take the lighthouse keeper's boat straight across the Sound and surprise the occupants of Camusfearna.

For boats of this size the crossing is quite without hazard in calm weather. On this occasion there was hardly a ripple. Slowly the squat lighthouse at Sandaig grew in size while the graceful pillar of Ornsay shrank until it was no bigger than a candle on a first birthday cake. A slight swell met us near the end of the crossing and rolled us gently into Sandaig bay. I think we both felt rather proud of ourselves in having thus arrived, by water and unheralded.

I had forgotten that Maxwell was averse to unscheduled visits. He liked to prepare his house for visitors; it was necessary for him to adjust his mood to meet people at any time. He did not like people "dropping in" and he was never guilty of doing so himself. It was the most formal trait in his character. Now when he saw Joan and me fresh from the sea standing at his door, he just failed to conceal a look of aversion before an urbane expression took its place, "Well, well," he said, unenthusiastically, "come in and have a dram. I am glad to see you both, but I'm sorry that I can't offer the hospitality I should have liked. Jimmy is ill and in bed. I wish," he added with a cold smile, "it had been any other day."

Poor Jimmy was in bed with stomach pains. I thought perhaps that Brewster had poisoned him—there seemed no other explanation for the boy's high spirits. He greeted Joan and me politely, handed us our drinks and seemed quite a different person. He offered his help to pull the dinghy up the beach above the rising tide, and we took a Jeep and went down to the boat. A short rope was attached to the tow bar of the vehicle and tied to the mooring ring of the boat. Brewster then drove gently away while I held the stern as upright as possible. Although I was not to know it then, this is a bad practice. The weight of a large wooden dinghy being pulled in this fashion produces huge stresses along its length. Unlike a prisoner on the rack, the dinghy cannot shout "I recant" and thus bring its agony to at least a temporary halt. An old boat may easily fall to pieces by being thus treated. This one, which was not old, didn't, but as it slid heavily over sand and gravel there was a sudden crack. A concealed deeply-embedded stone had gored its side and smashed two planks. I knew nothing about the scope of boat repairs and had a guilty conviction that the boat was ruined. What would the lighthouse keeper say?

Gavin had now warmed to our presence, and he gave comfort to my troubled spirit by assuring me that the damage was much less than mortal and could be repaired at little expense. He urged me to telephone the lighthouse keeper at once. That gentleman showed none of the anger I had expected, but asked that I return the boat as early as possible in the coming week as he would need it for his own use. Gavin said he would ask Alan MacDiarmid to effect the necessary repairs on Monday, and, since it was now Saturday, he would be delighted for Joan and me to stay at Sandaig, which would give us all an opportunity to discuss the project.

It turned out to be a most pleasant weekend.

Gavin, who had been worried by Jimmy's illness and confused by the sudden unexpectedness of our arrival, seemed otherwise to be in the midst of a calm period of sunny optimism which had even softened Brewster's disruptive attitude. Like others of a determined will whom I have known he could project his mood far beyond the confines of his skull, and either poison or exalt the atmosphere of any house he occupied.

Now he was happy, and smiles, friendly nods and sighs of relief were the order of the day. In this amiable climate a number of plans were confirmed and some new ones were brought up for general discussion. I now learnt that a party of tenants had actually been booked in for a date early in August. This disturbed me a little; doing anything to a time schedule makes me agitated, but Gavin's apology gave the impression that this rather premature arrangement was something outside his control and he laced the bitter medicine with a great, sweet lump of sugary praise. His power to flatter and charm was, I believe, an honest quality which resulted from a true appreciation, and was not a deliberate insincerity as it sometimes appeared to be; his reason for giving presents, on the other hand, was often spurious—a cold discerning eye for the future rather than a grateful heart for what had been done.

Alan MacDiarmid came to Sandaig on Monday morning and confirmed that the damage to the boat was slight. Unfortunately he had no suitable planks, and said it would be a day or two before the boat was ready to return to its owner. Jimmy, now quite recovered, drove me back to Isle Ornsay.

Here there was considerable activity. We had applied to the GPO for a telephone link some time before and now things were on the move. By Monday evening the engineers arrived at the cottage door at the head of their cable, having laid nearly a mile of it through sand and silt, rock and bog, in next to no time, and all for the standard connexion charge of £10. The man in charge carried a little box containing the instrument and laid it at my feet. "Where do you want it to go?" he asked. It was like getting a birthday present. Gavin thought so too when I 'phoned him in a self-explanatory announcement, for he loved telephones and their proliferation gave him joy. I have no particular affection for the instrument in my own home, but at Isle Ornsay I found it an unmixed blessing. No one who has family or close friends likes to be beyond the range of urgent human call.

The long days of late June made it possible to work far into the night and the changes in the house were becoming quite dramatic. But I had one baffling problem. With a complete system of plumbing now installed in the house I could not get sufficient pressure of water at the end of the long lead pipe that led from the well, high on Ornsay Island, to fill it. Not a drop went into my tank in the roof, although it gurgled in a listless dribble at sink level. I could only suppose that somewhere in the three quarters of a mile of deeply buried and invisible pipe there was a hole. It was a miserable suspicion. The fact that within six weeks the house would be occupied by a party who had paid a lot of money for the privilege of doing so gave that same suspicion a nightmare quality.

I rang Gavin, much more for comfort than advice. Apart from remarking obliquely that water always finds its own level and saying how sorry he was that I should be faced with this difficulty, he had nothing to offer, but went on to say that Alan had now repaired the lighthouse keeper's boat. This gave me a sudden bright idea of the kind that often floats high on the turgid waters of frustration—a call to action.

"I shall come across and collect the boat. The lighthouse keeper wants it."

"By road?"

"No"—very firmly—"by sea."

"In what?"

"Why not in the pram?"

"The pram? You can't come in that. It will stand no sea at all—"

"There isn't any sea. It's dead calm. Please don't destroy my tiny confidence—it won't stand much. Of course"—half-hopefully—"you may forbid me its use. It's your pram."

"Damn the bloody pram. It's your life I'm thinking of, but if—as I imagine—you are determined——"

"Yes?"

"I shall give you, assuming you arrive, the biggest dram you have ever seen."

"Right. Within the hour."

Ten minutes later I was on my way. For a few hundred yards a feeling of misgiving competed successfully with a growing excitement, and only my boastful assertion to Gavin kept me from turning back. To increase my safety I had extended the tiller of the outboard engine so that I could steer while seated in the middle of the boat. The pram was only eighteen inches longer than I was, and my weight added to that of the engine in the stern tended to lift the bow right out of the water.

Thus trimmed we sped along, and Ornsay tower grew small.

My fears diminished with its shrinking outline and by the time I was half-way across the Sound they were replaced by a keen enjoyment in my sturdy movements through sun and sea and air, and the proud thought of my coming entry to Sandaig bay. But pride is sometimes the forerunner of a fall, and my confident glance at the approaching Bay of the Alders suddenly revealed something which I had not seen before—a wide belt of rough, corrugated water which splashed whitely in the bright sun. It was plainly some ill-begotten offspring of wind and tide, something with which I had become familiar in the homely waters around Ornsay Island in the sturdy, wooden rigidity of the lighthouse keeper's big dinghy. But here and now it told a very different story.

I briefly debated whether to chance it, and decided that I could always turn out of it if it seemed too dangerous. I suspected that it probably was, but by now I had built up a pretty strong determination to carry out my intention and a certain amount of risk would add a nice touch of drama. I hoped that Gavin had me under observation through one of his pairs of powerful binoculars. To lower the centre of gravity I lay down in the bottom of the boat, put my legs over the centre seat, reduced speed and waited to see what would happen.

It came on quite suddenly. One moment the pram was slipping gently through flat water, the next she began to bump, sway and pitch and toss in all directions. The whole scene was in miniature, none of the waves exceeded six feet from trough to crest, but they were short, steep, random and vigorous, and they threw the tiny craft about as though she were a leaf. A strong wind was now blowing and it whipped the bubbling crests into froth and spray which, from time to time, formed a curtain above me. A lot of sea water came into the boat as opposing waves slapped their wet hands above my head, and I recalled with a curious disinterest the fact that I had carelessly left the baler on the jetty. Indeed I was by now pretty frightened, and had a strong suspicion that I was in grave danger: yet the pram seemed quite equal to the task. She tossed and pitched, turned and twisted, all but played ducks and drakes as the wind tried to prize her off the breakers, revolved as though in helpless mirth, bored deeply and swung high, and always emerged with confidence to shake herself as if it were all a great game. And as quickly as it started it ended, we were back in calm water—and Sandaig bay was much closer at hand. I had not consciously steered through the turbulence—indeed the pram had completely revolved more than once—and I imagine that the south-west wind had taken a hand and blown the light hull along as though it were a sail.

A few minutes later we chugged gaily up to the beach. The first thing I saw was the lighthouse keeper's boat riding pleasantly at anchor, the next was Gavin. He rose cautiously from behind a sand-dune, a large tumbler of whisky in his hand, and gave me an ironic salute. I was pleased to see that he had his binoculars. "Well, well," he said, "I wouldn't have done that. Not for anything." Such praise has always been music in my ears, for I am a great exhibitionist, but he was a much bolder man than I—although I suspect that we both suffered from an excess of imagination which makes heroism very hard going. I remember that he once told me of the time when he was training with the Special Operations Executive and made his first parachute jump from a captive balloon. He said he was so paralysed with fear on the way down that he landed rigidly and seriously fractured an ankle. The injury was bad enough to render him unfit for any further descents and he spent the rest of his service as an instructor. He added: "That ankle hurt me like hell for weeks, but I never ceased to bless it. It was the only honourable way I could escape the prospect of something which absolutely terrified me."

I know, however, that had it not happened to him he *would* have gone down into enemy territory—terrified as he was— which is the mark of the truly brave man. Much later I was to see him re-establish rapport with the otter Edal, and this seemed to me to be a very dangerous thing from which he might have received serious injury. It is true that he had been the only person she had never attacked during the spate of outrages that had led to her exclusion from close human contact, but this had been so long ago that it was impossible to tell how her confinement might have affected the unpre- dictable animal's behaviour. I certainly didn't know and I do not think he did, for I saw his confidence wax and wane as he prepared himself for the entry into her pen. He gave me a stick—"just as a precaution"—and with a grim smile, that had just a hint of melodrama about it remarked that whatever happened I was not to let the otter out. The meeting was a success and nobody was hurt, but it had taken a lot of nerve, more especially because it had not been undertaken lightly or on the spur of the moment. He had given a lot of thought to the possible consequences, and by then I knew him well enough to realize that his imagination was working overtime.

However, this incident was still some years away. Now we both stood on Sandaig beach on a lovely June morning, drinking whisky in the warm sun. I was slowly beginning to like him then, but I was not so naïve as to overlook the possibility that his amiable mood resulted from a sense of indebtedness to me for my gratuitous labours on his behalf. As we strolled companionably towards the house he continued to heap undeserved praise on my head for what he called my insouciance in the face of danger. I told him—with as much fervour as my basking ego would permit—that such performances as the one I had just managed to survive were undertaken by accident or through ignorance, and that I was only prepared to test myself to the limit in spheres of adventure in which I was accustomed to operate, and then only after a very careful assessment of the odds. At this he smiled slightly and with a flattering disbelief.

On arrival at the house we retired to his study to continue the small celebration in my honour, and to discuss the latest developments at the lighthouse cottage. From time to time tousled boys knocked at his door; they were young pupils from a progressive school in Fife, to whose headmaster Gavin had offered outdoor facilities in which to practise his theories of natural education. Gavin was, at that time, a fervent supporter of the work of Dr Robert Mackenzie of Braehead School, and he soon began to deliver a treatise on this theme. As with any subject that attracted his serious interest he had assimilated its every facet, and I am sure that Dr Mackenzie himself could not have presented a more comprehensive picture of his own philosophy of education. I am at the best of times a slow learner, and now the combination of alcohol and self-satisfaction completely closed my mind, so that at the end of his admirable lecture I was little the wiser; but the fault was mine. Presently we moved into the living-room. Here quantities of boys were milling around and Gavin was much in demand. I noticed that they treated him with lusty infor-

mality and not with the deference due to a man who was their
headmaster's contemporary and also their host; this policy of
under-rating authority was, I believe, a cornerstone of the
school's system, but in any case Gavin always went out of his
way to put young people at ease. He was, as the saying goes,
very good with children.

After some time I found myself rather at a loss—my host was
enveloped in an unruliness of boys—and I decided that I had
better be on my way. I approached Gavin and told him that
I was about to go. He asked me in a casual fashion to stay the
night, but his heart was not in the proposal—like Hamlet, he
had found more attractive metal—and I relieved him of the
obligation to press me further by remarking that the lighthouse
keeper needed his boat at once. After promising to telephone
him to tell of my safe arrival, I went out into the bright sunlight,
and a trifle unsteadily walked down to the bay.

Minutes later—with the pram loaded upside down across its
bows—I steered the lighthouse keeper's boat out into the
Sound. In that hot June afternoon the wind had died away and
the sun blazed down upon sparkling blue water. My immediate
destination was not Isle Ornsay but Kinloch on the north-east
side of Loch na Dal; here the lighthouse keeper spent much of
his time. Propped up in the stern of the boat with my feet on
the centre seat I was luxuriously at ease with the world. A
summer's day always upsets my sense of values and banishes
all my immediate problems; now, still glowing from a sense of
achievement and stimulated by much spirit, I had become a
feckless fool, firmly believing at that moment that everything
was going to be all right for ever. I blessed the day on which I
had met Gavin and the processes of Fate through which I had
been introduced to this new and enchanting life. I began to
mutter poetry and make singing noises as is my custom on
such occasions, and thus creatively occupied I was almost
unaware of my progress over the quiet sea. Only when the
dinghy grounded on the shore at Kinloch did I fully leave the
lotus land of whimsy to return to the no less beautiful world
around me. The way to Kinloch Hotel from the sea leads
through a magnificent avenue of rhododendrons, then in full
bloom. Their scent was glorious, strongly evocative of childhood. If, as Jefferies said, rushes have a green scent, surely the
great red and white blooms have a smell to match their flam-

boyant magnificence? Overcome entirely with nostalgia I sat down in a quiet glade and indulged in a riot of day-dreams. It was there that the lighthouse keeper—who had watched my journey from Sandaig from an hotel window—came across me. Good, kindly man, he mistook my flat-eyed stare and staggering gait for the result of exhaustion, and prescribed the true Scots remedy for that condition. Leaning over the bar later I found that I could not admit to him to what use I had so recently put the pram.

It seems strange, but the next thing I remember is being back in the rhododendron grove. Lighthouse keeper, hotel bar and the army of whisky glasses standing like toy soldiers on its counter—all had become a distant dream. In fact many things had become pale and fragmentary, and perhaps a little odd. The sea bulged like a great blue eyeball. Only the massive blooms, hanging like lamps in the golden evening sun, were real. A small part of my mind, acting like a guardian, said, "Come on, man. Pull yourself together"; but when I wobbled to my feet the sky spun above me despite my attempts to steady it. I crawled over to the pram and pushed it out, only remembering the engine when the boat drifted to a halt. Finally I fitted it fumblingly to the pram and motored away.

We spun along. The pram gave expression to my mood. Going in the general direction of Isle Ornsay, whose lighthouse tower glimmered in the heat haze about a mile away, I made local variations in my course; the most popular was an exuberant figure of eight. Before long I tired of this and tried to hold a steady line for the tower, but a great tiredness extended to everything now and my eyes would no longer keep open. I slept.

To this day I do not know how long I remained asleep. I woke with a great jerk and an aching head. The sun was several degrees lower in the sky and I was going away from Isle Ornsay in a wide sweep; yet my position did not seem to differ from when I had been last conscious. The reason was not hard to find, for I had been half lying on the tiller and had held it at such an angle as would produce a circular course. By the amount of petrol left in the tank I concluded I must have been revolving for nearly an hour. As I sat digesting this fact—alarming in retrospect—confirmation came in the form of a great shout of applause. Through a break in the trees along the main road about half a mile away I saw a quantity of people who were apparently observing me with tremendous glee. I thought what a good story it would make on a beery evening in some London pub. I waved, and the applause redoubled.

I now remembered my promise to telephone Gavin. By this time he must be getting alarmed, I thought, and he will probably let the coastguards know; and all manner of people—including my wife—will become alarmed and despondent. I made for the cottage as fast as the pram would go.

Gavin was sour and miserable, strongly resenting my delay in communication. In these moods he exactly resembled my mother, who, if she felt herself to be overlooked, would create a mood of pained martyrdom. He now did what she would have done, and disregarded my story in favour of his own trivial complaint that hordes of boys had been running in and out of Sandaig all day, thus disturbing his writing. After an interminable recital along these lines he abruptly changed the subject and asked why I hadn't 'phoned him earlier.

"I couldn't; I was drunk in charge of a pram," I said, without elaboration and rang off as soon as courtesy permitted, knowing that in his present mood he was not likely to laugh. But long after I had replaced the telephone on its rest the waves of his bored depression and small hurt still reached me across three miles of twilit sea.

3

SUCCESS AND DISILLUSIONMENT

A FEW DAYS later I solved the problem of the water supply. The lead pipe was very ancient and countless tides had jostled it where it lay in a shallow trench of shingle below the smaller inlet. If not actually cracked it had become porous, and the additional pressure of water required to prime my new system in the house caused it to weep copious fresh-water tears. I saw that there was no way of repairing it, and rang up Jimmy Watt to ask if he would bring me an equivalent length of alkathene pipe. This material—one of the better modern miracles—did the trick in double-quick time. I laid it on the surface of the ground from the well to the cottage, except where it was necessary to dig it in below the tide. Within a few hours of starting the job, all the taps in the house were running merrily.

By the beginning of July most of my work was complete; the day on which the Raeburn stove and the furniture were to arrive was being considered. Almost all the rooms had been painted or distempered in white. This décor made use of any light there was on dull days, while, when the sun shone and the sea sparkled, it produced the most subtle reflections inside the house. The only thing which caused me annoyance was the ubiquitous damp. The whole fabric of the building was permeated with salt, from the air, the sea spray, and no doubt the sand which had been used in the construction. This salt did horrible things to paint, causing it to weep, discolour, blister and finally flake. There seemed to be no known cure and all one could do to palliate the situation was to scrape down the surface and repaint it. As soon as the humidity increased it activated the salt and the whole destructive process began again. The house was most vulnerable when unoccupied: there was then no heating, and the windows had to be closed.

I had still to fit a large plate-glass window in the space where the second door had been—an innovation decided upon by my masters at the ambitious height of their May meeting—and complete a number of smaller things (which became more numerous as the time went on, as happens), but it seemed reasonable that the Raeburn and furniture could now come. I spoke to Joan and Gavin and a date was decided upon.

Murdo Mackenzie landed his cargo on Eilean Sionnach at the second attempt. The operation was complex and called for impeccable planning coupled with good luck. Firstly, Murdo and his boat were fully occupied at Kylerhea during the week and were free only on Sundays. Then the tides had to be considered—the ferry boat might only land at the island jetty on the flood, for fear that an ebbing sea would leave her high and dry. Furthermore the lorry, whose 60-mile trip had originated at Drumnadrochit, had to be at Kylerhea at a pre-determined time to meet the helpers who had agreed to be responsible for loading and unloading throughout the trip. With careful planning these conditions could be met, but the weather was the imponderable factor without whose blessing all would be set at nought. On the first attempt this is what happened, and the partly-loaded ferry boat had to be relieved of its cargo when a rising north-easterly wind perusaded Murdo Mackenzie that the day was unsuitable.

In fact, with the notoriously fickle winds in the Sound of Sleat we were very lucky in conditions on the successful day, but even in the calmest weather the landing of so many items of furniture and equipment, much of it large, heavy and un-gainly, on a short and slippery jetty, called for supreme skill on the captain's part. Mackenzie controlled his boat as though she were an extension of his own limbs, gently, firmly and with an almost animal sense of touch. He edged her in foot by foot until the slightest shudder proclaimed her contact with the jetty. The turntable swung into place and down crashed the steel ramps. There followed a perfect surge of activity.

In addition to Jimmy Watt and Brewster, Murdo Mackenzie and his able assistant, "Tosh", and one or two other local men, some of the schoolboys who were still at Sandaig had been encouraged to join in, and in all we were a numerous company. Joan, whose day it was after months of detailed planning, supervised the placing of the furniture in the cottage. All the men and boys were now engaged in emptying the ferry boat as quickly as possible so that she could stand out from the jetty, and soon the path to the cottage was alive with staggering figures. Men began to leave the jetty bent double under crates of books and other impedimenta, discharged them at the door, and rushed back to the sea like lemmings. Soon the spacious turntable of the ferry boat was empty but for the solid, weighty Raeburn stove. At first it defied all attempts to move it: with a weight so great in relation to its size the four men detailed to lift it got dreadfully in each other's way. In the end a litter shaped like an H with a double cross bar was made and the stove loaded upon it. Six men haltingly raised the contraption to shoulder height, and climbed the slope at a funereal pace. They looked like pall-bearers at the burial of a fat midget.

I installed the Raeburn two days later and had my first hot bath in that very luxurious bathroom—now resplendent with a huge gilt-framed mirror, a pedestal wash basin and a tiled platform surrounding the bath on which stood a veritable garden of geraniums. My life assumed a certain grace and dignity which had previously been lacking: Joan's designs and her selection of furnishings gave a distinct air of opulence and good living.

There was one item of furniture in the house before Murdo Mackenzie's great delivery. It was a large Victorian wooden bed and Gavin had insisted—in the face of strong protest from Joan—that it should be housed in the cottage. He had spread the rumour that it had been the property of an admiral; how he had come into possession of it in the first place I cannot remember, but he held it in high regard and urged me to speak in its defence before my wife. Then one day when I had crossed to Sandaig for stores he asked me to take it back with me by dinghy. Crossings of the Sound were now commonplace, for I had been provided with a fine dinghy called the *Eider* which was larger than the lighthouse keeper's boat and very seaworthy. It was a calm day and I had no misgivings about my unusual cargo, except that it took up most of the length of the boat and overhung it on either side by several feet. It gave the impression that it might float, and I warned Gavin that I would have no compunction about pushing it overboard if the weather grew rough. A brave admiral goes down with his bed, I remarked.

Needless to say, as soon as I came into the area of Loch na Dal the north-west wind blew up a swell, and at each roll of the boat the sides of the bed dipped into the sea. That was bad enough but worse was to come. The bed was of box construction and its frame was honeycombed with drawers. There must have been over a dozen of various sizes and none of them had locks. As the pitching of the boat increased they began to slide out into the sea and float away. No sooner had I recovered one than another went in: there was no way to stop them falling out, for had I crawled to either side of the bed the whole thing would have tipped into the sea. In the end I turned off the engine and recovered them one by one with an oar. The whole idiotic operation took more than an hour.

Of course there was a low spring tide at Ornsay so that I could only take the boat to a remote beach behind the upper channel; from there I had to manhandle the abomination up to the cottage. I slept in it two nights later just to justify my labours, and spent a most uncomfortable night tossing and turning on a mattress that was as hard and unyielding as a wrestler's mat. When I told Gavin how damnable it was and how little it might be expected to appeal to a high-paying tenant, he suggested that we might spread the rumour that the admiral owner had been Lord Nelson. I felt moved to remark that had the revered captain of the *Victory* ever made love to his Emma Hamilton in that bed, the whole course of British naval history would have been altered.

For a few days after I had installed the Raeburn I allowed myself a holiday. I had worked steadily since May and I thought the time had come to enjoy the fruits of my labour and at the same time to explore my environment. My attitude to the sea had undergone a complete change, and now nothing pleased me better than to take the *Eider* out in rough weather. One day I edged her down the coast towards the Point of Sleat in the teeth of a strong southerly wind, making slow spray-soaked progress against the press of a huge rolling sea that had blown up from the Irish coast. When I had gone about five miles I turned and raced home with the wind and sea behind me, this time bringing the *Eider* daringly close to the rocky coves where the raging water sucked and spewed. She was a strong and solid boat with healthy timbers and a wide beam, and she made a fine nurse for my growing confidence.

During my brief vacation the weather alternated between uncanny calms and torrential rain, quiet nights when the sea was like polished jet beneath a canopy of velvet and the only sound the sudden squawk of a seabird, and noisy nights when nothing could be heard above the boom and rustle of the rain-soaked wind and the rhythmic rush of water cascading from the rocks.

I had never been to Knoydart and had planned to make a trip across the Sound to that remote, almost roadless peninsula. I savoured the idea for some time and its appeal grew; in order that it should come up to expectations I chose my day with care. Just after six o'clock on a late July morning I pushed the *Eider* down the slipway into a flat calm sea, and motored away to Knoydart, whose hills stood out like cardboard scenery against the rising sun.

It was a day to be remembered. From the moment I dragged the *Eider* high up on the shingle beach I cancelled my obligations to humanity and cut my moorings with the workaday world. My indolent nature makes it easier for me to enter a groove than to leave it, and a firm wrench is required before I can break with habit and custom. In the days of my youth, before the war, I never lost an opportunity to climb a mountain; if a week went by without it I was desolate; my fanaticism reached a point that was little removed from madness. I resented the war, which I spent in passive service. At the end of it my spirit committed suicide through self-contempt, and never again was I able to be whole-hearted about anything. I was a broken man, hollow, rather like Coleridge's mariner after he had shot the albatross. My attempts to emulate my steadily maturing contemporaries were a failure, and I became a veritable Peter Pan of a fellow, unwilling to grow up, who recoiled from a demanding present into a web of nostalgia. Sometimes this nostalgia becomes so potent that it assumes the substance of a great need, and then I must abandon whatever I am doing and go straightway to the hills. Thus it was on the day of which I write.

In retrospect details separate from general impressions. It took me until eight o'clock in the evening to walk about twenty miles; the sun shone throughout. It was hot in the valleys but a cool east wind blew over the ridges. And inside me there was a huge feeling of elation, such as I had almost forgotten, which ran through my every nerve and brought a new spring to my stride and a strong desire to shout for joy. I walked up a thick, flaring ridge that stood like a root against the solid trunk of the mountain. Below my feet the deep, springy heather and sun-cracked peat gave way to shortening grass which was soon replaced by the arid gravel of the high ground. Little alpine flowers winked brightly in their dull setting. I climbed steadily, hardly pausing for breath, until ridges and summits that had formerly dominated the skyline no longer held pride of place, and a vast panorama rose up behind me. Now the wrinkled sea was far below; beyond the low, green land of Sleat was an endless mystery of hazy islands. To the south of Loch na Dal the face of Skye was spotted with innumerable white cottages, while towards Kylerhea no habitation softened the dungeon-like gullies that fell from Beinn na Seamraig into a restless, fast-flowing tide.

Almost directly above the thin spire of my lighthouse rose the cracked and jagged Cuillin ridge where I had spent the best of my boyhood days; though thirty years had gone by not a single memory had vanished and the brightest of them had hardly dimmed. The sight of those mountains was like looking at time; its power of evocation was so strong that it brought tears to my eyes, for it opened the book of memory at the right page and showed what was clearly in the margin—the solid security of boyhood home, being in love for the first few times, and the exciting challenge of adolescent crusade, all played to the music of Gershwin and Kern. Unlike my new friend at the Bay of the Alders my boyhood had been unwisely happy—I mean, I had become so used to doing what I wanted that it did not seriously occur to me that there was any other course open. A few stumbling blocks set at random across an endless line of stepping-stones might, in the long run, have been worth their weight in gold.

In a long day that was never too long I saw a thousand things and nothing disappointed me. I began to appreciate the value of recent abstinence; it is not true to say that you cannot have too much of a good thing; even when I was young and at the height of my fanaticism my mountain mania occasionally burnt itself out. Now, after some months of mundane life, all that lay around me had both the warmth of an old familiarity and the excitement of new acquaintance. The streams that rushed and tumbled down polished rock into dark mossy channels sang no new song, yet their voices seemed sturdier than before, and there never was a silence so intense as that which made my eardrums ring in the high corries where no water ran and the winds were dead. Afternoon merged into evening and the red searchlights of the sun blooded the mountains tops, while long shadows began to stretch themselves like lazy giants on lower slopes. By this time I had wandered round to the coast again—some distance from my boat—and I sat on the top of a high cliff and looked straight down into the darkening waters of Loch Hourn. I would like to have lingered here to watch the white afterglow flare above the Cuillin, and to dream the old dream of blossom on ageless apple orchards in the heart of the sun's fire, but by now I knew that the tide—retreating when I had left the *Eider* nearly twelve hours earlier—would be high. I had still three or four miles to walk, and I did not want to find the heavy boat high and dry on the almost flat beach on which I had left her. I quickened my pace and reached the *Eider* just as the water was drawing away from her stern. On my way I had passed old houses, rowans twisted about their doors: there was an extreme air of desertion about them as if their occupants, in leaving, had forfeited all human rights to them and given them back unreservedly to the hillside on which they were built.

The next day Gavin Maxwell and Jimmy Watt arrived by road for a tour of inspection. The former was in a jubilant mood; I sensed that a run of good fortune had come his way. His praise for my efforts and the developing theme of Joan's design was effusive, but his satisfaction was plainly sincere: he did not sweep the possibility of criticism aside—as one would who offered thoughtless applause—but pondered each detail and apparently found no fault.

He had already confided to me more than once that he had no love for writing, and now the *Ring of Bright Water*'s great success had created a new supply and demand he was faced with a continuing need to carry out what had become an irksome chore. He reminded me now, as the three of us walked round the cottage still fresh with its new paint, that he had high hopes that the rental from this property and the other at

Kyleakin might allow him to have at least a rest from his pen.
He thanked me and asked me to give his thanks to Joan for
our part in making this dream possible.

By the end of the month little remained to be done, or so it
appeared. But unless one's thoroughness is absolute and each
piece of work is entirely completed at the time, loose ends
multiply in inverse proportion to the days left for their
finalizing. And the plate glass for the huge window which was
to look out over Loch na Dal was still in Inverness. I borrowed
the Land Rover from Jimmy Watt and went to collect it, some
necessary odds and ends, and my wife, who was intent on
spending the last few days with me before the tenants came
in the cottage.

The plate glass, from the first, seemed to attract disaster.
Securely crated, it was packed tightly inside the Land Rover
in such a way that only the most violent change of position
could destroy it. This extreme circumstance was almost
immediately provided. On our way back to Ornsay, some five
miles from the village, I had drawn into the side to allow a
lorry to pass. The Land Rover had been at rest for a few seconds
when suddenly it fell over on its side. The verge had given
way beneath the heavy vehicle. Joan and I, entirely unharmed
though in a state of great alarm about the safety of our precious
load, scrambled out and were soon able to get a message to a
local garage, who restored us to an even keel in less time than
it takes to tell. Unexpectedly there was no damage to anything.
We continued to Ornsay and crossed to the lighthouse rock on
one of the calmest and most beautiful evenings I have ever
seen. It was a gentle prelude to a week of considerable stress.

The next morning I checked the dimensions of the glass
against the frame which I had built into the opening, and then,
instead of replacing it in its crate, I propped it up against the
wall of the house in what seemed a safe position.

Ornsay Island carries a small sheep population: a very few
animals seem to prefer Eilean Sionnach to its large neighbour,
and more or less live below a large, deserted walled vegetable
garden to the south of the cottage. After a warm day they tend
to congregate on the long paving slab which runs in front of
the house, in order to enjoy its retained heat, as they do on
roads. That evening I left the front door open, for the air was
still and thundery, not dreaming for a moment that the

animals would seek territorial advancement. Joan and I had been diligently polishing and sweeping, and when we went to bed the little sitting-room positively beamed at us.

Next morning it was filled with sheep. There were at least six large woollen bodies, and might have been more, lying about in disgusting relaxation, like courtesans after an orgy. Wool and droppings were much in evidence. Snatching one of Gavin's stainless-steel harpoons off the wall (a piece of unusual decoration from his shark-fishing days) I prodded the nearest offender in the rump, causing him to give such a leap that his fright communicated itself to his companions and they made for the door in a concerted rush. There they stuck, jamming the entrance in their hurry to be gone. Helpfully I made adroit passes at them with my weapon until the door was clear, and the last of them went skipping with lambish abandon along the side of the house. The quiet of the summer's morning was suddenly violated by the high, sharp crack of splintering glass—— It was not one of my best days.

The next morning I was about to set out for Inverness to obtain a new piece of glass when I discovered that the water supply had failed. Apart from the fact that it was suffering from some form of embolism—air bubbles poured out of the valve which I had set in the lowest point of the pipe—it had become coy and mysterious, and the fact that two hours of work restored its efficiency did nothing to reassure me. If it had happened once it could happen again, and next time there would probably be no one to cater to its vagaries.

When I came back from Inverness that evening with the new glass a brisk sea was running and the tide was low. I would have preferred to wait for it to rise so that I could have avoided the rough waters to the north of Ornsay Island, but time was at a premium. I strapped the crate securely across the bow of the dinghy, and crossed my fingers with a short prayer to my guardian angel to take special care of me for the next 30 minutes. I can only assume that the gentleman thus addressed was either on leave, unconscious or dead, for although no harm befell the crated glass a sudden lurch twisted the outboard engine off the stern, and it disappeared with a despairing gurgle and a stream of bubbles in about 30 fathoms of water. Luckily I was near the jetty, for it was impossible to row the boat since the crate covered more than two-thirds of its length; using a single oar I laboriously punted the *Eider* to the island. I was most distressed to have lost Gavin's property in what was certainly a careless fashion, and I postponed telephoning him as long as possible, my moral fibre being more than usually flaccid. But I should have remembered that with Maxwell spilt milk was *spilt*: there being nothing more that can be done, neither tears nor recriminations were in order.

I 'phoned Sandaig. Jimmy answered, and having heard my news remarked that Gavin was in the bath and that the engine was not the first of its kind "to suffer a sea change". This whimsical conception of its metamorphosis did not alter the fact that I would now have to row whenever I wanted to go anywhere. Gavin, by now out of the bath, seemed to be in almost hysterical good humour. "I hear you've joined the club, Richard," he shouted without a hint of displeasure, and went on to explain more soberly that the "club" was an informal body to which everybody belonged who had dropped an engine in the area. I was comforted to hear that it had a substantial membership, and even more so when he told me that the engine was fully covered by a clause in the insurance policy which dealt with "dropping off" as a hazard.

The next day I introduced the plate glass into its frame. The only damage which took place during this part of the operation was to an imprudent sheep who approached during a critical stage, and came within accurate throwing range of my hammer.

The day before that of the tenants' arrival Gavin and Jimmy came over, and with Joan started to make an inventory of the contents of the cottage. These were increased by Gavin who had brought with him a quantity of knick-knackery which he determined to impose upon Joan's already balanced design, and which only served to produce local states of incongruent clutter. It was an odd trait in his character which made him make such a show of his possessions and quite paradoxical when one considered his substantial family background. He brought with him a number of exquisite photographs of young Arabs which he had taken on the Tigris marshes. Beautiful they certainly were, but I felt that they need not have been so prominently displayed high up on the bathroom walls. From then on I was always embarrassed when lying on my back in that enormous bath with all those dark, lustful eyes in their brown and secretive faces staring down at me through the geraniums.

The inventory took much longer to prepare than we had expected, and our two friends decided to stay overnight. We sat down to a pleasant meal, and when it seemed that we had left nothing undiscussed about the morning's arrangements bed was suggested. Jimmy and Joan were both tired and excused themselves without more ado, but Gavin sat steadily on and so did I, for I thought it would be churlish to leave him there with only his whisky for company. In fact he had been quietly drinking all evening and there was a hint of unsoberness about him, but his mood was cheerful. I suspected that he wanted to talk, and this was confirmed when he said: "Richard, if I go to bed now I shan't sleep. Could you find it in your heart to stay up with me a little while?"

"All right," I said, "I'm not tired, and it's very pleasant to relax over this drink and in good company."

"Thank you," he said, coming to the point at once: "I wonder if you would be so happy to sit down in the company of a murderer?"

I was taken aback. This man was full of surprises, and I hoped that he was joking. "A murderer?" I asked cautiously. "Depends, of course, but probably not. Er—where does this come in to it?"

"It doesn't," he said without conviction, and as a change of mind: "But I am a homosexual. Does that worry you?"

"This I think I knew—it is, after all, common gossip."

"And it doesn't worry you?"

"Why should it? Several of my friends are, or claim to be. It is not unusual, is it? I am not in any way, but this does not put us on different sides of a fence. In fact—if I may say so—I have much sympathy for you in this. Your situation has little popular support. A man can take a woman, providing she's willing and legally over age, and the world smiles with a greater or less indulgence. The physical expression of your love is still considered pretty sinister."

This annoyed him. He took a long swallow of his whisky and lit a cigarette, looking glum. He exuded an aura of hurt. I was sorry I had said that; at best it sounded pompous, at worst unkind. He went on:

"I think you associate yourself with people who think it sinister, you are much too heterosexual to try to understand us." Now he was both angry and hurt.

"Not at all, Gavin," I said, "I have a simple philosophy. I believe in pleasure and happiness; but not just mine. Two grown people—men or women—aware of themselves, knowing what they want, what comforts them, can decide, and the world can go hang as far as I am concerned. But when it comes to young boys—or girls—who are persuaded for an adult's gratification to do something that is unnatural, that is a different story. And I repeat the word unnatural," I added, meaningfully, for he had half raised his hand in protest as I said it.

"To this you object," he asked, in quiet anger.

"To this, in any physical form, I object," I answered firmly.

"You are a prig," he stated, "and in some ways ignorant. You do not know Morocco, so I shall tell you that there it is a custom, an accepted thing, that young men of position spend some years in the houses of elder men as adopted sons. In return for love and affection that they give, they receive advancement and worldliness. No harm is ever done to the boy who, as a married man or in later life, looks back upon his sponsor with feelings of affection. What is wrong with that?"

"Nothing—in Morocco," I said, "but this is not Morocco. Isn't that the point?"

We went on talking for hours. The heat had gone out of our argument as soon as we had clearly stated our separate standpoints. My attitude to the subject was modified when I had heard all he had to say, and over the years of our association I came to accept what he said with understanding, if not with approval. I came to realize that, in this relationship as in the other, it is individuals who set the moral values, and that no general ruling has much relevance.

As morning grew in strength the conversation became discursive. Maxwell, comfortably unsober, went on talking, but now it was a monologue to a sleeping audience. What had given him fire had quenched me. I could no longer keep my eyes open. After a brief doze I woke with a start. The Tilley lamp had gone out, but the grey dawn, peeping through a fog of tobacco smoke, had sneaked in upon our privacy while the empty whisky bottle, which stood on the table between us, looked like a man who had gone to sleep on his feet.

Finally I rose in protest at my companion's garrulity, and so tired was I that it was as much as I could do to remark: "We must go to bed now, Gavin. It is morning, the light is bright and it will be a busy day," but he answered: "You go, Richard —good night!" and stubbornly sat on in the thinning twilight.

I took my chilled body and weary mind into the bedroom, and as I felt my wife's warmth, a wave of compassion swept over me for the man I had left alone. Later I heard him go outside, and when he did not immediately return I went to the door to see if all was well with him. He was standing quite still on a rock above the sea, his eyes apparently fixed on the red dawn flaring over Camusfearna.

Yet, in the later morning, after the briefest of sleeps, he was himself again, the rather introspective mood quite put aside. We took mugs of coffee and rolls out to the grassy ridge on the island's top on a gracious summer morning of hot sun and a scented seabreeze, and we were pleased with ourselves and with each other. Gavin thanked us both again for the "mammoth task" we had accomplished, and said quite simply to Joan, "You are a genius". Being against nature, however, a state of bliss between people is impossible to maintain, and it would have been well had we parted there and then and left the island to go our separate ways. Unfortunately there were still things we had to do which would keep us together, and since the peak of mutual congratulation had been reached there was nowhere left to go but down; and on that stony slope, uninspired by the sight of the summit and tired after the struggle to reach it, the backward glance was not rewarding. To add to that, it is no less bad to drink on an anti-climax than on an empty stomach, for both turn the wholesome alcohol to poison.

Deterioration set in when Gavin claimed he did not want to meet the tenants. "Leave me as a famous name," he joked, "they may find me disappointing!" He was therefore quite unprepared for the meeting when he bumped into them in the local hotel. Chance encounters held no charm for him, and he always liked to acquire a little Dutch courage for scheduled appointments. There was nothing for it but to invite all the tenants to join him in the bar. After they left he stayed on, drinking quietly and gloomily.

Joan and I stayed on at the cottage to form a reception

committee for the newcomers. Jimmy, having left Gavin at the hotel, was to bring the tenants back in the dinghy. After an unexpected delay—brought about by Gavin's unexpected meeting—the boat reappeared round the point and bored its quiet way through a calm sea. I thought to myself how fortunate we were to have such weather; it might just as easily have been blowing great guns beneath lowering grey clouds and an hysteria of salt tears.

Even so the four people who stepped from the dinghy—there were two couples—showed some apprehension about an environment that was obviously strange to them (it would have been to most people!), but they were enchanted with the cottage. At first I imagined that they would cling to it as a haven in the midst of an inimical waste of rock, sea and sky, and leave it only when their holiday was ended. Jimmy and I instructed the men in the use of the outboard, and showed them what precautions to take to prevent the boat being broken up by the tides and wind. We asked that they pay particular attention to a framed chart that had been our joint creation. It showed how to approach the island at various states of the tide, and here and there short warning captions had been inserted, such as: "Here be quicksands", "Bay dries out at Low Springs", "Sewage slick" and the ever popular "Foul Fround" which sounded sufficiently forbidding because of the total obscurity of its meaning. When we left them it was, I think with universal misgivings, but we are a seafaring nation and in each of us, even the least likely—such as myself—there is a deep-seated instinct for survival in wild waters. And so it proved for, by the end of their holiday, our two couples, adaptable and indefatigable, were ranging the restless waters of the Sound of Sleat with the carelessness of buccaneers.

Joan, Jimmy and I landed, and went back to the hotel. Gavin made us all sit down and drink with him. This failed to rekindle the recent spirit of mutual goodwill; that boat could not be launched upon a falling tide. Gavin soon cornered the reluctant Joan and force-fed her a tale from a gloomy episode in his life. She was in no mood for such a recital; she had worked well for the successful outcome of his scheme, and saw no reason to celebrate it like a wake. Before long she was forced to the conclusion that for some reason of his own he was trying to distress her, and she grew angry with him. Unaware, no doubt, of the cause (was the Ancient Mariner aware of the hatred the Wedding Guest felt for his interminable tale?) Gavin flinched from her scorn, and at that moment communication between them temporarily ceased.

I was annoyed to see any contention between people on a lovely summer's day. I always believe that disputes should be set aside in good weather and only brought out when the barometer is low. Not when the sun is shining; war is incongruous then.

After a short time we arrived at Tormor. Gavin was lending us the Land Rover to take us home. We were still on speaking terms, but our parting was a little less than cordial. By now the weather had caught the general mood; a thick yellow overcast had spread across the sky and a few sullen drops of rain began to fall. So the conversion of Isle Ornsay cottage came to a rather uninspired completion.

4

CRUSOE AND MAN FRIDAY

I THOUGHT THAT this might have been an end of it. The clash of moods on the day of the tenants' arrival at Isle Ornsay is the sort of thing to impede—or even halt—the growth of a friendship; after such it requires a fresh impetus, or a decline in relationship sets in. It crossed my mind that Maxwell might take advantage of this small hiatus to justify the abandonment of the second conversion which, after all, he was in no way able to afford. In thinking this I did him less than justice.

We seldom heard from him now, but Jimmy Watt kept us informed of how things were going with him. We heard that Brewster had finally broken Maxwell's patience, and had been sent away on an Outward Bound course, for which Maxwell paid. The first tenants finished their holiday and another party took their place. Everybody was pleased, including Maxwell, for as the weekly cheques for £60 began to make their modest contribution he spoke (we were told) of what Joan and I had done to make this possible, and what, perhaps, we might do elsewhere. During one of these talks with Jimmy I asked him just how much money Maxwell needed to keep his little empire going. He told me about Gavin Maxwell Enterprises Ltd (whose northern manager he was), which had been created as a practical move to deflect the impact of heavy tax claims arising out of the inflated income from *Ring of Bright Water*. What was a quasi-legal device Maxwell took most seriously, speaking of it in grandiose terms as though it were a vast commercial undertaking. Nobody else took it too seriously—except, one imagines, that august body which it had been formed to placate, but in the early days it was a practical thing which absorbed tax into its corporate body at a rate no individual could have survived. It had another purpose. Ever since Adam hinted slyly to God that Eve had started on the apples, Man has needed a scapegoat for his weakness. If Maxwell had a hangover after a spending spree, or was warned that there was insufficient money for something he particularly wanted to do, he would speak darkly of "mismanagement of company affairs" which relieved him of complicity without actually indicting anyone else.

But while in the days of opulence it allowed a high standard of living out of tax, when the bonanza was over and the flood of money became a modest flow the company was still there but the means of meeting its demands were not. A comparison is too obvious to name, but Mary Shelley wrote about it. Gavin, Jimmy affirmed, hated retrenchment in any form, so that now he, and not the tax man, was the sole provider for GME Ltd's voracious appetite. His agent, Peter Janson-Smith, as clear-headed as his author was vague and impractical, made no bones about it and told the reluctant writer that his output must be no less than one substantial book a year if life were to maintain its quality. Gavin hated the idea and hoped his rents would help, but by his own accounting—or by his interpretation of his accountant's—Sandaig was costing £7,000 a year to run; my own arithmetic failed to make any sense of this situation, but I did not see how he could afford the cost of converting another cottage until the first had proved itself by at least a year's letting. It was therefore with some surprise that I answered the telephone in late September, to hear him ask Joan and me if we would pay him a visit and discuss the Kyleakin venture. He hastened to remark that this time our services must be adequately rewarded. We did not deny this and promised to listen to his plans and proposals.

Gavin said he was pleased to see us again, and he was on his very best behaviour. Such a mood may have been a precaution against our reaction to his proposals. The sum he suggested was not a striking one in view of the amount of work and planning which would have to be done; Joan was both angry and hurt, for she felt a need to maintain professional status which acceptance of such a small amount must have degraded. When we were alone she disinterred the memory of Gavin's fair promise to her earlier in the year, and I smiled a superior smile for, deny it as I sometimes do, there is nothing that pleases me more than being able to say "I told you so". But, oddly enough, both our opinions were shifting, for I did not see this outcome as arising from Gavin's lack of integrity, but from caution on the part of his accountants, who had no doubt said, "Thus far you can go, but no further," in calling a halt to some over-generous offer he had suggested. He made no attempt to suggest the terms were adequate, and in fact seemed acutely embarrassed at their meagreness, stoutly maintaining that his hands were tied. It was a clear case of "mismanagement of company affairs"!

The outcome was that Joan declined any involvement and I agreed to do the conversion for the amount of money offered to us both, but this time to Gavin's design. From every point of view I would have liked Joan's participation, not least as this new situation contained a slight sense of disloyalty to her, but the objections were insufficient to over-rule the advantages. I was, as usual, painfully short of money and the amount promised, though not large, was not insignificant either; it would bring comfort to my creditors, if not to me. Also, although so short a time had gone by, I had already felt a nostalgia for the rough and tumble seas and the solitary charm of island life, while the idea of the work itself was a fresh challenge, which to me is important, like climbing rocks.

I had already looked over the Kyleakin cottage, and was well aware of its current state. It was in much worse condition than Isle Ornsay had been, excessively damp with some of the floors rotted right away. Alan MacDiarmid had done some inside demolition which had covered the rooms with dust and given them a look of complete dereliction. In late autumn with the long nights lengthening it was bound to be a depressing place, and I was delighted when Gavin 'phoned me a few days before I was due to start work to say that he had arranged for Terry Nutkins to be my assistant. This surprised me. I had not known that they had come together after the fracas at Sandaig two years earlier, although Gavin was not a man to hold an extended grudge and Terry's bright and open nature would never have denied a reconciliation. However it had come about, I welcomed it. I had always liked the boy. Although at this time he still had a life to fashion, he was tough, amiable,

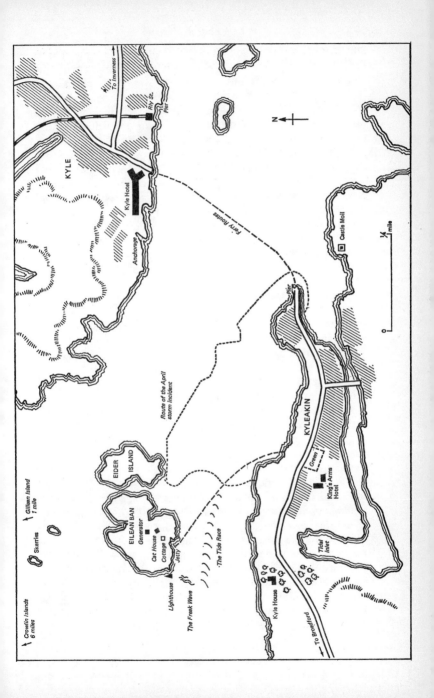

amusing, a good cook and an excellent seaman. He intended to bring with him his bitch, Compass, the daughter of our Dalmatian Hedda by our neighbour's Labrador, and Gavin had gladly given him permission to house on the island his two very unusual pets—a male and female wildcat which he and his woman friend had reared from kittenhood, in defiance of the pundits who said that such a thing was impossible.

Before we settled in at Kyleakin, Terry and I paid a few days' visit to Isle Ornsay cottage. My object was to check the house for deterioration and pull out and sell the old lead water pipe which had given me so much grief. Having done this and made a handsome profit—which I split with the company—I felt the new undertaking had started well. On a lovely late September day I motored the *Eider* through the Kylerhea narrows and by evening had my first view from water level of Eilean Ban—the White Island—lying low, dark and sharp-outlined against the sunset.

I met Terry on the shingle below the King's Arms Hotel. He had driven over from Isle Ornsay in his venerable Ford with tools and provisions. We transferred everything to the *Eider*, including Compass and the cats, and within a few minutes had crossed a short stretch of calm water and landed at a jetty in a shallow bay beneath the lighthouse cottage. This is situated to the south of the ridge which forms the highest point of the island, an infelicitous arrangement in some ways because the ridge prevents the sight of the magnificent seascape to the north and at the same time acts as an amplifier for every sound that originates in the suburbia of Kyleakin opposite. In calm weather it confuses the ear like a miniature Tower of Pabel.

We pulled up the boat to a safe place above the tide and unloaded it. A steep path led up to a long pavement in front of the house. On the way we saw a dead rat lying on the verge, its sightless eyes fixed on the mainland opposite. It gave the impression that its latest thought had been escape. It depressed me, and when I saw the house I was cast down even further. It was open, and Alan had removed all the steel sheets that had sealed doors and windows, as had been the case at Isle Ornsay. Before the front door there was a great pile of discarded masonry over which we clambered. Inside, the brownish plaster dust invested everything with the close intimacy of a shroud, while the coffin shape of the long room and the dark, tomb-like entrances of the bedrooms enhanced the illusion of death and decay. It was by far the most depressing place in which I have ever expected to live, and even Terry's volatile spirits suffered a rebuff, while the dog, Compass, whined and squeaked and seemed loath to leave her master's shadow.

We all but dug our way into the kitchen, scrambling over débris. There was a ragged hole in the far wall as though a cannon ball had gone through it, but otherwise the room was intact; we established it as our working headquarters. From it we made exploratory forays to other parts of the house. Much of it was like Isle Ornsay as it had been in early May, though some parts were much worse: it was like going back several stages in evolution, and a sobering reminder of what had been done at that house and what now must be repeated here. The two buildings were much the same in external shape; inside there were minor differences, such as a small bathroom—for which water was not available—in a room that had been a bedroom at Isle Ornsay. In the front Alan had knocked down three brick partitions to form one long room.

The Calor-gas stove which I had used at Isle Ornsay until the march of progress made it redundant had been summoned back from retirement, and on it Terry made a strong cup of tea which we drank in reflective silence. This made us feel happier and we lit two Tilley lamps and started to clean up the room in which we had chosen to bunk down. This one was in good condition and almost free from damp stains. We agreed that a fire in the small iron grate would promote a cheerful going-to-bed atmosphere, and ignited a few pieces of broken lath. A merry crackle turned into a throaty roar; unaccountably the chimney had caught fire. Clad only in our shirts and in extreme discomfort and misery we clambered on to the roof with a kettle which we repeatedly emptied down the pot. Soon the fire was out, but a soggy multi-coloured rag protruded from the flue. We pulled it out for examination. It was the pennant of the Northern Lighthouse Board depicting a tall, graceful tower emitting flashes of light. It was quite spoiled, but later on we found another up a second chimney, and I gave it to Gavin. He flew it from the flagpole at Isle Ornsay until the rough Atlantic winds blew it to shreds.

Terry and I were now cold and covered with wet soot. We were very sorry for ourselves. We could not be bothered to re-light the fire and rolled ourselves in our blankets as we were. Disturbed by the unfamiliarity of the house I could not sleep. It was much noisier here than on Eilean Sionnach. The wind and sea were dead, and in the vacuum of their silence every domestic noise from across the water tapped on the window panes, but inside the house the still, cold air was petrified.

We woke up to a grey, cold morning with the south-westerly wind gusting strongly. The Indian summer whose gracious days we had enjoyed on Eilean Sionnach was dying at last, and in the rising rain-laden wind we foresaw the topsy-turvy pattern of rough days and nights ahead. The short stretch of water that divided us from Kyleakin had seemed of no account a few hours before; now the long, green rollers toppled their heavy heads against the tide which swept inexorably through the channel and underlined the fact that this, unlike Eilean Sionnach, was a full-time island and we would only be able to leave it on the sea's terms.

We spent much of the day in Kyle of Lochalsh introducing ourselves to tradesmen and suppliers and gathering materials for general repair work. Gavin had promised me that he would drive over to Eilean Ban within a few days of our arrival, bringing detailed plans of what he wanted me to do. Between Joan and me a strong rapport has built up over the years, and she is able to give definite shape to an abstract notion by a wave of her hand in thin air or a momentary image traced on a table top, but with Gavin I could not expect such a casual transfer of information to be effective, and from him I should require much more indelible guidance.

The next day was calm and cold, there was new snow on the Skye mountains and the world glittered. It was a good day to collect the things we had set aside in Kyle. We made several trips and by evening a big pile of building material and general gear lay stacked upon the jetty. In the clear, frosty twilight we carried it up to the cottage, warmed by the activity and cheered by a feeling that the operation was getting well under way. I was glad to have sturdy Terry at my side as we plodded up the steep path. Later, when he was no longer with me, I was to remember with nostalgia the sight of his big body, bent under the weight of planks or cement bags, as I staggered up from the jetty with similar impedimenta. Later, with the first real frost of winter lying grey on the island, we wrenched old boards from the ruined floors and made a great fire in the bedroom. We sat on our bunks, drank huge mugs of tea and watched the salty timber green-sparking in the red heart of the fire. All at once the whole prospect of the conversion appeared in a more cheerful light. The initial strangeness was wearing off and the house was becoming familiar: we had really arrived.

Gavin brought with him not only a collection of detailed plans but his water-colour impression of how he conceived the long room would look when finished. This impressed me so much that it gave me a strong incentive to provide an exact replica of his illustration. His ideas were interesting, neat and functional, but I suspected that some aspects were borrowed from Joan—possibly subconsciously, for however he regarded her as a woman he had a genuine admiration for her prowess as a designer. In the painting he had so placed the furniture as to give it a sense of individual dignity but, knowing his fatal preoccupation with clutter, I did not think this spacious arrangement would long survive in its illustrated form.

He also had a special fondness for Eilean Ban which he preferred to Eilean Sionnach. I could never understand why. Gavin told me that the rough heathery ridges reminded him of the terrain around his Wigtownshire boyhood home, but nostalgia apart, there was no reasonable comparison between remote, desolate Ornsay cottage standing on its moulded turf, and ragged, thorny Kyleakin's knee-twisting undergrowth. When he eulogized about the narrow vista of Lochalsh to the east he seemed oblivious to its frame of poor quality suburbia, and although he plainly deprecated the littoral jerry building opposite his windows he would spend hours looking at it with a kind of forlorn fascination. It was all the more strange because he hated ugly housing and he found mankind in the raw mass oppressive. He told me once that he thought Skye "was a faery island, with houses built by unscrupulous goblins".

Be that as it may, he was obviously excited at the prospect of a converted Kyleakin, and I sensed that he had entered into a competition with Joan's Isle Ornsay, which did not surprise me. It would give him a feeling of sexual one-upmanship to make a better job of something than a woman had done— especially when he openly conceded her excellence. I wondered if his attitude to me would alter now that I was not only a friend but an employee, but there were no signs that this would happen. In fact, with a delicate courtesy he brushed aside any hint that there had been a change in our relationship, by saying casually that both he and I were employed by his company in whose affairs he had practically no say. He had obviously forgiven Terry for being whisked away from under his nose and their conversation was affable and unstrained. He was enormously interested in the two wildcats—now housed in an old laundry building adjacent to the cottage—and gave Terry unilateral praise for the difficult task of having reared them, which was predictably unfair to their absent joint-owner.

As the days went by Terry and I got into a very good rhythm of work and relaxation. In order that the claustrophobic limits should not become too oppressive we would often make a night visit to one or other of the Kyleakin hotels for a drink and a chat with the locals. The brief voyage over the dark and unpredictable channel had a spice of adventure about it. The trip to the mainland was usually uneventful; we chose our weather and our time, and since Kyleakin beach provided a wide target navigation was unimportant. On the way back it was not always so easy. Although we left our Tilley lamp burning on the jetty we still had to thread our way through the serpentine entrance to the bay, which was fringed by a ring of rocks. One such night we shall not easily forget. There had been a fresh south-westerly all day, and we waited until later than usual for it to drop with the turning of the spring tide. By nine-thirty it had become a race against closing-time and as the sea had settled down into a steady, thrusting swell we decided to set out. There was the tiny slip of a new moon and the sky was speckled with stars. On arriving at Kyleakin we tethered the boat to a steel bar just above low-water level; by the sideways rush of the water we knew that the tide was flooding strongly. Dashing off a brace of whiskies we called it a short night and ran back to the *Eider*. We had only been gone a matter of minutes, but already she was swinging in the tide from a rope two feet below water level. We cast off at once and were instantly wrenched away by the tide which was rushing and bubbling through the channel like a mill race. The village lights reeled away behind us as we started the engine and pointed the boat at right angles to the shore. We knew that the tide would do the rest.

It took no time at all to reach the area of the jetty bay. Here the water was running over the buckled surface of waves that stood stock still against the drift. I took a glance at the Tilley lantern standing on the end of the jetty about forty yards away and was about to turn in when: "Richard, don't turn! Head into it! Look at it—it's just not true!" shouted Terry, and automatically I swung the engine back in line with the boat. I could not believe my eyes, nor steady the frantic beating of my heart. Standing steeply in front of us was a wall of water at least fifteen feet in height; its centre was silently advancing while its landward edge collapsed in a torrent of spray on to the ring of rocks outside the bay. The forward movement of the mass was slight but the opposing tidal water rushed over its hump so fast that I could plainly see tiny pieces of phosphorescence rising out of the sea-bed like tracer bullets. To me this sight was a diabolical confrontation with a life-long phobia: in many a restless night I had dreamed of this wave and woken in quivering terror of it.

It is fortunate that the need for urgent action tends to cancel out fear. We both knew that nothing we could do would get *Eider* out of the way, so a frontal engagement was the safest and most dignified course open to us. The boat joined battle with a wild rush; her bow buried itself deeply, but the quarter decking saved her from being swamped, she was heaved into an almost vertical climb, the face of the wave met her bottom squarely with a mighty slap, I saw Terry darkly silhouetted against the stars hang on for dear life to the mooring ring and there was a great clatter as all the loose gear fell down the length of the boat into the stern. I kept her straight on and I gave the engine every ounce of power. We were pushed backwards even as we were pulled over and suddenly, unbelievably, we were on top of a long, trembling ridge which ended in a foaming hole to landward where the great wave had sucked the water from the bay. Now I panicked, for I had a dreadful fear that there might be more to come, and I turned *Eider* towards the light of the Tilley lamp, careless of what might lie between as a child in fatal ignorance dashes to its mother across a crowded road. We were lucky. The great flush of water that filled the bay behind the wave carried us to safety, we struck once, twice, but only as glancing blows at gunnel level, and we were in. We tied *Eider* up without a word. It was only after a whisky or two from Terry's half-bottle that we spoke of it at all, but after that we went on talking for most of the night.

Terry's wildcats were undeniably impressive, even magnificent, but in no sense of the word could they be described as pets. All men and women were their enemies and though male and female they seemed to regard each other with a mixture of suspicion and fear. When I sometimes accompanied Terry into their den I always wore a heavy plasticized waterproof with attached hood, for I had been warned by him that the cats were not above dropping from the rafters (where they spent a lot of time) on to one's unprotected head. One glance at their massive paws and razor sharp claws told one what would happen then. In contrast to the wildcats' implacable irascibility the dog Compass—so named by Joan on account of a revolving habit of puppyhood—was one of the most warmly affectionate creatures I have ever met, and she adored Terry who nevertheless ruled her with a rod of iron. Thus the bitch had both affection and respect for her master; a state of affairs that was very sorely tried one November day.

It was such a warm pleasant day that we ate our meal outside, seated on boxes on the pavement. Terry always did the cooking; he was very proficient, and his services in this direction were invaluable. At Ornsay I used to lose a lot of time in cooking for myself. Now he came out of the cottage with two plates heaped high with what appeared to be fish. I gave him a questioning glance while Compass with an air of meal-time optimism stood at a polite distance. "Herring!" revealed the cook in the voice of one who has just made a discovery, and added: "Salted, bought in Kyle yesterday, certainly cheap and said to be excellent. Try one." "No, you first, Terry," I said politely and with a certain caution, for I had noticed that parts of the fish were thickly coated with a whitish substance that I didn't understand. Obediently Terry selected a large portion of the reputed herring and popped it in his mouth. About a minute later he swallowed with some difficulty. A frightening change came over him, his eyes closed, his face contorted, tears ran down his cheeks and his limbs appeared to stiffen. I thought him in a fit, but bravely he controlled his condition and made the understatement of that or any other year in a thick, strangled voice: "'Fraid bit too much—oh!—salt—sorry —try that corner of the plate—better?" Spurred on only by loyalty to his reputation I selected a relatively unencrusted portion and attempted to despatch it as one would an oyster. It would not go down and at once a scalding sensation spread through my mouth and my lips went numb. "Oh, Terry," I groaned, "what is it? Battery acid?" at which he looked so unhappy that to please him I swallowed yet another bit. The shock caused me to double up. While Terry and I lay there helpless Compass mistook the situation and concluded that we had finished our meal; as was her permitted custom she approached the plates and cleared them at a gulp. Like Lot's wife she became momentarily a salted pillar then fell over on her side, frothing at the mouth and whimpering quietly to herself. Terry could not bear to see his bitch's affliction and rested a reassuring hand upon her head, but she gave him a look of fear and doubt and he said sadly: "She thought I was trying to poison her!" After a few minutes we had recovered sufficiently to go round to the slate tank where the humans drank water direct from the tap and Compass from a bucket.

Later we spent our customary evening at Kyleakin. As I luxuriously sampled a long, cool pint of beer I noticed that Terry was in deep conversation with a local man. As we returned to the *Eider* he seemed to be digesting some food for thought. I asked him what he and his companion had been talking about and he answered defensively: "Salted herring."

"Oh, I see. Did he want some?"

"No, he was telling me about it."

"What about it?"

"Oh, how to cook the damn stuff!" said Terry, sick of my inquisition. "First you soak it in water for hours to get the salt out and then——"

"What did *you* do?" I persisted.

"Well, in the first place I didn't even wash it, and in the

second I *added* salt. I thought it looked a bit off, and that the salt would help!"

We both dissolved into helpless laughter as we pushed the *Eider* out into the channel.

We had now been on the island for over a fortnight. It was time to go home for a few days to check up on the outside world. We shut the house and left the next morning.

5

AN ISLE FULL OF NOISES

WE WERE ASTONISHED to find Brewster at Drumnadrochit. He had graduated in his course of adventure and was by his own reckoning a reformed character who looked back upon an aimless life with profound regret. He had asked Joan if he might stay the night with us before catching his train south, and she in the Christian charity with which she is over-endowed had agreed.

Certainly he was polite, helpful and pleasant, and one or two friends who drifted in and out of the house that night commented upon his manners. In the morning he asked me for a job at Kyleakin, remarking, with apparent sincerity, that such an opportunity would confirm his personal improvement. He undertook to work hard and be polite, and swore that if I allowed him to come I would never regret my decision. I told him that the decision was not mine to make but that I would ask Gavin about it. In truth, everyone likes a reformed prodigal, and I further felt a sadistic satisfaction that if a moral relapse did take place he would be answerable to me, and me only. Kindness be damned! It was no way to improve him.

When I told Gavin that I would have Brewster on the island he was amazed. "But you *hate* him," he said. "You can't want him to work with you."

"I know," I replied, "it surprises me too. But I'm really impressed by the improvement in him. If we reject him and he goes back to those influences—that background—all the good will be undone."

Gavin regarded me narrowly for a moment and then laughed: "You're taking the mickey out of me, Richard. That's my argument; you don't believe half of it. If you want him he'll be your responsibility. As you know, he's on probation, and you must square it with the authorities."

I did so, and Brewster joined us in December. He was never allowed to forget that he was there on sufferance. He was an improved worker. There were plenty of necessary and monotonous jobs to do which gave him time to reflect on our wise benevolence. Filling the water tank was one of these. Unlike the Isle Ornsay cottage this one had been sold to Gavin complete with an internal plumbing system. We had a bath, a boiler which provided hot water, and a sink; but someone had removed the pump which raised water from a well low down on the island to a tank near its highest point. The tank had also disappeared. Until these things were replaced we could only have hot water by charging the usual roof tank by bucket from the rainwater containers outside the house. This meant that probationer Brewster would fill his bucket, climb a short ladder into the loft, and treading with the delicacy of Agag approach his destination along a narrow duckboard laid across the joists, all in pitch darkness. We warned him that if he fell through the ceiling we would throw him into the sea, and he knew we meant it. It took about 50 trips to charge the system, but we were not merciless, and if Brewster carried out his task smartly and without resentment Terry or I would allow him to use our filthy bath water after we had finished with it.

Therefore, by the use of a certain amount of prep-school bullying, we moulded Brewster into some sort of civilized shape. If he showed signs of reverting, Terry would simply administer a few good thumps in the privacy of the bedroom and the matter would be dismissed.

Before Christmas the weather became furious with almost daily storms from the south and south-west. The two boys did the shopping together, leaving me in the cottage to work. Neither Terry nor Brewster was afraid of the sea, but the former had wide experience coupled with common sense, while Brewster was still untried. One afternoon a sudden storm blew up while they were away. I imagined that with the responsibility of the younger boy Terry would not set out from Kyle in such conditions. With the amount of rain and spray flying about outside, and an unbroken white line of surf on all the north shores, it looked very hazardous. Thinking about it

I was no longer sure that Terry would not have made an attempt to return; despite his caution he was a very capable operator in rough water, and a strong sense of duty coupled with a well-developed sense of the dramatic would bring him back if it were at all possible.

On Eilean Ban the rain spattered the windows in fury, the wind rolled and roared in the chimneys. There would have been a joy in walking on the island in the warm, wet rush of the salt, south wind but I was now filled with anxiety for the two boys, and stood at a window anxiously scanning the tossing grey water to the east. They did not return that night. The south wind grew even more violent; it rushed across the channel, screamed up the island, and barged full face against the cottage so that the windows bulged and rattled. It was impossible to sleep so I worked and read until three o'clock in the morning, when the storm suddenly ceased and only the splash of waves broke the silence. Then I went to bed.

Though tired, I slept badly. Subconsciously I was worried about the two boys and twice I thought I heard their voices outside the cottage. It was still dark and I wondered uneasily how they could have reached the island. The second time, the sounds were unmistakable, but something unusual in the cadence of the speech—unlike the carefree and bantering tones I should have expected—made an anxious thought run through me that this was not Terry and Brewster returned, but others to tell me of their fate. I went to the window and shouted loudly, but only the sound of water dripping from the ridge and the echoes of my voice came back to me through the darkness.

When next I woke it was broad daylight; the house was still empty. Great was my relief to see a small, unmistakable shape edging out of Kyle harbour. When they arrived they told me how they had made repeated attempts to leave Kyle pier but each time the engine had been swamped by rain and spray. The storm had been growing, they had conceded defeat and spent a comfortable night in a local lodging house.

Christmas was close at hand. We had made a good start, the floors were repaired, I had built two large, stone fireplaces and doors were filling the gaping entrances to the long room. There was still plenty to do but the final pattern was becoming clear. I ate my Christmas dinner with a sense of satisfaction.

We were back early in the New Year through a world that had grown white overnight. On the high ground at Cluanie the deer were nosing anxiously in the deep snow; Terry's venerable car ploughed uncomplainingly through it or skidded spectacularly on the white ice underneath. The winter was here and with it came a feeling of isolation. Though the coast was below the worst of the weather, sleet and frost made the unavoidable trips to Kyle unpleasant. We had no fuel other than occasional driftwood and old timber from the house, and this we hoarded for an evening blaze in the bedroom which would at least send us to bed warm.

It was about this time that Terry decided to leave us. His reason for doing so was Gavin's refusal to allow his woman friend to visit the island to see the wildcats which they had brought up together. He had not forgiven her for persuading Terry to leave Sandaig. Recalling her stay at that house— which he maintained had been uninvited—he gloomily prophesied a similar situation on Eilean Ban, and asked me whether I thought it reasonable that he should ban her from his property. Believing as I do in the sanctity of private property I had to answer "No" to this, but I am also a great compromiser and I saw in Gavin's denial of this simple request the seeds of further trouble. And so it proved. Terry, charging his anger with high principle, demanded his inclusion in the ban. Quite apart from his decision, which if put into effect would leave me with the rather ineffectual Brewster to minister to my needs, I felt that no harm at all would come of this small placatory gesture. The woman also had her pride and I felt sure she would not wish to linger on the island for any longer than it took to see the cats.

So I persuaded him without too much trouble and the next day the visit took place. I had thought that this gesture would satisfy Terry and in doing so I had underestimated the boy's sturdy spirit. He would have none of it. The incident had reminded him of the days when he was under Gavin's direct control and how he had bucked against his autocratic rein. Now he had the power of absolute decision he used it rightly, and after some initial coldness a new and adult relationship grew up between them which lasted until Gavin's death.

With Terry gone, Brewster's heart began to fail him. He

took over all the other boy's duties, and although he tried his performance left much to be desired. He was a poor cook and no food was safe in his hands. In order not to hurt his feelings I suggested he was doing more than his share with both the cooking and the washing-up. I became cook. His activities in the cold water of the kitchen sink so shocked me that in self-defence I had to re-wash up behind him. He was finally redundant in every sense of the word and he was also unhappy. I was not in his age group and we had nothing in common. He missed Terry whose strict attitude seemed to have given him a sense of security. One morning he told me that he no longer enjoyed the job, and it was with relief and no ill feeling that I offered to release him. Apart from the job there was a quite different reason why Brewster, for his own good, should leave Eilean Ban, but it is one that only he, I and a few others past and present will credit without scepticism.

Brewster was terrified because he had come into range of the island's psychic wavelength, and his subconscious mind had been invaded. Gavin had already suggested that Brewster was the embodiment of poltergeist activity at Sandaig—witness to which I had been on several occasions—but here his link-up with the unnatural was of another kind. The time-locked army on Eilean Ban were making themselves known to the boy by the echoes of voices that had died 1,200 years earlier. His was a primitive mind and uninhibited; as such it was both vulnerable and unable to rationalize the interruption in his thoughts, or the meaning of those distant sounds that welded sleep to the first moments of wakefulness. I was all too conscious of the same phenomena, but my more sophisticated mind was able to adjust to it in an uneasy acceptance that it was one of those things of which there are more in heaven or earth than Horatio (or anyone else) dreamed of.

But Brewster was panic-stricken and at night he would not be left alone. He followed me about like a shadow. When I went down to the boat for its final adjustment to wind and tide he would be with me, often in pyjamas, for he would force himself to keep awake until I had performed this nightly task. Even in the house he would not happily sit alone, but would often leave the comfort of the bedroom fire to find me and reassure himself that I had not gone outside. I had every sympathy for his situation which I determined should not be unnecessarily prolonged, and two days after he had asked to leave I took him to Inverness and packed him off home. We parted on good terms and it gave me genuine satisfaction to think that Brewster's sojourn with us seemed to have done him a power of good.

Before leaving Kyle we had pulled the *Eider* up a steep, rocky bank to a point at which I thought she would be safe from wind and tide. My judgement was badly at fault and while she might have survived one or the other, the combination destroyed her. A Job's comforter in Kyle gave Gavin the news and he telephoned me at home. Again he had no word of blame for me—although it was obvious that I had acted unintelligently—and simply suggested that I should commute with the island by hiring a local boatman until another dinghy could be procured. I was miserable, for I had adored the *Eider* which had been my first grown-up boat. I went to Kyle the next day to find out what the sea had done to her.

She lay untidily on the slope where we had left her, like a discarded toy. Her oars were gone and she was covered in seaweed. As I approached I saw some rocks inside her, and concluded that they were there to prevent her being lifted by the tide: then I realized that they were part of the slope and that all her bottom planks were gone. She was plainly beyond repair. Sadly I turned away to find a man of about forty wet summers regarding me with speculation. He annoyed me unreasonably.

"Yes?" I said, challengingly.

"Your boat, was it?" said he, in a soft, duplicitous West Highland drawl, and as I nodded: "It was very foolish to leave her there, what with the spring tide and all."

"I know." It gave me no comfort to have it confirmed.

"She had no chance. Murdo MacKessock and I watched her break up; aye, t'was on the Sabbath."

"Yesterday? You *watched* her? Could you not have done something to save her?" I exclaimed in outrage.

"Ach no. As I said, it was the Sabbath," he repeated with what may well have been genuine regret. I turned my back on him in disgust, for I knew he had obtained a wrecker's pleasure in the death of that boat, as his narrow bigotry absolved him from all responsibility to help a fellow human or protect his property on the day which, according to Christ, was made by God for man.

I decided to stock up and stay on the island until the new dinghy came. I was marooned at three o'clock that afternoon, and by evening felt an oppressive sense of isolation. Brewster was no soul mate but he had been contemporary (unlike my other timeless companions) and there was no escape from the island after dark. I decided to work through the entire night. This was not onerous, but I cannot sleep during the day: by the following night I was in a daze wandering round in circles and not knowing where to start. Sleep was plainly a necessity, and damn the captive echoes. I had refused Gavin's offer of a new assistant, so it was pretty obvious that I must come to terms with that nonsense. The presence of a boat—just in case —would have helped with that process. However—there was no boat and my eyes would keep open no longer.

I made myself a hot drink, went to bed and five minutes later was fast asleep.

Something hit my nervous system a massive blow. I think I was awake: I know I was not far from it. My whole body was poised as though at the last moment of breaking orgasm: my eyelids and my fists were tightly closed, my back rigid, my toes curled and my heart fluttered like a bird's. There was a single high-pitched clang which echoed in my ears and flashed in front of my closed eyes. I waited with a detached curiosity, feeling safe in the house because the house was in an inexplicable fashion innocent and uninvolved: I slipped down a few rungs on the ladder of consciousness; I did not go to sleep. As the minutes whispered by I waited uneasily but not in fear. The voices came with the rising of an old moon—the face of the ridge turned yellow-grey and a long bridge of glittering light joined Eilean Ban to Skye, cutting the sea that compressed the island like a tourniquet.

They were plotters' whispers, low and sibilant, breathed in urgent chorus; moving whispers, moving like invisible moles who tumble the soundless earth before them, creeping towards the east through the shadowed gully between house and ridge; there were the voices of creeping men, crouching men, low in the grass and brambles men, angry and violent men who had locked up all the fury of their violence in an echo that had vibrated for a millennium. After that first real, full experience

I learned to live with them and control my awareness of their ancient drama. Boredom and a blank, unconcentrated mind would bring my actors hurrying to their stage and in my exhaustion they would give their best performance. A continuous preoccupation with constructional problems, a well-written thriller at bedtime or a keenly constructed sexual fantasy were sure protections against the psychic invasion, as was a hopeful state of mind.

During the fifth day Simon MacLean—ex-lighthouse keeper on Eilean Ban and now island postman—brought a telegram from Gavin. It told me to expect a dinghy. Shortly afterwards Jimmy Watt and Noddy Drysdale—a Braehead boy who had taken Brewster's place at Sandaig—banged on the door in high spirits. "We've brought you a boat, Richard," shouted Jimmy. "Remember the pram—this one is even smaller!"

This one was called the *Assunta*, an ex-ships' lifeboat, displacing about half a ton, high, wide and handsome. She looked old and probably leaky but her dimensions would make her incomparable in rough weather. This was her great advantage, as was her carrying capacity; but the fact that she let in water made it impossible to leave her out on a running mooring for any length of time, and to pull her up on the shore called for both strength and determination coupled with pulleys and rollers.

Shortly after she arrived I took her to Kyle. The weather was bitter and a chance meeting with a coalman in the village led to an increase in my load which already included two hundred-weights of cement and four large bags of sand. After my return to the island I left her tied up and still unloaded while I drank some tea and changed my wet clothes; I had not taken into account the fact that she would leak twice as fast when low down in the water. When I came back to the jetty she was gone. I thought she must have drifted away but there were her ropes, going straight down into the sea. I looked over the edge of the jetty wall. She was seated comfortably on the bottom, in ten feet of water, carrying two bags of cement, three bags of much needed coal, the sand, and an engine which would take a night's work to dry out. To crown it the tide was just beginning to ebb so she would be "dry" in about five hours' time—i.e. midnight—and that was inescapably the time I must attend to her needs.

I dutifully returned at midnight in torrential rain with my baling bucket. I couldn't use the bungs because the tide didn't go down as far as I had hoped, her gunnels were almost flush with the sea so I had to stand on her centre seat and bale out about three hundred gallons of water. My only light was the feeble glow of the Tilley lantern which stood on the jetty. It took me three hours to refloat her and unload what was left of her cargo. I don't think I had ever been so miserable in my life as I climbed the path to the cottage and I still had to dry out the engine.

With the beginning of February came the most wicked weather I had ever experienced on the island. Night and day the south-westerly wind howled through the channel and huge, truncated waves sloshed into the jetty bay. The tides were getting smaller so that the *Assunta*, pushed and dragged up the jetty on two rollers, lay above the sea's venom. For some time I had been collecting a large amount of planking to build a single floor in the long room and I had recently brought a companion to the island—our Dalmatian bitch Hedda, large with pup. So with plenty of provisions, an amiable friend with whom I could discuss my problems without fear of argument, and a clean, satisfying piece of carpentry to occupy me, I was happy to ride out the storm. There was a special pleasure in watching the unmatching surfaces steadily giving way to an expanse of white floor, and I began to feel something of the contentment that one sees on the faces of those who work all their lives with good wood. Unfortunately I can never do anything in moderation if I can do it at all, and despite my satisfaction in the work I could hardly wait to see it finished. At four o'clock one morning with only a few planks left to secure, a chisel skidded off a knot and made a six inch incision in my left forearm. I looked at it in shocked disbelief as the wide mouth slowly gaped a bloody smile, and I began to feel very much alone.

It was not serious. A torn up sheet took care of it, but no more work would be done that morning. "Come on, Dog," I said, giving her fat belly a playful prod, "it's past our bedtime." We retired. I had a fire burning with coal and some peat I had dug from the back of the island, and it was quite a pleasant room.

Hedda had a bunk that had formerly been Brewster's. I had wondered how the dog—traditionally sensitive to such influences—would react to the voices, but in all the time she was to spend with me on Eilean Ban she seemed oblivious to them. At any rate that night she had other and more pressing problems to attend to. In the dark morning I woke to find her a proud mother with half a dozen Labratian puppies on her bunk.

6

UNGILDED GINGERBREAD

THE LIGHTHOUSE COTTAGE was no place for a nursing mother so the next day I took the new family home. My arm stiffened as the wound healed and it did not seem sensible to go back to work until full dexterity was restored. When I came back towards the end of February the great storm was over and there was a tiny hint of sweet spring in the air.

My constant presence in the house had obscured what had been done there: a fresh glance showed a well-advanced situation. I had every reason to believe that my contract would be completed by the end of March, leaving only the arrangements for electricity and a working water supply to be attended to. These matters, outside the original scope of my undertaking, were discussed between Gavin and me when he visited the island a few days after my return.

I had lit a great fire in one of my new fireplaces in honour of his visit. He had not been to see me since he had brought me the plans three months before, although we had been in contact by the telephone. I made a fine show for his benefit, cleaning up all my débris and so arranging unfinished things as to give a clear idea of how they would appear on completion. I love praise, it is food and drink to me, but I am also honest enough to feel little satisfaction unless it is merited. Now I wanted Gavin's thoughtful applause; on congratulating me on what he saw, it would please me to think that he was fully aware of the wettings, freezings, traumas, exhaustions, confusions, night horrors, and even woundings that I had experienced in order to arrive at this point. He did not disappoint me. He explored each piece of work with gratifying thoroughness and pronounced his absolute satisfaction. His flattering comments began in the hoped-for way: "How on earth did you get that up there?" or, "Surely no one man could have done that?" which elevated my uncertain self-esteem to a high point.

After about an hour the paean died down a bit and we began planning. We decided that a self-starting diesel generator would be the best means of providing electricity, both to supply the house and to drive the water pump. I had obtained some catalogues of a well-known make of machine which I showed to Gavin. It took him no time at all to choose one of the largest and most expensive in the range; it cost well over £500 even where it was. I suggested that we could do with something smaller and his attitude grew cool. "No, no, no!" he said, almost angrily: "*Never* settle for less than the best. We must maintain our prestige." It still worried me to think that the company (for which I felt some sympathy, as one does for any dead donkey which is being flogged) should suffer this new burden; it was no concern of mine except that I was already owed some money; but I thought that in decency I should pursue the point. I said: "Gavin, I am sure that the smaller ones are just as good. Do we really want all this power?" "We might want it, Richard; yes," he said, nettled, "if I decided to live here one day." It was the first time he had mentioned *that* idea.

The next thing was to wire the house for electricity: then to decide where to install the generator. I had little knowledge of this trade but I bought an illuminating *Do It Yourself* book and soon learned the essentials. It took me several weeks in and out of the dark confines of the lofts to complete the circuits, while outside spring began to take a grip on the countryside and a mass of unexpected daffodils brightened the slope below the cottage. Engineers from the local agents for the generator came to inspect for a place to site it. They dismissed the suggestion that the big machine should operate in the coal-store (which was part of the house) on the grounds of noise and vibration: they were keen to put it in a broken-down stone shed about 50 yards north of the house. This crumbling ruin was much too small as it was, but by taking off the roof and heightening the walls a sizeable building could be created. It would mean a lot more work, but I was glad of it; the weather was fine and warm, it was a pleasure to be outside. I told the engineers I would have it ready within a month, by which time the generator might be expected to have reached Kyle.

Knowing what they wanted I started to collect materials. I was glad that I had occupied Brewster in the rather penal exercise of striking the old mortar from the hundreds of used bricks that had come from the partitions inside the house. Cement worried me. I had often been unlucky in bringing it to the island, but now I took the matter seriously and built a sturdy framework of wood across the *Assunta*'s gunnels, which enabled me to carry half a ton of this formerly ill-starred commodity in two uneventful trips.

Simon MacLean had become my good friend. Although no longer resident at it he still maintained the lighthouse apparatus for the Board, and I used to look forward to his visits. He told me all manner of interesting local things and pointed out where I could obtain fine sea-sand without having to go too far afield for it. It did not worry me that the sand would be salt: the concrete made out of it would not require decoration. The hidden cove on Eilean Ban's neighbour, Gillean Island, to which Simon directed me was a fascinating place. Hidden behind a broken spine of reefs it penetrated deeply into the low, rocky back of the island. Its gently sloping narrow floor was thickly covered with beautiful shell sand which was easily obtainable at all states of the tide except high springs.

For three days I crossed and recrossed the half mile of sea between the two islands with three large tea-chests, a shovel and my faithful dog, now once again my companion. At the end of that time there was a mountain of sand on the Eilean Ban jetty. I had been liberal with my estimate, because once started on the building I did not want interruption of that process by running short of sand. To make assurance doubly sure, and with some daylight left, I decided to make one last trip and call it a day.

The best time to load the tea-chests was on a rising tide. The boat settled under the weight but in a few minutes the deepening water took her clear. This had always happened before; now it did not happen. The tide was near its peak and a strong wind had suddenly arisen and blown *Assunta* well up the cove. When I tried to push her clear after the customary pause she was immovable. There was still some tidal gain, so I took

Hedda for a walk round Gillean Island and left Nature to get on with it. Twenty minutes later she was just as fast and the tide was as high as it would get. Waves were running up the cove and sloshing over her high stern, no doubt soaking the engine. Action was called for. Taking off my Wellingtons I waded distastefully into the freezing water as far as the *Assunta*'s stern, which I pulled from side to side. She came free, but as I was easing her round a big wave knocked her into me and I tripped over something on the sea-bed. I went flat on my back, right underneath the boat, and through a welter of spray I saw the blunt line of her steel keel-strap hang above my chest, apparently supported by nothing more solid than foam. Somehow or other—too quickly for accurate memory—I caught a part of the boat and half-pulled, half-pushed myself clear before she descended with a whoosh to within a few inches of the sandy bottom. I returned to the shore to recover and reconsider my situation, remarking to the dog, who regarded me gravely, that it had been a near thing. I sat down feeling angry, then cold, and the cold fed the anger; suddenly I was filled with it, and I ran down into the sea, grabbed the *Assunta*'s stern and pushed with a strength charged with mania. She came free then all right, and down the cove we went together; as the water reached my neck I let out a Neptune's war whoop and hauled myself over the stern where I lay gasping like a stranded fish. The engine started on the first pull of the rope and I took her out into deep water, baling madly as I did so, for I have never seen a boat nearer to sinking. She had about six inches of freeboard left and for five minutes it was touch and go. Then before I had time to breathe a sigh of relief at my hard-won success a petulant sound above the roar of the engine reminded me that I had forgotten the dog.

An open boat is never a cosy place, even on the warmest of days. When you are soaked to the skin, tired, hungry and in a state of near shock, you feel there is no comfort or warmth left anywhere in the world. And the dog was out of her wits; she seemed unable to understand the simple thing required of her. Time and time again I brought the *Assunta* into one rocky point after another, swerving off again into the safety of deep water as Hedda, convinced that I was in playful mood, danced away wagging her tail with delight. The night was thickening and, even conspicuous as she was by her spots, I began to lose her in the gloom as she ran from point to point in her keen enjoyment of the game. I dared not bring the heavily-loaded boat against the rocky edges for more than a few seconds for the strong wind and surging water would have splintered her old planks like matchwood. Slowly I withdrew to a safe distance in search of a sandy bay or beach while the dog, suddenly frightened by my change of tactics, rushed along the ridges like one demented.

I had reluctantly decided to go right round into the lee of the island when Hedda overbalanced, shot down a slippery rock and fell into the surf. "This way, you stupid bitch!" I shouted for fear that she would drown in the turbulent sea, but I need not have worried. For her the game was no longer a game but a matter of survival—and she knew in which direction her salvation lay. In the few seconds which it took to pull her aboard we drifted within feet of destruction, but I was able to use an oar to push the heavy boat back to a safe distance. On the way back to Eilean Ban we shivered together in the stern.

With the contents of 50 tea-chests forming a miniature mountain by the jetty, my cement stored safely in the coal-store and a formidable pile of bricks on the site I was ready to start. Famous and far more worthy men than I have enjoyed bricklaying but I have always believed that, next to gardening, it is the purest of human pleasures. Enjoying every moment of my task in the fine spring weather I laid layer after layer until the walls stood ten feet high. Between them the grave-like excavation—into which the concrete forming the engine base was to be poured—grew deeper until I struck solid rock. Hedda hated that hole, and would not come near it; she sat at a safe distance and grinned encouragement to me every time I passed with spade or barrow, as only Dalmatians can. Soon the block was finished and the walls had reached their final height; a door, a wooden, felted roof, and suddenly it was all ready for the final touch, a wash of cement all over the brickwork near the top of which I inscribed my initials RBF in the month of May 1965. It had taken me twenty days from my first trip to Gillean and I was proud of myself. I waited just long enough to see the generator landed on the jetty and the engineers start their task of hauling it up the slope—a Gargantuan task calling for the secret ways of the pyramid builders for its success. Then I went home for a well-merited rest and a great brag about what I had been doing.

Four days later I came back out of curiosity. I expected it would take at least a week to set the machine on its block, but there it was, as large as life, and almost ready to start. I will never know how they did it.

My moment of truth was approaching. I should soon know how accurate (or otherwise) my work in the dark lofts had been. I had misgivings, for I could not believe that in all those hundreds of feet of wire there would not be a fault of some kind. After all, the budding electrician had been in the dark in more ways than one.

Unbelievably when the generator thudded into life for the first time no faults could be detected. It was a triumphant moment. I turned lights on and off like an ignorant savage, chuckling with glee at the magic of it. The toaster clicked, the electric kettle bubbled, a radio shouted its head off—I had done it all, I was God. There was just one little, undetected error which remained concealed for several weeks. I had set twelve pretty double sconces in the long room and in one of them a live wire was in contact with the body of the fitting. Gavin was entertaining some friends at the time. I was not there, but I am told that the story is true. As will be related at the end of this chapter Gavin and I fell out when the job was finished; I fancy my name would not have been mentioned much by him. Jimmy Watt, however, remained faithful to my memory. It is said that in the numerous toasts that were being tossed off he managed to include one to me for bringing, among other things, the "blessing of electric light" to the cottage. To steady himself as he raised his glass he placed his free hand upon the offending sconce from which he received such a powerful shock that he was thrown to the floor and rendered briefly unconscious.

The height of irony.

May and June are traditionally Skye's best months; that year they came right up to expectations. It is the time of the eider and the cuckoo, but looking back to that quiet interlude I must add the incongruous note of the generator to complete a nostalgic picture. Eilean Ban in the hot, summer weather was a pretty fair imitation of what we think Heaven ought to be like; while the transition of the house from a place of wet and cold and crumbling decay to a pleasant, functional haven was dramatic. There wasn't much to do before the promised date of completion but what there was still had to be done. After the murderous pace I had set myself I had lost momentum and had little interest left for unspectacular touches. For a few days I did nothing at all but float about in the dinghy or lie in the sun on the silver sand of Gillean Island. But Mediterranean conditions produce Mediterranean attitudes, and after a spell of delicious euphoria the prospect of returning to the dull, uninspiring tasks remaining was intolerable.

As luck would have it Gavin chose this moment to offer me an assistant. He did it with delicacy, knowing that I might resent someone who came along at this late stage when even the shouting was getting pretty faint. It so happened that I did feel it, briefly, as an intrusion on my proprietary attitude to the work, but common sense soon convinced me that I was becoming over-sensitive and that an extra hand would be just the thing for me. Noddy Drysdale had pleased Gavin by his work at Sandaig and was now temporarily redundant there. I could have him for a month.

Noddy was seventeen, cheerful and willing. He did not have to be asked twice to do anything, and he made no demands on me, for he had a compact personality and an infinite capacity for amusing himself. He did the routine things that had begun to weary me and left me with more heart to attend to the finishing touches.

In the second week of June, Gavin went to Iceland with Jimmy Watt to study eider-duck farming methods. He wanted to start an experimental colony at Ornsay or Kyleakin, the latter being the more favoured place. He had often spoken to me about it. Before they went, he paid me a short visit, the first for some time. I had small misgivings that he might have some new ideas at this late stage. In this way he was not unreasonable, but he was given to quick enthusiasms; he would disguise his wish in a passing suggestion and by repeated affirmations of confidence in my ability he would inflame me to a point where not to go ahead would seem cowardice.

Fortunately he was so full of his coming journey and the plan to start the eider colony that he had no room for further ideas for the cottage. In fact I found his lack of interest rather chilling, although his manner was friendly in the extreme: with satisfied glances and words of praise he dismissed my offer to show him the latest work and only remarked that he would be grateful if I would have everything ready for a small party of friends whom he wished to entertain in the cottage at the beginning of July. As this occasion had the flavour of a house-warming it did not occur to me that he would fail to invite Joan and me.

She joined me a few days later. Despite her declared intention to give Gavin no help with this house he had subtly persuaded her to choose a design for the long room's curtains, and having roused her interest he lost no time in feeding it. My daughter Jane—baby of the family at six years old—came with her mother. It was not her first visit, and she regarded a few days on Eilean Ban as one of the highlights of her young life. She always assured us that it was her favourite place. Vivacious and full of adventure she loved the sea and, in contrast to her father, had a joyous preoccupation with big waves which she called bouncies. She very soon learned to steer the big *Assunta* and to stop the engine; it took all her energy to start it. "Can I drive, Daddy?" she would ask, dressed in her little girl's oilskin and junior lifejacket, and only in the most turbulent seas would I consider it prudent to deny her wish.

On 21 June we invited two friends to stay on the island. Hardly anything remained to be done and the weekend had a happy carefree atmosphere about it, which only received a chilly check when Gordon Mackintosh saw the apparition of a man on the Cathouse path. Gordon later gave his account to Gavin who included it in *Raven Seek thy Brother*, and those who have read the book will be sufficiently familiar with it. I am convinced that this manifestation was on quite another psychic level to that of the "voices", but its shock to our friend was potent and lasting.

The longest day faded into a pretence of night—the brief twilight of the north when the sun changes into a silver-gold cupola on the horizon before sweeping up to another dawn. The outline of Beinn na Cailleach above the dozing village was clear and fine-drawn, blurred only on a high shoulder by a warp of mist. I lay back in a comfortable chair in a state of great good humour, filled with food and drink and with my friends around me. In the pretty, cheerful room—to which Joan's brilliant curtain design had given a crowning touch—proudly gleaming with its new paint and gay with its red-bonneted sconces, there was nothing to remind me of the dark and dirty cavern which Terry and I had first penetrated seven months before. I only wished that he had been there to appreciate the moment with me. I breathed a long sigh of satisfaction.

Gavin, back from Iceland, dashed in a week or so later. His expedition had been a huge success, and he was brim-full of information about eiders. His power to assimilate facts never failed to astonish me. In a week or so his knowledge of eiders, their environment, their habits and how to manage them, had become encyclopaedic, and his enthusiasm suggested that he would put all this information to good use. My own grasp of a new subject is indifferent, largely because I do not possess the habit of enquiry. I would have made an abominable journalist.

Gavin rushed round the cottage with uncritical satisfaction, apologized for the lack of time, and shaking me firmly by the hand dismissed me with: "Well, this *is* fine. I must go. I cannot thank you enough for all you have done here. I only wish I could repay you." He went.

Later that night I decided I was not pleased. He had not invited us to his party. Perhaps it was a trivial pique, but I had worked hard here. Neither of us received proper recognition for what we had done for him at Isle Ornsay. Through the long night I brooded upon this theme; did he take me for a workman? Our social equality could not be upset because he had paid me; he had always been careful to emphasize this point. At any rate, and for whatever reason, I felt we had been slighted, and in the early hours, when the forgotten hosts outside began their sinister prattle, a less than whimsical thought flashed through my mind that in those far-off days men knew how to settle injuries. Such satisfaction was denied me, but a few days later I was able to make my point.

Sadly now, in a mood of ungilded gingerbread, I did what

still had to be done, closed the cottage, pulled up the *Assunta* and went home. I was depressed, feeling like a triumphant runner who, amid the plaudits of the crowd, falls over the finishing tape and has all the wind knocked out of him. And two days later who should 'phone but Gavin. Offering him a neutral voice as I confirmed my number, I waited for him to start the conversation. He was in a low mood, and complaining. That I would not have. I hardened my heart, and listened. It seemed that a party had gone to Kyleakin in preparation for the stay, and had found "so much unfinished" there that it had delayed their return. Due to this—he inferred—the tides had been wrong at Kylerhea and the launch *Polar Star* had grounded. She—the vehicle on which he had hoped to make a regal approach to the cottage with his guests—was *hors de combat*, her port drive shaft twisted. Having heard my absolute refutation of any responsibility for his loss, he grew more friendly and presently asked me if I would care to do him a great favour. Deciding against it on principle, I waited to hear what it was. Well, it seemed that an engineering firm in Inverness would do a quick repair to the shaft and if it could be collected and returned to Sandaig the boat would be ready for his guests. Would I, in my Jaguar, do this for him, all expenses paid? Despite my rejection of the idea in advance, I believe I would have softened and agreed, had it not been for the mention of "expenses". This stuck in my throat. An errand boy?

"Wait a minute," I said, putting my hand over the mouthpiece to prevent my thoughts getting into the wire. It would have been so easy to say "Yes". A fast run in my powerful open car on a fine July day. It had an heroic quality like that of bringing the good news to Ghent. But I remembered our sense of anti-climax after the Isle Ornsay affair, the suspicion of rejection now. Our status was equal to his. In view of all this, to give him any further help would be obsequious. I would deny him.

I removed my hand, and spoke: "Gavin, I couldn't do that. It isn't convenient for me, not in the least. I'm sure any of your friends will be delighted to help you."

I thought he would understand me, and he did. Even then we had rapport, although hardly friendship. That was to come. He realized that my refusal contained a protest about something quite different. I imagine he even knew what it was. There was no room for any further words.

He put down the receiver and there was a silence. That silence lasted for many weeks. I settled down to a measure of peace, and a measure of boredom, equally mixed.

7

RESPITE

WHILE I WAS indolently settling down again to my aimless life Maxwell was having a rough time of it. Soon after the *Polar Star* incident he was afflicted with a savage abdominal pain which demanded a wild rush into Inverness, and hospital. An ulcerous condition had been whipped to frenzy by the continuous insults offered to a long-suffering stomach—much whisky and little food. The surgeon sternly advocated one or other of two courses of action, and mentioned a third. Our hero had little stomach for the first, and would have had less if the surgeon had had his way, which consisted of a prompt partial gastrectomy; the second called for a long stay in hospital under observation and treatment; the third, which Maxwell chose, was to go home after a few days and re-enter hospital in the following November for surgery. Considering the post-operational hash which had followed his lumbar sympathectomy so short a time before, and his inbred hatred of hospitals—in which he had spent more time than most people—it was a predictable choice, and one which was further supported by a telephone call from London. This spoke in bleak terms of a major crisis which had struck his sand-based company: a new broom had recently been elected to the Board and was sweeping away with an aseptic thoroughness. This broom, a gentleman in retirement from business, had noted in shocked surprise a widening gap between income and expenditure and had revealed a growing mountain of debt.

His cautious counsels did not go down well at all, and were regarded as spiritless and unheroic. "Sell the assets, every one of them." he advised. "Though we have nothing left, at least we shall owe nothing." To Maxwell, to whom retrenchment was the dirtiest word of all, this was heresy and treason. He would have none of it. The gentleman's seat on the Board, hardly warm, was whipped away from under him, Maxwell discharged himself from hospital, went back to Sandaig and his dissolute and ulcerating habits, took over the managing directorship of the company and made a good, if temporary, recovery both medically and financially.

When I heard this I was, to use a good old Scots expression, fair chuffed. This was indeed admirable insouciance. It showed a fine aristocratic disregard for the misgivings of others, coupled with the confidence and ability to put things right in his own time. To be sure, in a burst of conventional morality he applied a personal legacy to his company's debts; the money was gobbled up at once and he was left a sadder and a wiser man. In writing of this impecunious time in *Raven Seek Thy Brother* he laments that his quixotic gesture brought him close to the position of a friend into whose house a surly sheriff-officer entered to do diligence. His description of the law agent's archaic relish is only slightly embroidered: I should know, for I was the friend.

He now took a long, hard look at Sandaig expenses. These he trimmed rather than pruned, and on the whole it was a rather superficial snipping, and uneven. While he lopped off small twigs he gave the bigger branches no more than a hearty shake. Economy, to put it bluntly, was not in his nature, and if his living standard—and that of his Sandaig dependants— faltered, it was only to have a brief rest. Yet he survived to comfort his creditors and amaze the medicos who, when they examined him again in November, were unable to find any cause for urgent alarm and no reason whatsoever for an operation. It was somewhat unfortunate that the completeness of the one cure did not extend to the other; financially it was no more than a remission.

He had been told that salvation might lie in obtaining mortgages on the two lighthouse cottages, and to this end he bent all his efforts. At first he seemed to succeed, for his name and literary record gave him an assumed wealth, but when those whom he had approached detected an inappropriate urgency and saw the skull beneath the skin they prevaricated and finally withdrew. The two cottages, for a variety of reasons connected with their insularity, did not commend themselves to lenders. They would have probably raised money had there been more money behind them, but standing as solitary breakwaters against the flow of insolvency they were not worthy of serious consideration.

These were his circumstances when, in late November, after a mutually appreciated intermission, he approached me again. His true situation was by then very bad, chronic rather than acute, for his personal acknowledgement of debts—which I am sure he blamed on "mismanagement of company affairs"— would have had a staying effect on the ambitions of creditors. Of course, what was most alarming of all was the fact (unknown to me at the time) that his literary income, which a few years earlier had been "almost indecently large", to quote his own words, had now through imprudent anticipation halted altogether. Apart from a very small sum spent on the purchase of the two cottages, and an indifferent village house he had bought for Alan MacDiarmid's use, no money had been invested; and he had no private means.

He chose this inauspicious period in his affairs to ring me up and tell me that he was sure that the accommodation at Isle Ornsay ought to be increased so that the cottage might house twelve rather than eight people. He spoke brightly of spending a happy hour at his desk considering what physical alterations in the structure were necessary to make this possible; he added that the place would be much more appealing if it had electric light. I could not believe—knowing what I did of his condition —that these were other than academic and wishful imaginings, and when he asked me if I would be prepared to do them for him I seriously felt that he must have gone mad. In fact my amazement at his untimely suggestion and the complete lack of reference to the coldness of what had been practically our last conversation led to a suspension of my rational thinking to such a degree that I agreed to it without a single detail being mentioned. Asking myself why, later, I could only suppose that I had become such an addict to island life that its call overcame reason. It surprised me that I was no longer concerned over what I had felt quite deeply at the time, or worried that it might happen again. In truth he had his good side and his bad, and no perceptive man could deny that there was a certain persuasive magic about Maxwell.

8

ORNSAY REVISITED

THE MOON, LIKE a golden football, flew through the wild scudding clouds, while a huge, amorphous bank of mist bunched up on the horizon, like a monster bent on consuming the earth. The small black dinghy probed a cautious course through the falling tide which was sucking the water away between Skye and Ornsay Island. All afternoon the wind had blustered from the north, a bitter, breath-taking edge to it, but after a day spent closely in the confines of the cottage we had decided to brave the cold and take advantage of the sheltered channel to make merry at the Ornsay Hotel. Like Burns' immortal Tam we found the contrast between its warm interior and the "rattling blasts" outside sharpened by the effect of mine host's whisky, and we put prudence aside and relaxed like lords. When finally we were reminded of the time and tide a wild rush had ensued to push the dinghy down into the fast receding water. The tide was going out like bath water down a drain plug. We started the engine and raced across the choppy bay into the channel. Here we were brought up short as the propeller performed a rotary copulation with a great frond of seaweed, and stopped the engine with a grunt. We cleared it and proceeded with renewed caution.

The north wind harried us with paranoiac violence, whipping up a confusion of waves against the long, black sweep of the tide. Ornsay Island was black-pitted as a pool of moonlight drifted across it: it redoubled the darkness that came in its wake. Now only a few white shapes of sheep were to be seen on the hill and a line of spectral spray blossomed on the shore. I hoped the bar which separates Ornsay Island from Eilean Sionnach, the lighthouse rock, would not be dry. I had no wish to go round that rock against a great, black stormy sea, but there might be no choice: we could leave the boat nowhere but at the island's jetty where the winch would pull her up to safety.

My companion, David Ward, was sitting huddled in the bow, a baling bucket in one hand and a torch in the other. The boat leaked vilely and our sea-boots were filled with water. As we nosed into the bar David shone his torch down into the seabed; its sharp beam bored through the clear water to reveal yellow sand and shingle and long fronds of seaweed streaming out like the beards of old, drowned men. Under David's guidance we crept over the low shingle ridge with about a foot of water beneath us. Immediately there was a mighty commotion all round, as the turbulent sea driving in from the north bay clashed angrily with the withdrawing underflow. The tossing wave-crests exploded in spray, streaks of phosphorescence outlining their abrupt shapes. We were no more than a hundred feet from the house, from whose windows two Tilley lamps gave out a cheerful glow, but we might have been in the middle of the Atlantic for all the comfort the proximity gave us. Our progress across the tiny bay might well have been destructive if we mistook the position of the two rapidly drying reefs in the darkness. The racing moon now dodged thoughtlessly behind the corner of a fresh storm-cloud, and at the same time a heavy shudder proclaimed that we had struck the smaller of the reefs. Fortunately we bounced away none the worse, but the engine stopped. I told David I would row, and he, half-drowned with spray, peered into the shallow, treacherous sea with his torch. We eased around the larger reef, found deep water and slipped into the jetty. We winched the boat up, out of the hungry sea.

Such small adventures had become almost a pattern of the winter sojourn at Ornsay. We had been here for a fortnight. Despite my original intention to be alone on the island I had accepted David's offer to come and help me for the first three or four weeks. He is one of the few people I know who do not intrude upon my introspective nature, and as such for me is a near ideal companion. And, from a purely practical aspect, it would have hardly been possible for me alone to have completed the work in any reasonable time, for the winter days were very short and dark and the demands upon one's energy were many and varied. With no shop nearer than Broadford we were dependent for our food supplies upon visiting vans which arrived in Ornsay village at set times. Ornsay being a semi-tidal island, it was always necessary to decide whether to walk around the muddy bay or take the boat, so the collection of stores was left in David's hands, leaving me free to continue with the building work. David also did the cooking and attended at intervals to the great piles of fallen masonry, as I bored my way destructively through the massive wall which divided the kitchen from the lobby.

Looking back it seems to me that the most trying feature of this conversion was the fact that the cottage was fully furnished. With every room in the house filled to capacity—Joan's spacious arrangement topped up by Gavin—there was nowhere to move anything into, and the extremely wet weather made it impossible to leave anything outside even for a moment. As each massive block yielded to my sledge-hammer and crashed on to the mounting pile of débris the dust from the old lime mortar rose like a grey fog and penetrated every nook and cranny in the house. It went into the food, into the beds, it even found its way between the pages of the books we read when work was over for the day. Nothing could bar its insidious progress and gradually a universal greyness fell over everything, while we choked and spluttered as though in the final throes of silicosis. No sooner was the jagged gap opened in the kitchen wall and the stones and masonry removed hurriedly outside, than I set about the demolition of the two corridor walls including, to my sorrow, the arch designed by Joan, so that this dirty part of the work should be finally concluded and not returned to at some later time.

During these days we saw nothing of Gavin. The constant storms and the hopelessly unseaworthy boat would have made a trip across the Sound suicidal, although David and I would have thoroughly enjoyed an evening at Sandaig had the circumstances been different. We viewed him once through my telescope, walking pensively with the huge white dog Gus up the track above the house. Even at that distance we could see that his gait was not that of a buoyant man, and a telephone call confirmed that impression. I had asked his permission to buy some additional material. He accepted that my request was reasonable and that the stuff should be bought, but went on to tell me, as though I didn't know it, that his finances had taken a grave turn for the worse.

The comforting promises contained in the letters he had written to the company's creditors had lost their reassurance with the passage of time, and many people were again becoming actively anxious about their prospects. None of the good things he had hoped for had so far come his way while as rumours of his decline proliferated among solicitors and trade-protection agencies their clients, many of whom had been prepared to wait in silence for their turns, lost confidence and began to threaten.

He had sensibly abandoned any further attempts to mortgage the cottages and had given up hope that this could happen. It seemed to me that the situation had become sufficiently desperate to require a desperate remedy—the prompt closure of Sandaig, dismissal of his staff and disposal of the two famous otters. I knew equally that to even suggest such a drastic course would be to incur his scorn; it was the unthinkable thing, like asking an ardent Catholic to dispute the existence of God with his parish priest. Apart from anything else it was Jimmy Watt's home and his living, and Gavin's affection and consideration for that young man would have caused him to retain Sandaig as an active proposition even in the absence of any other reason. It was Jimmy himself who was shortly to offer him a chance to break with a situation which in a way had become a tyranny.

Gavin rang me a week later, towards midnight, on a night of excessive storm; the sea was exploding whitely on the lighthouse rock and hurled flying spume against the dripping tower, but the night was no more bedraggled than his mood. At first I could not hear him, he was muttering vilely with long pauses between his inaudible words. "Speak up, Gavin," I shouted, "I can't hear you. There's a hell of a wind over here. It's a dreadful night."

"It is a dreadful night, Richard," he answered; "and a dreadful night for me as well. I have just spoken to MacFerret (or some such name) about his account. The little bastard was keen enough to have my custom when he was starting up; now he can't wait to put his lawyer on to me. But I'm growing used to this although it still makes me angry. But"—he paused interminably and drew a long melodramatic breath—"now Jimmy wants to leave, and I just can't go on."

Suddenly I realized that this was real tragedy for him, and

Gavin Maxwell with otter.

Gavin Maxwell with Andrew Scot and otter.

Gavin Maxwell with deerhound Dirk at Sandaig. Colin Jones, *The Observer*

Maxwell at the wheel of his open topped Mercedes Tourer, with Jimmy Watt and his unidentified companion on track leading to Sandaig.

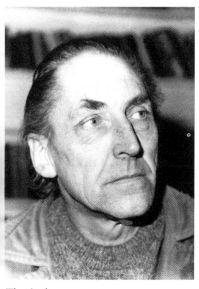

The Author.

Edal 1967.

Andrew Scot and otter.

Above: Gavin Maxwell at his desk.

Sandaig in winter, 1961–62.

Gavin Maxwell with deerhound Dirk at Sandaig

View of Sandaig showing otter house extension with Maxwell's Pyrannean mountain dog Gus.

Sandaig after the fire.

Maxwell's launch *Polar Star* at Sandaig.

the knowledge took the shallow flippancy out of my mood. Jimmy had been with him since he was thirteen and had grown up in the post-Mij period of Camusfearna, to become a part of the place as the place had become a part of him. If he went he would take much of the spirit from the Bay of the Alders, and I did not think that Gavin would quickly or readily return, or if he did he would not stay long, if the boy were gone. Using hindsight I was aware that I had noticed that Jimmy, though he returned Gavin's affection in full, offered a mild but stiffening resistance to Gavin's possessive attitude. He wanted to spread his wings and make a life for himself beyond the periphery of the older man's benignant influence. Looked at from any point of view it was an unhappy situation which admitted of only one moral remedy, that the possessed be released, and I hoped that in the process no more emotional pressure might be brought to bear than was necessary. I sympathized with Gavin because he was out on a limb and very vulnerable, and I comforted him as best I could.

What did not occur to me—or if it did I could not find it in my heart to mention it—was that this was the very moment for him to cut the lesser ties that bound him to Sandaig, to rid himself of the whole, intolerable burden of debt and live a comfortable life elsewhere as his uncluttered income would then allow him. But the moment passed in which I might really have been of use in putting my shoulder to a wheel that had perhaps begun to stir, and our conversation ended on a note of sterile gloom.

Yet he was nothing if not resilient, and in a strange way his resilience was contagious; a change in his mood not only activated the humours of his companions but incredibly stimulated events. In the two days before I next heard from him the whole immediate pattern of his life had altered. He told me that Peter Janson-Smith, to whom he was wont to ascribe superhuman ability in money-raising, had done it again and had obtained a sum of some substance by way of a further advance from his publishers. Jimmy had agreed to postpone his decision about leaving until the general situation grew more settled, and I was requested to make no comment upon the matter while it was *sub judice*—at least, not to Jimmy. These two events added up to a bright sunrise. Though hardly convinced that all was right with his world I was pleased that he had obtained a breathing space, and felt it might be an appropriate moment to ask for a new boat.

The *Black Dinghy*—by which sinister description it was known to the company's insurers—had been our only form of marine transport at Ornsay since we started there. It was a wet boat. A very bad thing had once happened to it which made the fitting of an entirely new bottom and keel necessary, and thereafter it never ceased to leak copiously. As a patient rejects his transplant heart so did this perverse dinghy refuse to accept its new planks, and it continued to be a trial and tribulation to those in peril on the seas until it was literally torn to pieces when being towed in a great storm at Kyleakin two years later. David and I were heartily sick of it, for, apart from the constant necessity of baling, it was not a good seaboat, having too narrow a beam for safety in the steep seas we often encountered.

Gavin was sympathetic and helpful, and admitted that he had just purchased two boats, one new and the other second-hand but in excellent condition: it was this latter that he gave us. It was a great relief to us both. He told us that Jimmy would bring it over to us by boat-trailer that very afternoon. It was arranged that we should all meet at the Ornsay pub at opening time to have a quick drink together and to take delivery of our new boat. Unfortunately in the early afternoon a sudden squall whipped up such a rough sea that we thought it unwise—with salvation so close at hand—to risk our lives on the journey round Ornsay Island (a low spring tide made the channel out of the question), so we missed Jimmy. He, in better spirits than I had known him for some time, rang us up from the appointed place saying he quite understood the reason for our absence, that he would leave the boat in a safe position above the high tide to be collected at our convenience, and that he would like my permission to charge to my small account at the pub the cost of the large whisky he knew I would have bought him had I been there. Doubled up by this delicious piece of Wattish whimsy I just failed to catch his parting words which took the form of a postscript. The only thing I heard sounded like "bung-ho" which as a salutation between drinking men seemed entirely appropriate.

Between five and six o'clock the wind dropped suddenly and the moon rose rapidly above the tide-swollen channel. It seemed as good a time as any to collect the boat and I was impatient to see what she was like—for her seaworthiness was going to make a big difference to our lives—so I called David and proposed this plan. He demurred—which was quite unlike him—and asked me to excuse him on the grounds that he thought himself poisoned by eating a traditional mixture of choice seaweeds which he had pounded into a pudding and thereafter boiled. I had fortunately declined to do more than taste this concoction, which was greenly and lividly spotted like Lorenzo's decomposing head and smelled slightly of urine. I excused him and set out undeterred.

The night was beautiful as the *Black Dinghy* chugged down the channel on what I fervently hoped would be her last voyage, but the inevitable storm cloud soon stood up in the west and started to spread its slow stain across the starry sky. I reached Ornsay bay in good time and drew the dinghy up beside a brave shape which was plainly the new boat. She was quite splendid lying there, with a good beam on her and a fine pair of oars which made the splintered stick we used on the *Black Dinghy* look very shabby and inefficient. I walked over to the pub, paid for Watt's drink, charged two more up to him and having changed the engine from one boat to the other set out on the return journey. By now the moon had gone, as well as most of the stars.

The seaweed I struck at the entrance to the channel was as tough as new rope and nearly wrenched the engine from the boat. I decided that in the dark it would be easier to row. As I removed the engine I realized to my disappointment and disgust that the boat was nearly full of water. It sloshed deeply and as I staggered forward I feared that she would dip her bow into the small waves. She was obviously sinking, and sinking very fast, and there was nothing I could do about it. The water seemed to be coming in from two large holes at opposite ends of the boat: I could hear it gurgling quite distinctly. Grasping the oars I rowed as hard as I could in the direction of Ornsay Island, but I had only taken a few strokes when her nose submerged and she was full to her gunnels. She sank slowly in about four feet of water and I, drowned in misery and disillusionment, went down with her until the icy water froze my genitals and brought my breathing to a gasping halt. I walked about on Ornsay Island to keep myself alive until the tide might go out sufficiently for me to go dry-shod across the bar. It was now raining steadily. After an hour or so I noticed that the boat was becoming high and dry, and with time to spare before I could walk to the cottage I thought I would investigate the condition of this abominable craft. I bent over the gunnel and ran my frozen fingers along the bottom. The planks seemed solid enough. Suddenly I found a hole, small and round and quite certainly there by design. At the other end of the boat there was a second hole. I felt below the thwart, searched around for a few moments and found what I was looking for—two corks of the appropriate size. A deep sigh escaped me as I inserted them, pushed the boat back into the sea and rowed quickly round to the jetty. As I approached it a torch flickered dimly and David, pale as any birch and shaking like an aspen, came to the path to greet me. He had been alarmed at my long absence: a telephone call from Jimmy had not relieved him. I emptied my boots with some ceremony, and asked casually: "What did he want?"

"He wanted to confirm that you had heard what he said."

"What did he say? And when?"

"When he 'phoned from the village. Said he thought you grudged him his dram too much to listen. It was about the bungs."

"The bungs?" I murmured, peeling my socks from feet devoid of all sensation.

"Yes. He took them out because he thought it might rain at Ornsay and if we didn't collect the boat for a few days it might fill and burst. He says it's absolutely watertight. He also said he hoped you heard him."

I removed my trousers, squeezed them carefully and handed them to him: "Have them cleaned and pressed for me by morning, Jeeves. And now run my bath. God knows I could do with one. Bung-ho, indeed!"

We did not savour the delights of the new boat at once. David and I decided that it would be much better maintained if we kept it constantly in the water, thus avoiding the stresses and scrapes of winching up, and we had arranged a "running mooring" to a small fixed buoy off the jetty. This simple device consists of an endless rope running in two pulleys, one fastened to the buoy and the other to a steel pin cemented to the rock. A short length of rope is plaited into the endless one and attached to the bow of the boat which can then be drawn out to the buoy and retained there until required. The morning after my misadventure with the bungs we put the boat on the mooring.

By evening the wind had begun to rise again and David went down to the jetty to confirm that the boat was safe. All was well. By midnight a hurricane was blowing, as strong a wind as any we had experienced on the island. We put on our waterproofs and struggled down to the shore. At first we could not see her at all, for the light from our torches was diffused by sheets of spray, but just as we were becoming really worried I caught a glimpse of her shape, vague and spectral, in the raging sea. She was riding high and bucking like a mad thing with a rhythm that had almost a gymnastic precision about it, and she was as helpless as any puppet. Fortunately we had great confidence in the mooring. Nothing should go wrong. It was, however, patently impossible to recover her while the storm lasted; she would have been smashed to pieces against the jetty or the surrounding rocks.

The storm lasted for four days, and each day it grew colder until the brown hills around us were covered in a mantle of snow. One night the wind dropped, the sharp stars glittered overhead, and a sudden frost drew a skin of ice across the island. We foraged for driftwood to burn in the open grate and lit a cheerful fire. Thinking the storm was over we left the boat where it was, but by morning the temperature rose again and with it the wind. It blew hard for two more days. The boat sank at its moorings as the storm was passing, overwhelmed by the accumulation of rain and spray; we collected the oars and bottom boards as they were washed ashore. She was unharmed, and soon we were able to ease her ashore. By then it was the first day of December.

I was anxious to be at home for young Jane's birthday which was the next day. I 'phoned a still cheerful Gavin to tell him that we would be away for a day or two, and he applauded my reason. He ascribed great importance to keeping faith with children, and would have been the first to urge me on my way to keep this important engagement. He was very fond of Jane, and she of him; they got on well together, and he seldom

failed to give her a handsome present on her birthday, or at
Christmas, which was usually of a book inscribed with some
amusing and appropriate message.

We set out early, for a glance at the icily sculptured peaks
above Glenshiel pointed to difficult road conditions below,
although the wet, black roads in Skye tended to lull us into a
sense of false security. Things changed as we climbed towards
Cluanie; the hard surface soon vanished beneath sandy slush
which itself became hard and ridged as we neared the top of
the glen. I was driving an Austin Mini and while its powered
front wheels were just the thing to pull us over the increasingly
slippery surface, its small clearance began to provide a problem.
The big wheels of larger vehicles had bitten deeply into the
snow and had left a high central ridge polished hard by many
sumps. Without warning there was a loud grating noise and
the engine raced. David and I sprang out in alarm. The Mini
was grounded and its four wheels hung uselessly just above
the ruts.

We had been near the middle of a queue of cars. Just
behind us came a shooting-brake with four burly fishermen
anxious to get home. Their leader hailed us in a tone of cheerful menace—"D'ye ken you're in the way?"—and the rest
sprang out and half pushed, half lifted us, for about 50 yards.
Here the snow was shallower and our tyres were once again on
solid ground. We set out in hope, but the hope was short-lived.
This time the fishermen were noticeably less cordial, much
more urgent. Without pausing for permission each took hold
of a corner of the Mini and lifting it clear of the ground
deposited it gently in a snowdrift on the side of the road.
"Ach, weel," said the biggest, "ye'll be fine the noo. Ye'll no
be in onybody's way there." This was small comfort. The
fisherman apologized in his bleak Aberdeenshire way for lack
of space in the brake, but expected that we would not be long
in getting a lift.

As it happened we weren't. The last car in the queue stopped.
It was of German make, rear-engined, and the driver was a
wild-eyed gentleman in a blue serge suit. "Care for a lift,
boys?" he asked rhetorically. Our benefactor was a council
official from the Western Isles. He was friendly, discursive and
going to Inverness, but what we shall remember him for was
his total lack of road sense. We soon settled down to a steady

60 miles an hour on the ice-bound single track road down which the car guided itself with the fixity of a railway train. Our man—who wasted no time in unnecessary concentration on the road—kept turning to us to emphasize a point in conversation (to this day neither of us can remember the subject of it) and each time he did so some stiffness in his joints caused him to press sharply upon the accelerator. I was hoping against hope that we would catch up with the slow-moving traffic ahead before some fatality intervened—even this Hermes could not expect to overtake as things were—when to my horror I saw the narrow headlights of a Land Rover approaching. "Blue serge" was in hearty discussion with a preoccupied David upon the spreading evil of the drinking habit in South Uist when I gave him a nervous tap on the shoulder. He turned his head towards the road. The only practical sign he gave of the approaching peril was an attempt to urge his car to climb a bank of sheer ice on the left of the narrow lane: he slowed down not a whit. Fortunately the Land Rover driver was more *au fait* with present reality, and his vehicle more able to cope. He was reduced to a crawl and half off the road when we struck him a powerful but glancing blow and were thrown up and over the ice hummock on our side.

We landed at right angles to the road, pointing downwards. "Blue serge" uttered a deep sigh of resignation and made a notable remark while I switched off his ignition: "Boys, I am told that I am probably the second worst driver in the world." We were never able to understand why he had been allocated second place.

For myself I was not unhappy to remain where I was, it was quite warm and relaxing and I was busy with my prayers. Mercy, usually withheld, should always receive due recognition. David, also, seemed quite averse to continuing the journey by car and whispered to me that if we walked strongly we could be home in about five hours. "Blue serge" was made of sterner stuff. He quickly organized the next few cars to come in our direction (the Land Rover, damaged as it must have been, had preferred flight to further involvement) and before long quantities of hands were busy at our reinstatement. Morally we could not ask for a transfer.

Off we went again. The incident had in no way sobered

"Blue serge". He bowled along with the wild abandon of a high-speed toboggan. As we reached Loch Ness-side, conditions were much improved with only occasional patches of black ice and belts of mist. Then it began to rain. He took some time to find the switch of his windscreen wiper and when he did one of the blades fell off. He drew up with a hideous squeal of tyres in the middle of the road between two blind corners, and went to recover it from where it lay on the bonnet. David was sitting in the back of the car, in front of the engine. I could feel the heat from his sweat.

"Blue serge", back in the driving seat, mused: "Why is this *always* happening to me? Not worth getting a new one. Won't keep this car forever, you know, boys." We were still standing in the middle of the road. Lights flashed suddenly behind us and the outraged hoot of a horn sounded a few inches away as a car brushed by and vanished in the mist. David briefly fainted.

And yet we reached home intact. "Blue serge's" last remarks were in the nature of a veiled apology. "I never had a test, boys. Was driving before they came in. Wouldn't pass one now, would I?" He was given to rhetorical question.

We walked unsteadily up my drive. Here the mother of one of Jane's little friends nearly ran us over. David muttered something about being killed after the armistice. It was still only about five o'clock. We met a welcome of bright lights, cheerful music and children's voices. We were glad to be alive. A shout went up as we entered the door and people fussed around saying they had almost given us up. My little daughter ran up to me and kissed me: "Daddy, just in time to cut the cake."

I did so, with a trembling hand.

We spent a few days at my home and then returned to Ornsay after recovering the Mini, none the worse, from a shrunken snowdrift. The weather had now entered into the quite customary period of pre-Christmas calm, that tantalizing time of bland days and nights with only the bare trees and the deadness of the yellow grass to remind one that the late northern spring is not so close as it would seem. For most of the next fortnight our little island lay like a black smudge upon a mirror, the wind hardly stirred the sea around its rocky coast. This was the time when an old grey seal paid us a visit and poked his curious bewhiskered nose out of the water each time either of us went down to inspect the boat; he always gave us a solemn glance before slithering off his usual rock into deep water. At night the seabirds shouted loudly in the unusual stillness.

We decided to visit Gavin and Jimmy by boat. Gavin had asked me to collect a small number of articles for the next tenants of the cottage, and this seemed a good moment now that we had both a safe boat and gentle weather.

We found the two friends in a merry mood. From their mutual ease and affability it was impossible to detect any trace of the emotional tug-of-war of which I had heard. When Jimmy spoke of Sandaig affairs it was as though he always expected to be there and Gavin gave no hint that he believed it could ever be otherwise. They were—as I had first and subsequently known them—the heart and the soul of Camus-fearna, a strangely perfect relationship within a brightly-coloured vacuum, and yet, because life is what it is, it could not carry the stamp of permanence.

As always we ate well and drank in a lordly fashion. The evening went by all too quickly. At around eleven o'clock I said that we must be going and even Gavin, the eternal worrier, could foresee no grounds for disaster on that dead calm sea. He had kindly offered us some comforts—including a bottle of whisky—from ample Sandaig stocks, and while David and Jimmy were getting these together he asked me to join him in his study for a nightcap. As he poured my drink he seemed to have aged by ten years, and suddenly his voice was flat and tired. "My God, Richard, I'm exhausted," he said; "keeping up this front is hell." At my questioning look he went on: "Jimmy doesn't know how bad things are. He knows most things, but I'm keeping the worst to myself. I don't want him to think that we can't afford him—just when his decision about staying is in the balance. Promise me that you'll keep what you know to yourself."

David's help had been invaluable to me and I began to look with concern to his departure around Christmas. By profession a composer of highly intellectual music, he earned my undying admiration by pursuing his complex art form amid falling masonry and dust which rose like the death of a civilization.

He was also at this time fascinated by the character of Marco Polo and would read to me long passages from a definitive book on the intrepid explorer and the strange sights he saw. This kept the mind from narrowing, for ours was nothing if not an insular existence.

The year ran out with a quiet dignity after the excesses of early December. I was well ahead with the building programme, there was plenty of time in hand to do what had been arranged without rush or stress; we shut up the house a few days before Christmas and went home. Gavin was making plans to go back to Africa in February for final research for his *Lords of the Atlas*, so it was clear that Jimmy would still be in control for some months whatever his final decision might be. I had undertaken to finish my work by the end of March, which would give a month's grace before the letting season began. It seemed without point to return to Ornsay before the New Year when I had so much time in hand, especially as I would be going back without either David or Marco Polo. So we had a happy Christmas and the year 1965 like so many others came to an uncomplaining end.

Even into middle age I have retained a whimsical belief in the ancient significance of that point in time when one year changes into another. Once I saw it happen on a mountain top in a flurry of snow and an unholy darkness that was punctuated with flashes of St Elmo's fire. It had been the first day of 1940 and not, in its way, inappropriate.

After the chimes of Big Ben we made our usual phone calls to absent friends. By about twelve fifteen it was Gavin's turn to be greeted. "Happy New Year!" said I happily. He sounded glum in the extreme as he replied: "By all means have a happy time, Richard. I shall not. I am alone in this house. Jimmy has gone to the village with friends. I feel the time has come to be realistic, for I cannot go on like this——" He paused, and I swallowed. Never had there been a man able to knock the sun out of the sky so quickly. He went on: "I am now quite sure that Jimmy will leave when I return from Africa. I should not blame him: I suppose he must have a life of his own. I think you should take over control of this company. You know everything about me and no one is better fitted to it than you are. What do you say?"

I answered with a strained sobriety which must have sounded

pompous that it was kind of him to think of me in these terms, but that I must have time to make a decision. I said I would think about it. And, as the morning wore on I kept my promise, and disappointed the festive friends, to whose houses we went, with my thoughtful and serious air. For it seemed to me, knowing him as I did, that this association must be more than just a business one, nor might it ever be terminated. I could foresee that I would become his confidant, his co-conspirator, his *alter ego*, for though there was much about him that, in earlier days, I had not liked I could not deny that a strong understanding had grown between us that had nothing to do with friendship. Yet I could only guess to what extent he would try to impose his personality upon me, or condition my mind to a ready acceptance of his changes of mood. I knew that he would monopolize my time beyond the terms of any contract we might draw up, and he being a wilful man and I an indolent one there were few indignities I might not suffer if I were to oppose him.

Having in my cautious fashion examined one side of the coin I turned it over to see what was to my advantage. A salary, certainly, for knowing my sparse resources he would not offer me an honorary position. This, in all honesty, was a sure inducement. Beyond that—well, let me admit that I was flattered to have been asked to eat my bread in the company of a clever and famous man.

As the January dawn grew grey in the sky and the celebrations flagged, I made the decision required of me. Considering the occasion I was remarkably sober.

9

ON COMPANY BUSINESS

I FINALLY TOOK over the management of Gavin's company in May 1966, although my agreement to do so had been made five months earlier. He had made it clear that my assumption of the post was entirely contingent upon Jimmy's voluntary departure, and to this I had no objection. I had no other plans for employment. Jimmy, not surprisingly, found it hard to break with the life pattern into which he had been moulded during eight of his most formative years. He was like an unfledged bird who teeters on the edge of the nest, unwilling to remain in the cosy security he has all but outgrown yet overawed by the unfamiliar expanse below. I suspected that Gavin's influence upon the young man's development had been extensive, and had Jimmy not been possessed of a stubborn streak it might have been absolute.

Once he had made up his mind to go Jimmy agreed to postpone his departure until 21 May: on that day I should take his place. Gavin went to North Africa in February and did not return to London until April. During this time I finished my work at Isle Ornsay.

On his return from North Africa I met Gavin in London. He did not intend to come north for some time—as I had rightly guessed, the idea of Sandaig without Jimmy made him sad—so we had agreed to exchange his Mercedes roadster which was in Glasgow for the Safari Land Rover which had been to Africa with him, and would now be my personal transport. In his Chelsea flat we spoke at length upon the problems I should be inheriting in a few weeks' time and I was relieved to note a slackening in his determination not to retrench. While I had formerly thought of his inflexible attitude as heroic, now that I was about to be involved in his affairs I found the idea of compromise even more appealing. He spoke seriously of sending the two otters, Teko and Edal, to a zoo, thus making it possible to shut down Sandaig, and I began to wonder where I should fit in if this programme were to be carried out. At this particular moment it was contingent upon suitable zoo accommodation being offered by one of the many establishments to which he had written, and until this happened no change would take place.

In the meantime the financial situation was extremely difficult, but the promise that this major relief would be brought, even at an unspecified time, might make it possible to bluff one's way through the difficult months ahead. Literary income would no doubt come to our aid before long. Gavin had also admitted, when pressed by me, that he would *in extremis* sacrifice Isle Ornsay cottage by way of sale, but he was determined to hang on to Kyleakin. All in all the situation was not bright; but there were rays of hope.

We parted the best of friends and mutually satisfied, I think, with our new business association. He went back to his attempts to find a suitable zoo while I drove north in the sand-coloured Safari Land Rover with which I was to become so familiar in the years to come.

In the middle of May I went over to Sandaig to learn the details of my new work. I was taking over not only from Jimmy Watt but also from a young man named Michael Cuddy whom I had met from time to time: he had been in charge of the London office of the company where he had carried out the functions of public relations, secretary and much else. Gavin had relieved him of his command—or, rather, liquidated the command itself, leaving Michael standing at the head of a vanished troop—when he had carried out his celebrated trimming the previous year. Michael was a very punctilious young man with as keen an eye for detail as I have ever seen; perhaps too much so, for in his close scrutiny of the bark he had failed to notice that most of the trees had fallen down. He was vastly indebted to Gavin who had seen him through a difficult patch, and he ascribed to his London office a dignity and a much greater importance than was its due. He was in fact a company man—in as apt a sense as this term can be used—in so much that he believed in GME Ltd as a child believes in faeries, and had become an executive in a make-believe world.

Michael had come to Sandaig (which he loved, for he was a countryman at heart, and its sea and its solitude suited him) to add his quota to my instruction. On the planned date the investiture took place and with small ceremony I became the new incumbent of the office of company manager. With my predecessor's help I loaded up the Land Rover with a dustiness of files, office equipment and adjusted records and made for home to set up headquarters in Drumnadrochit.

As the days went by my sense of authority grew. As my prime function was plainly to foster economy I began to talk to Gavin on the telephone along these lines and to send him small written reports on the progress of my axe-work. As I fancied would be the case, Gavin himself was the biggest stumbling block in the way of my attempts to cut major expenditure.

Just after our meeting in London, and unknown to me, he had engaged a youth called Sinbad Jones to operate the ill-fated *Polar Star* and bring the male employee strength at Sandaig back to two. Noddy Drysdale, of whom I had formed a good impression at Kyleakin, was the other boy. I told Gavin that in my opinion the boat had become an impossible luxury and, considering its record, a potentially dangerous burden which was reasonably safe only on its steel cradle until a total change of circumstances made its return to the sea permissible. He argued spuriously that potential tenants (or buyers) of the lighthouse cottages might be taken there in speed and style, and that this would more than justify the extra expense incurred in keeping an additional boy at Sandaig and the boat in the water. This was nonsense, of course, as far as *Polar Star* was concerned, but his contention that a second boy was necessary was not. There were too many risks inherent in the everyday work at Sandaig—danger in driving down the precipitous track, mishap on the sea or injury from the otters, to name but a few—to allow one to leave a boy there on his own without misgivings. Despite this it was still not necessary to employ Sinbad Jones, for yet another person was on her way.

Catherine Baxter was a woman of thirty or so, living apart from her husband. She had met Gavin from time to time and had typed the manuscripts of some of his earlier books. Recently she had asked him if he would allow her to use one of his houses to store her furniture in until she was ready to buy the house; and it was agreed that in the meantime she would stay at Sandaig and look after its human and animal occupants. She had been expected to arrive before Jimmy and Michael left but had been delayed by a car accident. I understood from them that Mrs Baxter was an excellent housekeeper, had a small daughter and kept one or two dogs. She seemed an extremely good idea to me.

I was sure that my first need was to get *Polar Star* safely tucked away on her steel cradle—at present she was moored uneasily on a buoy to the north of Sandaig lighthouse—and Sinbad sent away as a redundant sailor. Gavin did not agree to this now, but I suspected that I could bring him round to my way of thinking.

As company manager I had arranged my working week in such a way that there would always be a free day to visit Sandaig; the rest to be spent in office work at my home. My first task was to advise uneasy creditors that there had been a further change of management, that I shared my predecessor's concern at the number of unpaid accounts in my files, and that they might rest assured that I was not treating the situation lightly. I implied, of course, that there had been mismanagement of company affairs which by now was traditional and expected of me. The evening before my first routine trip to Sandaig, Noddy Drysdale rang up to say that Mrs Baxter would be grateful if I would pick her up at Inverness station the next morning.

I was alarmed to find Catherine Baxter still on crutches. Sandaig was no place for a cripple. Seeing my concern she explained that her injuries were almost cured but she had brought the crutches just to be on the safe side. Her halting movements and the hastily concealed expression of pain as I helped her into the Land Rover belied her words. She was an attractive woman with striking blonde hair, a practical person of great determination and immense vitality. She had promised Gavin (of whom she was obviously very fond) to look after his boys and otters, and the mere incident of a motor accident that could well have been fatal was not going to deter her any longer than was necessary from doing so. Her young daughter was a pretty child, intelligent and self-sufficient—the latter a necessary quality where she was going. When we arrived at Tormor and turned off the main road on to the appalling track that leads by way of precipice and quagmire to Camusfearna, Mrs Baxter saw that I was uneasy about driving down the two last hills and said: "You wouldn't take the car down if I wasn't here, would you? I'll walk"; and nothing I could say would dissuade her. The journey down the rough track in her condition must have been agony, but immediately on arrival at the house she brushed aside my offer to make coffee and said, "Woman's work. I'll do it," and within minutes gave me a steaming cup. Catherine Baxter was of such stuff as heroines are made.

Under her influence as my deputy Sandaig began to run smoothly, and as economically as its awkward isolation allowed. The two boys ragged her and did little to help. At Kyleakin I had found Noddy a serious, conscientious worker but Sinbad was a singularly idle youth who used all his energy in impassioned reminders that he had been hired to look after *Polar Star* and nothing else. Noddy caught on to this trades union attitude and would do nothing useful after five o'clock except under violent protest. Although they agreed on how work should be limited, in all else they were at odds. Noddy felt (not unreasonably) that Sinbad had usurped his job, for he had hoped to be in charge of *Polar Star*, and his protest took the form of a general surliness and lack of interest.

This was the situation when Mr Bruno Dereham, an executive of a leading estate agency, came to inspect the cottages at Ornsay and Kyleakin to give an opinion whether his firm would undertake to sell them. Gavin's idea was that this inspection would give us an informed valuation of the cottages and a chance to sell Isle Ornsay: he was still determined to keep Kyleakin. Mr Dereham, an ex-army officer, declared that he found both properties most interesting propositions and felt that they would have a strong if limited appeal. He was a little worried by the difficulty of access of which, in the case of Isle Ornsay, he had personal experience by the time he returned to the south; of Kyleakin his experience was to come later. But now we took him there by *Polar Star*, an impeccable door-to-door operation which would have delighted absent Gavin. The same afternoon—Dereham's time was limited—we re-embarked for the short trip to Ornsay, four miles away. This time *Polar Star* gave a characteristic performance; within ten minutes of setting out a propeller shaft failed and on one engine in a rising sea it would have been mad to continue. We disembarked and I drove Bruno Dereham and Mrs Baxter to Isle Ornsay village. At the time there was no boat there and with the tide coming up behind us our visit was made at the double. Neither Catherine nor Mr Dereham was brisk: she because of her temporary disablement still limped painfully, while he was somewhat out of condition. After a quick examination of the cottage (helped by a ration of coffee and biscuits, prepared by Catherine) we turned back to Ornsay. With three inches of sea-water rippling above the bar I knew that we were going to get wet in the main channel, and I urged my two companions on mercilessly. Catherine soon fell down and twisted the better of her two injured legs. Bruno slipped on seaweed and collapsed on to his broad back with military precision. I was beginning to feel unpopular.

The water in the channel was about three feet deep. Mr Dereham didn't want to cross. I told him that it would soon be much deeper, and he went. I helped Catherine across; the cold water helped the pain in her legs. Two hours later we were back at Sandaig. Hot baths, whisky and a good meal purged Mr Dereham's memory of the worst incidents of the day, and seated round a cheerful fire we were glad to learn that he considered the sale of Isle Ornsay cottage perfectly feasible at a good price.

That day's main mishap had beneficial results. The *Polar Star* was out of action. There was no way of examining her shaft in the water so I told Gavin that I must take her up on her cradle. He could do nothing but agree. Catherine remarked to Sinbad that since events had now made his function obsolete he could help her in the house where there was plenty to be done. This offended his trades unionism to such an extent that he immediately offered me his notice which I instantly and gratefully accepted. I was not so pleased, however, when about a fortnight later Noddy did the same.

I was never entirely clear as to why he decided to leave us. He complained that Catherine bossed him around and he didn't like taking orders from a woman, that he missed Sinbad and his male company, but I think he was depressed by the obvious running down of the place. I had told him that it was only a matter of time before we should close Sandaig with the departure of the otters for a zoo. He was also upset, I think, by the accidental strangling of Gavin's huge Pyrenean dog, Gus. Catherine had arranged a method by which the dog—a suspected sheep-worrier—could travel up and down a fixed wire, thus obtaining some of the exercise he needed. Unfortunately the line was so situated that its nether end crossed a stone dyke and it was over this that poor Gus fell to his breathless death. Both Noddy and Catherine thought the other had brought the dog in for the night and in the morning when he was discovered it was too late for anything but burial. I was told that Noddy's attitude as he dug a great hole for the dog was coarse and unregretting, but I knew enough to realize that this was his way of disguising his true feelings—especially from a woman.

At about this time the otter Teko developed a strange paralytic condition and we all wished Gavin was with us to give the benefit of his personal knowledge of the animal. I was there when this happened, for it was the day we had chosen for the dry-docking of *Polar Star*, always a complicated and prolonged operation. It called for the lowering of the boat with the falling tide upon the cradle which had previously been towed into the sea, only possible in calm conditions; then the whole thirteen tons of boat and cradle had to be winched inch by inch to a point safely above the highest tide. It took hours; Noddy and I started in the early evening and finished at two o'clock the following morning. Noddy had postponed his departure in order to help me bring the boat up, but he intended to leave the next day.

All that long summer's night we had been conscious of poor Teko lying half-paralysed in his hut and of the sound of the outside telephone bell as Gavin rang repeatedly for news. Apart from the fact that I had recently begun to find something fetching about the animal and was distressed to see it laid so low, I was worried that it might die; so soon after Gus' death it would be a bitter blow to Gavin, and would certainly reflect upon my management. With the boat in her final position high on the sand dunes Noddy and I felt that we had done a worthy job, and that we would benefit from a cup of tea followed by bed. We walked over to Sandaig.

Catherine was asleep in a chair, worn out by her anxiety for the sick otter, but she woke up as we came in and gave us the good news that Teko was back on his feet and well on the way to recovery. She insisted on cooking us both a large meal. Noddy was tired and went straight to bed after he had eaten. Catherine, now wide awake, brought me a large dram from a bottle she kept hospitably for friends—she never drank anything—and we sat talking quietly until the dawn was strong in the sky. She had known Gavin for longer than I had thought, their paths had crossed first in his needy, struggling days and she sketched in a picture of him at that time which came as a surprise to me. She held him in great affection, thought him a fool in the way he managed his life, and was fully aware of his leanings of which she spoke with the utmost frankness. She believed that he would never let a friend down and cited her present situation as proof. She now asked nothing more than to be able to help him the way she was doing; anxious to save his money yet privately hoping that some break-down in the plan to send the otters zoo-wards would allow her to care for them indefinitely. I could not agree with her dream, for I could see no salvation for the man for whom I was pledged to do my best until those millstones of expense were taken from his neck, and he was able to live an uncommitted life elsewhere. Nor did I expect any alteration in the almost completed plan. Gavin had chosen Aberdeen Zoo as a home for his famous creatures and its management was enthusiastic; many arrangements still had to be made, but the stage was set.

Meanwhile I, as manager *pro tem*, had a pressing problem. By the next night there would be—as a complete reversal of our agreed safety policy—only one effective person at Sandaig, a woman still recovering from severe injury who had a small child to look after. I came to the point. Both Gavin and I were extremely concerned that she was to be at Sandaig on her own, and he had asked me as a matter of urgency to employ another boy. She would not have it for a moment: "Certainly I can manage. My legs are almost cured. You know I don't take any risks with the otters, and we're on the telephone. Catriona" (her daughter) "is a great help. You can't have another of those idle louts here who sit on their backsides with feet on the table when we're entertaining one of Gavin's business friends." This was a reference to the discourteous performance of the unlamented Sinbad Jones. I had to admit that, if she could manage in safety, it would be an excellent thing for the exchequer. She went on: "I want to save him money. He doesn't need his silly boys. He's been so good to me, just letting me stay here. It's the least I can do."

And we left it at that.

At Isle Ornsay tenants came and went. We had decided to say nothing of the possible sale of the cottage but to play the situation by ear. The cottage was fully functional, and had we been able to wait selective advertising would have built up a good clientèle. But the money pressures were gaining in strength and time was something we did not have.

My practice was to spend a day at Ornsay to attend the outgoing tenants' departure and to welcome a new party in. One occasion in late July provided one of the longest days I can remember.

It all began when Gavin offered the Kyleakin house to Bruno Dereham's family for a holiday. On hearing of this *fait accompli* on the telephone I remarked surlily that we had more than enough calls upon our purse without giving grace-and-favour holidays to business acquaintances. Gavin disputed my attitude by saying that Dereham would be better able to sell one of our houses if he first captured their authentic atmosphere. To me this seemed a trivial reason, but since nothing could be done to alter the arrangement I took my son Richard—then on school holiday—to Kyle with the object of installing the Derehams. This was about a week earlier than my tenant duty at Ornsay.

It was a hell of a day. It was blowing a Force 8 southerly and the rain was sloshing down in bucketfuls. Bruno had arrived by car and was waiting for us at Kyle. We launched the *Assunta*—now powered by a seven horse power outboard—and had Bruno under cover in the cottage in double quick time. His wife and three sons were expected to arrive from Inverness by the afternoon train.

We spent an hour or two in the cottage drinking sturdy drams to give us some heart for the next move, then re-embarked in the *Assunta* and made once more for Kyle. I have seldom seen such rain. It came sweeping along in front of the howling wind in an unbroken curtain, almost hiding the

Skye shore from our eyes. We were blown into Kyle and skulked in the lee of the railway pier.

When Mrs Dereham and her children arrived my heart failed me at the prospect of taking them in an open boat into the teeth of the wind: I suggested that they should take the ferry boat to Kyleakin, after which we should carry them to the island. Richard and I, freed from the additional responsibility of a woman and children, slammed out into the oncoming sea, still warmed and inspirited by Mr Dereham's generous whisky. We picked up the family and soon had them safely in the cottage. While they were settling in I gave the house agent some advice about boats and local conditions. To do him justice he had warned me that he had no experience at all of small boats or of what they float in, and I fear that he found my instructions of little comfort, for even as I spoke his eyes kept flickering through the window at the tumultuous seas rising and bursting above the racing tide.

Not to my very great surprise a telegram arrived from him a few days later. By its content it was plain that it had not been sent from the mainland, and at some point in its hazardous journey it had become oddly corrupted. It read: "Marooned on island stop Engine broken down stop Have lost an ear stop Can you replace earliest stop."

Fortunately I had an engine in good order and the other items he wanted. I telegraphed him at once. In my mind's eye I could see Simon MacLean's face as he took the telegram to his boat. I had written: "Regret your predicament stop will bring engine and replacement ears two days stop"

Therefore when I set out from Drumnadrochit on that memorable July day I had a full programme and a loaded Land Rover. Apart from Bruno Dereham's engine and replacement "ears" I had a quantity of groceries for the new tenants at Ornsay and 3 cwt of coal for their stove. On the roof I carried the fibreglass pram which made me independent of the tenants' boat.

I was surprised to find the former tenants already gone. My plan was to load the wooden dinghy with coal and the pram with groceries and tow the smaller boat round to the cottage. There I would light the stove before returning for the new party—or at least for some of them, for there were no less than twelve (Gavin had at last achieved his full house)—in the wooden dinghy. The tide would be out when they came, so the youngest and fittest would be able to walk.

In the small bay that lies between Ornsay jetty and a concave shore the high shingle is hard and it is possible to take a Land Rover through a hole in the low sea-wall and down to the water's edge. From the back of the vehicle I slid the bags of coal into the dinghy and took the numerous boxes of groceries to the pram. Shortly, I was all set to go, but had overlooked the simple fact that the falling tide had allowed the heavy dinghy to ground heavily. I debated whether to wait for it to turn, but I was impatient to get the day's work underway. Starting the Land Rover I drove forward and then came back slowly at an angle. A patch of green mud passed unnoticed beneath my wheels. I felt a gentle check as the towing ball of the Land Rover made contact with the stern of the wooden dinghy. Preparing to shunt the boat into the water I pressed the accelerator gently when without warning the Land Rover heeled over as though its wheels had been knocked from under it. I jumped out and found the near-side wheels buried deeply in alluvia, green and fetid, which issued from a large round pipe further up the beach.

I saw at once that recovery of the Land Rover from this evil-smelling morass was going to be difficult and that I should need help. An attempt to move her under her wheel power caused her to sink more deeply, and the winch cable was not long enough to reach the top of the beach where there were many anchors for it. I scratched my head in alarm, then thought suddenly of Mr Macdonald, the amiable farmer who had helped Terry Nutkins and me with his tractor when we had pulled up the old lead pipe on Ornsay Island the previous year.

The tide was very near full ebb.

Luckily I found Mr Macdonald at home and enjoying his "elevenses". He took it for a social visit and before I could protest his kindly mother had set a pile of home-baked scones before me and pressed me to eat. Anxiety had dried my mouth and put butterflies in my stomach and I could make nothing of this hospitality until I had told my story to the farmer. Mr Macdonald set my mind at rest—he was about to use his tractor, would take it to the beach first and by offering it as an anchor for my winch cable we would have the Rover out in minutes. Much relieved I drank his tea and ate his excellent scones, and ten minutes later we were back at the sea.

The farmer backed his tractor close to the Land Rover—perhaps too close I thought—and we hooked my cable to the tow-bar. I engaged winching gear and let in the clutch. At once the cab was filled with the whine of powerful mechanism—the same sound that had accompanied the thirteen-ton *Polar Star* up Sandaig beach: yet the Land Rover did not move. But something had to go. I had been leaning out of the cab door watching the off-side wheels so that I did not immediately see the tractor had been pulled an appreciable distance towards me. Mr Macdonald was standing on his seat, the better to be seen, and gesticulated violently as the cable shortened between us and the back wheels of the tractor sank intimately into the gurgling sludge. My mind whimsically likened the distressed farmer to a faithful captain about to suffer with his ship, and I had an hysterical desire to salute him, although to have done so would have been sadly out of place.

I offered an apology but the farmer was in no way put out. He sent his boy for wooden rails which they strapped to the tractor wheels. It came out of the alluvia doing a butterfly stroke and was soon on dry land. Mr Macdonald told me that a garage in Broadford had a large recovery vehicle which would take care of the situation, and advised me to ring them without delay.

It took precious time to get in touch with the driver. I was told he was away for lunch. Panic swept over me in waves, and water was creeping up the beach. I wondered if the Land Rover insurance would cover overwhelming by the tide. I spent the twenty minutes removing perishable articles—Mr Dereham's engine and the inventory of the cottage, for instance—from the Land Rover and laying them on the bank. Then I went back to the telephone. The driver had returned from lunch, understood my predicament and would be with me as soon as possible. Another reprieve! I went in the wooden bar and had a much needed beer.

But half an hour went by and nothing happened. The sea had reached the Land Rover and was inches deep around its wheels. I began to believe that my cry from the heart had been taken with a grain of salt, when there was a distant sound like the rumbling of a tank on the road from Broadford and I knew that salvation was on its way.

The driver wasted no time. I waved him cautiously through the opening down to the beach. "Stop there!" I shouted, above the roar of his engine. "It gets soft further over." He couldn't have heard me, for he went on reversing slowly towards the alluvia. I saw what he intended; the big vehicle carried a short crane mounted on its back, and with this he would lift the Land Rover from the morass, thereafter driving both vehicles clear. In horrified disbelief I saw his four great rear wheels straddle the alluvia which held them up for as long as it takes to say "Oh God!" Then there was a hearty squelch and the heavy lorry sank about four feet deep in the mire, displacing a wave of sewage.

A titanic struggle began. The lorry lay in the same tide line as the Rover. There was potentially enough rise in the neap tide to cover the Land Rover completely, but the larger vehicle might just remain visible. On the credit side we had the great power of the lorry's winch, two 80-foot lengths of heavy cable, assorted shackles, and about an hour before the engines would be inundated: against us was the fact of the considerable depth to which the lorry had sunk, and the shortness of the cables. My companion began to feed the rope out while I urgently searched for an outstanding piece of rock round which to shackle it. They were few and far between. I noticed, out of the corner of my eye, that a few idle boys and girls had appeared on the beach while more mature citizens were beginning to line the quay. Everybody likes a Roman Holiday and I was quite sure that this was going to be one. At last I found, under seaweed, a rounded knob of rock over which I was able to shackle an end of cable. I waved my hand to show that I had established some sort of anchor and the winch began to grind. I stood well away and I was wise. The three-quarter-inch cable twanged tight like a giant's piano string, stretched noticeably and held. The lorry writhed and very slowly, very laboriously —like one who rises from a bed of sickness—struggled to free itself from the mud. Just as it seemed that victory was ours there was a crack like a rifle and a chunk of rock flew into the air and fell into the sea with a splash about 50 yards away. At the same time the sprung cable whipped across the beach, nearly decapitating a small urchin who had come to watch the sport.

A groan went up from the crowd, mingled with opposition cheers.

Our next two attempts led to broken shackles and then a cable broke. A huge boulder which we had used for an anchor lifted out of the beach and was of no further use. The only thing I could find below the blanket of seaweed was a blunt edge above a shoulder of rock but it seemed hardly likely to retain the cable. In desperation I stood on the cable to hold it until it bit into the edge, but it sheered off and I was thrown into the air and fell on my back among broken bottles.

The sea had reached the level of the Land Rover's doors. We had one shackle left, two had proved useless, and one cable. There was plainly little time left. The driver, routing in the seaweed, suddenly gave a shout. He had found a snout of rock which seemed part of the slabby floor of the bay. It looked like the answer, and it was. With the majesty of a woken Kraken the big vehicle pulled itself out of the mud, leaving a deep hole into which the sea rushed while most of the crowd, who had been looking for blood, murmured their disappointment at our success. With the lorry on indisputably solid ground I waded to the Land Rover and attached the crane cable. She came out with an almost indecent lack of fuss.

I shook the driver's hand and invited him to the pub. It was closed. I had all but forgotten the tenants until something happened to remind me about them. A young lout lounging on the quay shouted: "What about your boat?" He couldn't mean the pram. I had pulled that up out of harm's way. But the dinghy which had been the innocent cause of all the trouble was drifting slowly away about a hundred yards from the shore. I waded away as fast as the waist-deep water would permit to reclaim it. My course took me behind the Land Rover and I was heroically breasting the waves when suddenly, alarmingly, the seabed ended and I fell into a deep hole—the same that the Land Rover had so recently occupied. A wave of filthy water closed over my head and I felt my feet displace an obscenely treacle-like substance. I came to the surface and a riotous reception, for the crowd, fearing that it had been robbed of its sacrifice, had begun to melt away until it was seen that I had lost my boat. The sight of my immersion in that lavatorial place had restored their merriment to a new peak, and they slapped their thighs and shouted their approbation in unrestrained joy. Amongst them, most unexpectedly, like a face in a dream, was Jimmy Watt, grinning insanely. I had no idea what he was doing there but I made a quick mental note that, having recovered the boat, I would go over and hit him for his unseemly amusement at my expense.

In the event we greeted each other as the old friends we were, but there was still a subdued twinkle in his eye as he said: "I think these are your new tenants. Shouldn't you introduce yourself?" A rather severe looking young lady came forward and faced me. "I am Miss Smith," she said, "one of the new party. I've met Mr Watt—" here she paused and looked hard at the dripping, mud-stained, foul-smelling object in front of her—"and he *tells* me you are Mr Frere, whom we expected to meet." She added, suspiciously: "Have you had an accident?"

But they were nice people and kind to me. They helped me to restore myself to a condition in which I could once more face the world, and by seven o'clock all twelve of them were installed in the cottage. I got into my little pram and rowed back to the Land Rover, now drying out on Ornsay quay. At the cottage I had received an unexpected telephone call from Bruno Dereham who had managed to cross to Kyleakin with Simon MacLean. He wished to confirm that I was coming, asked me to buy him a bottle of whisky and added mysteriously: "This is a strange place and I have some most peculiar things to tell you. You won't pass us by, will you?" It was a plea rather than a request.

It took me two hours to start the Land Rover engine. At last it fired spasmodically and we got under way, but my clutch would only disengage at random. I wondered how I would manage on the ferry.

I reached Kyleakin village by about ten o'clock and quite by chance came across Simon MacLean. He was doing some work for the Lighthouse Board on the island and had seen quite a lot of the Derehams. He remarked: "Mr Dereham is not happy at all"; to which I replied that, having broken an expensive engine and lost an ear (at this Simon did not bat an eyelid), he had no reason to be overjoyed. Said Simon in his slow, thoughtful West Highland voice: "No, he isn't happy about that *either*," but would not be drawn any further.

I unstrapped the pram from the Land Rover's roof, loaded

the engine, et cetera, and rowed quickly across the flat-calm channel to where the *Assunta* lay at anchor on her running mooring. I landed, put down the engine and walked quickly up to the cottage. Owing to the soiling of my clothes I was reduced to a pair of shorts, a shirt and a white plastic waterproof with an attached hood. As I passed the first window I gave it a cheerful double tap and glanced inside. The effect of my sudden appearance was traumatic. The boys and Mrs Dereham were playing chess. At the sound of the knock they gave one look, but the sight of the white cowl framing a tired and cadaverous face was more than they could stand. They sprang to their feet: over went the chess board as the youngest boy screamed and buried his face in his mother's lap. Ashamed to have been the cause of such emotional unrest I ran to the door to identify myself, but before I had my hand on the knob it flew open to reveal a wide-eyed Bruno Dereham. He raised his arm to strike, but changed his mind in the conclusion that this was a psychic menace and converted the belligerent gesture into a pious sign of the Cross. "Dereham," I said quickly in my most comforting voice, "it is I—*Frere*," for I was sure that he was about to thrust a Bible in my face and bid me begone. Though partly reassured he continued to eye me doubtfully until the hood was off, for I think he still suspected some form of diabolical impersonation.

The story he told me of his experience was doubly strange because it was so like my own. He alone among his family was on the psychic wavelength that made reception of the "voices" possible, and the knowledge that in this he was set apart from his wife and children increased his distress. His fear —though unexpressed—had soon spread through the house like the half-heard whisper of thunder on a summer's day, and had made everyone nervous and upset. Gavin had said something to him—as I knew—but insufficient for him to concoct the details of what took place within his mind. I had never before heard the weird substance of the phenomenon described in such a way that I could say in all honesty: "Yes, that is *exactly* how it is"; but I said it to Bruno Dereham, and meant it.

They persuaded me, without much difficulty, to stay the night with them and I am pleased to think that my presence did something to reassure them. At any rate neither Bruno Dereham nor I gave any sleep away that night.

The letting season ended with the twelve tenants at Ornsay who departed satisfied at the end of their time; we never let either cottage again. The emphasis was now on selling Ornsay —and Kyleakin too, if need be, although Gavin was still firmly opposed to the idea—and Bruno Dereham's firm began to advertise on a national scale. Enquiries began to come in and by September much interest had been aroused. A young barrister and his wife, Mr and Mrs Jeremy Ashburton, had 'phoned Bruno Dereham to arrange a visit to the cottage towards the end of the month.

10

CATHERINE

Gavin Maxwell came back to Sandaig in late August of that year, and shared the house with Catherine Baxter and her daughter for four months. Considering the idea of women which arose out of his perversity, and the difference in their personalities, coupled with the lonely and claustrophobic situation—they seldom left the house and I was practically the only visitor—they got on remarkably well. Any disruptive moments were predictable, and did not last long. Gavin, who generally preferred the company of boys and men, could be at ease with women, but certain conditions had to be met. He was no spartan, and he liked his comforts, when they were available. I hasten to add he could also live as rough as any explorer: but that is not the present point. Catherine was the most domesticated of women, and no one could be more attentive. Gavin appreciated her ministrations, but recoiled from cosy intimacies. He often demanded solitude in which to write and she granted him this with scrupulous understanding, but at other times when he wanted only to be alone with his thoughts she would start a cheerful conversation. This upset him, he was too polite generally to deny her this outlet, but it rankled with him so much that he would introduce an acid theme into the conversation which soon upset her. This made her unhappy, and she did not know in what way she had offended.

Still, on the whole, all went well; but there was one issue right from the start. Catherine had only one child, the little girl Catriona, but she made up for her small family with a distraction of animals. She loved animals in the mass (which must be even less rewarding than loving your fellow men) and collected them. Gavin denied that he knew of her intention to bring her many pets to Sandaig, and made me promise that I would speak seriously to her about culling the numbers before he took up residence at his house. The dogs were numerous, and there were also cats, donkeys, a horse and a formidable gander. Added to Gavin's own deerhounds and the otters they made a large and distracting company, and the author envisaged a state of confusion in the midst of which any attempt to write a book would be so much wasted time.

I duly mentioned his feelings to Catherine. Usually the most reasonable of women, she was evasive and finally obdurate. If I remarked that the animal population was in a state of explosion she would give me a bright smile and promise to dismiss some of her pets before my next visit. On my return she would take pride in showing me that there were gaps in the ranks and that (say) Towser, Bonzo, Tray, Spot, Penelope, Glen, Lassie and Sausage were no longer obvious. Her subdued air suggested to me that some violent action had been taken to effect their removal and out of deference to her feelings I did not ask where they had gone. I was soon to learn that her attitude was guilt not grief, for as the days went by the absent ones came creeping insidiously back again from wherever they had been hidden, until the full complement was once again restored. I had no choice but to tell Gavin that Catherine was not taking his wishes too seriously, but he was in an amiable mood at the time and merely urged me to go on trying; a few days later he was low in spirits and expressed the fear that Catherine, like other women before her, might take over Sandaig. I said that I was sure that nothing was further from her mind and that she was the best thing that had ever happened to the place. I realized that a viable relationship must exist between the humans there if Gavin were to start his new book, and that nothing must upset his declared intention of sending Edal and Teko to Aberdeen Zoo on a date which had been provisionally fixed for late October. To ensure this I would unscrupulously sell all the concord I could think up, even if I had to invent most of it.

I drove Gavin to Sandaig after he had spent a couple of nights with us. He was visibly uneasy at the thought of the new incumbents there and had fully made up his mind that the spirit of Camusfearna had gone with Jimmy. Yet when we arrived the auspices were good, there was not a raven to be seen in the sky and mother and daughter welcomed him as a soldier who returns from war. His own mood appeared to match theirs and he simulated a delight in meeting Catherine's animals. Some of the smaller dogs were drawn from the most unlikely recesses and I began to get wise to the secret behind the conjuring trick which had been played on me. Of course the population explosion was both apparent and real, the dogs being particularly randy, and it is indeed fortunate that Nature has placed a limitation upon cross-breeding or Sandaig would swiftly have become a mutant's paradise. The otters Teko and Edal were, at that moment, in excellent condition: this genuinely pleased Gavin, but he was not so happy (although not a word escaped him) to find that Catherine had arranged the inside of the house as a woman would for a man, which was subtly different from the way it had been before.

During his stay with us Gavin had told me what he required of the Aberdeen Zoo in the way of new facilities before he would entrust the famous otters to their care. Some officials were already wilting at the scale of his demands, and I began to wonder if he was creating an artificial barrier in the same way that one puts an enormous price upon an article one doesn't really want to sell. We spoke about the lighthouse cottages, and he asked my opinion of the price we were likely to obtain for one, or both, and then added quickly that he didn't want to sell Kyleakin anyway: would a good price for Isle Ornsay get us out of difficulties? I thought it would, provided that Sandaig was closed down and he was living in a house that didn't cost the earth to run. He gave me an aggressive look and remarked that it wasn't necessary to include a proviso; we all knew it was going to be closed down and that was that. I repeated that, in that case, a good price for Ornsay would suffice. He was, I knew, vaguely thinking of living on Kyleakin Island, an expensive alternative to Sandaig, which merely meant we should take all our difficulties elsewhere, and I hoped that I should be able to dissuade him when the shut-down of the latter was ensured.

In the meantime Bruno Dereham's firm had printed a glossy brochure at considerable expense, which was beginning to find its way on to enquirers' breakfast tables but not, I fear, with any great result. The barrister Jeremy Ashburton was bringing his wife to see Isle Ornsay and a date had now been fixed. Gavin demanded that the *Polar Star* be launched for maximum prestige.

To the expensive grind of the Land Rover's winch I laboriously pulled her back into the sea, hoping, as I did so, that she would have the decency to keep going long enough for Ashburton's visit, or break down discreetly before he came.

Actually the trip went well, which was a good thing, for the Ashburtons had only one day to make it in. I picked them up in Inverness in the morning and drove them back at night. Under Alan MacDiarmid the boat performed faultlessly, and Gavin and Catherine were host and hostess on the trip. Gavin found something in common with the barrister who had been present at the hearing of the Aliata libel action, and had felt much sympathy for Gavin at its outcome. We were soon ashore on the island. The house, not long vacated by the last tenants, was dry and fresh, with none of the sinister smell of frowst and fungosity that could be such a deterrent. Ashburton, though his calling had made his thoughts immune from easy interpretation, seemed to approve of the cottage and was plainly pleased with its situation. His wife, of more overt emotions, was entranced with much she saw but retained a woman's caution, and showed a regrettably practical side to her nature. "Doesn't it get very damp?" she asked me, a question which I had schooled myself to answer dishonestly. "Not if it is lived in," I said; "and when you leave it keep the windows open." She murmured that they would only be using it during school holidays. Her second question had a rhetorical ring about it: "Won't my children fall over the rocks?" To which, being taken off my guard, I could only answer by saying: "Mrs Ashburton, I don't know your children but mine will fall over anything!"—which was not even true, for mine have all been good rock-climbers—and she only laughed for a few moments at my poor joke. I never have been much good at salesmanship.

The pace at which I drove them back to Inverness and their train did not encourage conversation but as I helped them from the Land Rover I said to Mr Ashburton: "Did you enjoy your visit?" He raised his heavy-lidded legal eyes and replied with unexpected candour: "I am keenly interested. Your solicitor will hear from mine." It looked as though good luck was beginning to come our way in the long term but, as it happened, the short term had not been neglected either, thanks to Catherine.

*   *   *

When she had asked Gavin to lend her a roof in the north in her hour of distress, with the possibility of purchase later, he had offered her a choice of two houses, both of which he owned. Had he known the condition of the smaller his suggestion would have been a cruel joke, for it was no more than a sordid shell standing on a desolate part of the Inverness road two miles from Glenelg. He had bought it at the height of his acquisitive period just because it was for sale and he had paid an insane price for it: so much so that I suspect he was afterwards ashamed to go near it. Catherine took one look. The other, a palace only by comparison, was within the scattered periphery of Glenelg village and went by the unlikely name of "Cremona". It was pretty unpleasant, but there were possibilities of improvement although its construction, position and the indefinable air of depression that went with it would defy dramatic change and ensure a permanent mediocrity. Alan MacDiarmid had done a lot of work to it during his tenancy but he had been gone for some time and the wild, wet weather played havoc with all the care he had put into it, the iron roof frayed and tattered at the edges while inside the black damp spread over the walls like grotesque ink-stains, and the unventilated floorboards rotted away.

Catherine, having no choice, chose Cremona, and asked Gavin if he would give her first refusal if it came up for sale. He was suffering from an attack of baseless optimism at the time and told her that he would be delighted, and that further she could have it at valuation whenever she wished to settle. I inherited this arrangement and promised to honour its terms, but as the financial showing of the company steadily declined I began to regret it. The matter came to a head when out of the blue I received a letter from a woman visitor to Glenelg who had heard that Cremona might come up for sale and coveted it. This seemed odd to me, but tastes differ. I wrote back asking for curiosity's sake what she would be prepared to pay, and her answer gave me disturbing food for thought, for she was prepared to give us immediately a full thousand pounds more than Catherine had been asked for. More money and much quicker, two fat birds in the hand and only a fledgeling in the bush.

I decided that I must tell Gavin and hoped that it would

not upset Catherine too much. What did a young and active woman want with a residence in this out-of-the-way Highland village? Our creditors were as restive as cats on hot tin roofs, and if an injection of cash did not come very soon the company coffers would be empty. Of course, having made his promise to Catherine my employer might wish to stand by it, and to do him justice he abandoned his integrity only with difficulty. "Richard," he said gravely, "as you remark our first duty is to our creditors. This is no longer my decision but yours. You have my mandate to do anything you think fit. My arrangement with Catherine Baxter has been overtaken by events. I know you will treat her with every consideration."

When I told Catherine what had come about she said little but the look in her eyes clearly expressed her thoughts. After a short silence she said: "All my furniture is there. I can't face another move. I will have to pay your price and if it'll help I'll let you have a down payment in about a week's time. That ought to please him."

She was as good as her word. A few days later I paid £2,000 into the company account and spent some time at my desk thereafter advising the more jittery creditors that all was far from lost, and that if they were pleased to do so they would find a provisional token of our esteem attached to my letter.

I worked out that I could now stem the tide of disaster until the end of the month when Gavin went to Africa and the otters to Aberdeen, and still leave sufficient to meet our day-to-day running costs. These calculations on paper took no account of the hypothetical sale of Ornsay cottage (which would solve all our problems until the build-up of literary income took over) although Gavin and I, with the weakness of wishful thinking, had both privately concluded it to be a *fait accompli*. And then a letter arrived from our solicitors whose innocent contents held the seed of poison fruit: it said they understood that Ashburton wished to have the cottage surveyed, but that he might be prepared to accept a warranty from its owner as to its good condition. They said that we should on no account give any such warranty, for it might lead to nothing but trouble. My heart sank, for I knew that a survey could well mean the end of all our hopes for a profitable sale—or indeed any sale at all, for the fatal flaw of the cottage's pervasive dampness could never be banished entirely, although it could be controlled by regular residence. Much as I longed to persuade Gavin to sign the guarantee I could not dismiss the possibility of a heavy claim for damages, if after a winter's absence, Ashburton returned to find fungoid growth on his fine furniture, and I added my disapproval of the idea to that of our solicitors. Isle Ornsay cottage would have to be put to the test. We agreed to the survey and waited for the other side to arrange it.

It took place in the third week of October. I spent two days in frantic preparation. The place was undeniably damp—not quite as bad as I had feared, for it had been a dry autumn—and the paint was beginning to blister where the hated salt crystals had prized it proud of the surface. I had no time to make a proper job and a quick rub down with sandpaper had to suffice, followed by a lick of fresh paint. I knew, of course —none better—where the really frightful places were, such as the innocently boarded-up cupboard bottom where dwelt the dreaded Merulius, or the plastered wall from which all the lath had rotted away and only the plaster was left hanging.

At the appointed time the architect rang up from Isle Ornsay village and I set out to bring him to the island. Through no fault of his own he was not welcome and did not merit the wooden dinghy: to dismay him I turned up in the pram. But the architect whose name, by some extraordinary prescience on his parents' part, was Gordon Carpenter, was made of the sternest stuff and would not be deterred by the overloaded toy boat, or by anything else. He seemed a humourless fellow, chunky, moustached, with large furry hands and comatose eyes. Apart from introducing himself he said nothing during the trip to the island, and apart from refusing some tea at the cottage nothing much as he commenced the survey. Though he was bulky he was brisk and he went through the house with the thoroughness of a hungry dog demolishing a bone, stopping only at the end of each stage to scribble his destructive comments in a cheap, red notebook. His cunning fully matched my own and try as I would to divert him from any suspect point he would return, within minutes and with renewed suspicion. Only once did his gravity forsake him—although not a hint of a smile went with the lapse—and that was when he was thumping a wall, presumably to find if the lath were rotten underneath. I said pertly: "You should be a doctor: what are you trying to diagnose? Pneumonia?" and he gave it an extra heavy thump causing a shower of plaster to tumble down behind before replying: "Too late, if I am. That was a death rattle."

Having broken his silence my black humorist became almost garrulous. "One gets to know," he said gloomily, "just where to look," and he pointed to a perfectly sound-looking piece of skirting-board, and added: "What would you think *that* is, poria or Merulius?"

"God, I hope neither of them," I groaned my reply.

"You would be wrong," he answered gently, and to my dismay but no longer to my surprise he broke a piece off the skirting board and squeezed it till the water ran through his fingers and it fell to bits as would a cheap sponge. "Poria, almost certainly," he concluded with tired triumph.

For technical confirmation of the damp he took from his case a little instrument with two prongs powered by electricity which he applied to surfaces throughout the house. Needless to say it registered its maximum reading which showed, no doubt, a moisture content exceeding that of pure water.

The agony of Isle Ornsay cottage went on for another hour. At the end of that time every nook and cranny had been probed, every fungus brought to bay and each damp patch traced to its point of origin. Carpenter closed his book with a snap and asked amiably: "Now, I'm off duty. How about that tea?"

Informally he was a delightful chap, filled with amusing accounts of the houses he had rightly condemned. But as junior partner in a firm which had a high reputation for integrity he explained that he could not conceal his findings, but he did not intend to emphasize any faults other than the damp about which his client was chiefly worried. He agreed that damp was a common feature of older houses along this coast. He said he was sorry about it, and he seemed so sincere that I took him back to the village in the wooden dinghy.

And if storm clouds were hanging over Isle Ornsay, a storm was about to break at Sandaig. Some years before, in circumstances of great coincidence, Gavin had obtained the otter Edal from a woman, a doctor's wife, who was now living abroad with her husband. The couple were in the country on leave and the woman had been anxious to see Edal again. They had come to Sandaig on the day of the Isle Ornsay inspection. The ensuing meeting had the chilly uncertainty of a reunion between a mother and a child adopted by foster parents. It might have been well had it not been for the fact that Gavin no longer intended to keep the otter. When he had taken the creature from her, the woman had been in no position to keep her; now the positions were reversed. The doctor's wife, unreasonable only in that she overlooked Gavin's commitment to the zoo, now called for the return of her pet. Gavin denied her, offering reasons other than that, which seemed to be spurious. I said nothing on my return to the house, for this pre-existing situation bewildered me; having been introduced to the doctor and his wife I seated myself inconspicuously, lit a cigarette, and helped myself to a large whisky.

It all grew rather emotional. Catherine, so often solidly behind Gavin, tended to support the doctor's wife in her claim. Implacably opposed to the zoo idea as she was, it still surprised me that Catherine would favour anything that would lead to the separation of the otters, or destroy the chance of their remaining at Sandaig indefinitely. Gavin was not a man to brook disloyalty and I knew that he must feel that Catherine was betraying his interests.

My only feeling amid all this claim and counter-claim was that the otters must go to the zoo as scheduled. I supposed that if only Teko were to be offered, the zoo, who had agreed upon a package deal, might reasonably change their mind. That would never do.

The meeting was nearly over, and an old friendship had sadly decayed. Soon the doctor and his wife appeared anxious to leave, and a few minutes later they left Sandaig with hardly a word to Gavin.

But I stayed on, and after a long silence he said to me: "Richard, hadn't we better drive them up the hill?" He had not forgotten his obligations as host. I said, "Yes," and started up the Land Rover, and found them up the first steep bit, stumbling in the darkness. At first the doctor would not accept my offer, but when he saw how broken up his wife was with the day's events he changed his mind, and I drove them up the hill and to their car.

Back at the house I found a distressed Catherine; Gavin had retreated to his study. He had told her how surprised he was that she supported the doctor's wife's claim on Edal, and he had inferred that in doing so she had let him down. I wondered if in the prevailing unrest it might be more prudent if I kept my ill news to myself until morning, then changed my mind and knocked on Gavin's door. He said: "Come in, if it's you, Richard." He was seated dejectedly at his desk.

I came to the point: "A bad thing has happened, Gavin. I think the architect will advise Ashburton against buying the cottage. Despite all I could do, he found it very damp. He was a critical kind of chap!"

He raised his head from his hands and said in the matter-of-fact voice he used for genuine setbacks: "We both know what this means, don't we? But Catherine is entitled to know. We've had a few cross words—but I'd be obliged if you'd ask her to come in." This I did gladly. Catherine brightened up at once. Over coffee—her anodyne for all the world's ills—the three of us discussed the implications of the new situation until well into the morning, united again in the face of this fresh misfortune.

I stayed at Sandaig for another 24 hours because, faced with the possible failure of the Ornsay sale, we had to make alternative plans. We telephoned Bruno Dereham who was in close touch with Ashburton. He gave us some reassurance. He did not think that Carpenter's report would stifle Ashburton's interest, although a reduction in the purchase price would probably be asked. Dereham, very much on the alert, had already discussed with the barrister the idea of seeking expert advice upon damp treatment, and our agent declared that such continuing preoccupation with ways and means was a very hopeful sign. Bruno was prepared to wager that if we were to knock £500 off the purchase price there would be no further hesitation. We would have to wait and see how the report was received, but he had the utmost confidence in the outcome.

This news produced a euphoric attitude in Gavin and a mood of cautious hope in me. There would be less money to go round but with Sandaig shut down and the otters at Aberdeen, Gavin could still expect a good living from his literary income if he lived in a reasonable place. Once again I began to see some daylight.

But as the day wore on I noticed that Gavin was sinking into a mood of depression. I should no doubt have guessed in what direction his gloomy thoughts were leading

him, and how he was setting the stage against the moment when
he might declare publicly the decision which I now believe he
had already taken in private. We had been drinking most of
the day but I still had the wit to realize that something was
about to happen.

Gavin got up and said to me: "I need some exercise. I shall
go for a short walk."

It seemed a long time before he came back and when he did,
looking wild as a scarecrow, he was urgently shouting for dry
blankets. I was bewildered, thinking that some harm had
befallen him. But we soon understood that on his way back
from his walk he could not resist the temptation to visit Teko
in his shed and had found the otter wet and in some discomfort,
the slates having blown off the roof. I knew at once that all
was lost—or gained—according to one's viewpoint, for Gavin
had sworn that he could not bear to have any contact with the
otters with their departure so close at hand. He told us then
that Teko had greeted him like a saviour in his hour of wetness
and misery, and was still fully dependent upon human contact.
In the little drama of that moment of reunion Gavin had found
the touchpaper to fire the cannon at last. I remember thinking
uncharitably that he had probably knocked the slates off the
shed himself. To do him justice, however, he had been quite
consistent in his doubts that Teko would settle successfully in
the zoo; he considered Edal, despite her record of violent
outbursts, to be the more phlegmatic of the two.

Now he raged at me. "That otter is not going to any zoo,"
he said defiantly. "I don't care if you are bloody angry with
me, Richard. That otter stays here!" He gave me a look of
pure hatred.

There was nothing to be done. I knew that in this I could
not move him. It had been apparent to me that he had long
regretted his former decision. He was, in his way, fond of those
two strange creatures and he looked upon them realistically as
the mainstay of his writing. Yet there was still no reasonable
doubt in my mind that only with the closure of Sandaig would
come financial salvation. I had to make some protest.

"Gavin," I said, "I am sorry but this cannot be done. Within
a few weeks if Ornsay isn't sold this house will not be tenable.
No electricity, no telephone, no food for otters or humans—
what shall we use for money, for God's sake?"

"I assume that you will stay with us," he said with entire conviction; and without irony he added, "so we shall have the benefit of your advice." I found it impossible to deny that assumption, and thus felt that even the power of decision had left me. Things were now just happening. I tried to trip his intention on the last stumbling-block I knew—"Who will look after Teko? Who will stay here with him?"

He made no immediate reply and in the ensuing silence I briefly closed my eyes, for my head was aching with the madness of it all. When I opened them I saw that he was not looking at me but at Catherine. Almost imperceptibly she nodded her head. Now I knew from what quarter the strength to make his decision had really come. Catherine had condemned herself to a hard and lonely winter, happy in the knowledge that she was wanted and that, in this matter, which he held to be of such importance, she had not betrayed him at all.

Gavin left for Tangier in late December. He was well out of it. The all but omnipotent Peter Janson-Smith had with great difficulty raised the money for Gavin's sojourn in Africa, for well he knew, as I did, that no book would be completed in the hand-to-mouth situation which must soon obtain at Sandaig. Two more smart blows set the seal on our extremity. The Aberdeen Zoo failed to satisfy Gavin's conditions for Edal's life there, and after some unpleasantness it was mutually agreed that she should be withdrawn. There may have been faults on both sides but my sympathy tended towards the zoo. Gavin had led them a merry dance. After months of complex instruction from him which they had done their best to carry out, they had been told without warning that they were not to have Teko. They had cause for complaint then for they had been promised both of Maxwell's otters, whose fame and attraction lay to a great extent in their combination. Much advance publicity had been arranged and much money spent and the zoo authorities had plainly been greatly embarrassed.

From Gavin's point of view it was no longer necessary to send Edal away, for Sandaig was to be kept open; the additional otter was without much economic consequence. So that was that, and there was certainly some argument for keeping the famous duo intact if only in the faint hope that by some miracle the old days might be restored.

The other blow—a much heavier one—was the collapse of the Isle Ornsay sale. After Bruno Dereham's optimistic assessment of our chances our hopes had gradually faded as Ashburton made no further move. Bruno, to do him justice, had miraculously kept the barrister interested even in the face of Carpenter's damning report and insultingly low valuation. Ashburton's agents then made an offer. It was too low for us to accept, and we tried to split the difference. That didn't work.

There was briefly a dead-lock, but it was broken by the reintroduction of the idea that damp-course specialists should be asked to quote for treatment. The other side proposed that we should be liable for the cost of the treatment and that *provided* their client was satisfied with the result they would then pay us our stated price. It seemed perfectly fair and at the same time perfectly hopeless, but in the absence of anything else we agreed to it.

I was at Isle Ornsay when the specialists were preparing their quotation. By the nature of the "cure" I knew it could not be cheap—nor did I think it would do much good. It consisted of a copper strip embedded right round the walls of the cottage, and earthed. It struck me that they were looking for the wrong culprit. It was not electricity we had too much of, it was salt.

Gavin and I had agreed that if the proposed treatment were to cost more than £700 we must drop the sale. The risk that Ashburton would still not buy was too great.

Right up to the day of Gavin's departure for Tangier no word had come from Bruno Dereham who was in touch with the damp-coursers. Gavin suggested that he postpone his departure until we had definite news but I assured him that he must feel independent of this outcome, it had no relevance as far as his next move was concerned. He insisted, however, that I 'phone him in London at the last moment before he boarded his plane.

Bruno Dereham found me at Sandaig two hours before Gavin's take-off. I had rushed there to mend a fault in the otter's water supply. Catherine called me in from the river to speak on the telephone. What I heard came as no great surprise: the estimate was in excess of £2,000. Bruno wanted clear instructions from Gavin (whom he had failed to raise on the 'phone) or from me. I told him without hesitation that the sale must be dropped at once, for if we committed ourselves to this enormous sum and Ashburton was still not satisfied we should be in the hottest of hot water. And if he did purchase the house at our price we still should not have enough money to settle with even our most pressing creditors.

I gave the news to stoical Catherine who shrugged her shoulders, gave me a sympathetic pat and suggested coffee. She was basking in an enchanted glow enkindled earlier in the day by an affectionate and grateful Gavin who had 'phoned her to say goodbye. Cynically I hoped that some of this glow would light her way through the long, hard and bankrupt winter ahead.

My employer spoke to me at exactly 5.30 p.m. as arranged. He was always a punctual man. I gave him the burden of my news. He at once agreed that a sale on these terms was unthinkable and added firmly: "Now I shall cancel my flight." He added: "I can't go away while you are thrown to the wolves." I said: "Bloody nonsense, if you stay we'll all be eaten. Your book is the most important thing for us all, and we agree that you can't write it here."

He sensibly gave in. His parting words were: "You are in charge and you'll never know how grateful I am. My thoughts will be with you in what is truly a rearguard action. We'll keep in the closest touch. Goodbye, and God bless you."

I should miss him, I knew, and I appreciated his words. But I didn't really deserve them. I hope he gave his thoughts and his blessing to the indomitable woman who single-minded, single-handed and courageous intended to carry on the legend of Camusfearna for him to its long and bitter end.

II

THE REARGUARD ACTION

EXACTLY ONE YEAR after Gavin's proposal to me that I should manage his company I sat down at my typewriter and began to ask our creditors' permission for its continuance. There hadn't been much promise in the New Year's dawn of 1966 but for me there had been the excitement of a new thing, a change in the rather hum-drum life I was leading at that time: now that year had ended in disappointment and apprehension. In the six months during which I had been in charge of affairs there had been a steady decline in Gavin's fortunes, and I could see no reason for the high praise he heaped upon my head.

Our lawyers had suggested that we ask our creditors for a moratorium. In doing so we should point out that our assets (mainly the two lighthouse cottages) still exceeded our liabilities by a comfortable margin, but that we must have time to realize them in a favourable market. We were also to stress that a panic sale would almost certainly result in a poor price and that those people whom we hoped to attract were little in evidence in early January. Those to whom we addressed our plea reacted in three different ways: some gave us a cautious vote of confidence; others remained silent, preferring not to commit themselves; while a minority, through greed or need, began to take legal action against us. At my wit's end for money, I invented extraordinary stories for the pacification of tradesmen, and many abandoned their immediate attack in the sure conviction that they were dealing with a madman. Others, however, persevered in their intentions and soon I was having to agree to make small, regular payments to the Court or face the consequences. The consequences, in these cases, meant "poinding" (a word Gavin heard about from me and immortalized in *Raven Seek thy Brother*) or seizing a debtor's goods. It is, at the best, a very shaming thing, and at the worst denuding.

Apart from old debts, I simply had to find money to pay the electricity bill at Sandaig: this was the prime priority. Nothing happened at Sandaig without electric current: if it went it would be a dead house. The telephone was also important. Catherine Baxter was doing quite enough for us already without having her only means of alerting the outside world denied her. Although both she and her child seemed to lead trouble-free lives I would have been filled with apprehension if I thought she had no means of calling for a doctor should an emergency arise.

And gradually a change was coming over her. It was as though she had used up all her reserve of strength and good humour upon Gavin, and now that he had gone she was less boisterous, much more withdrawn, and had taken to criticism of him for his behaviour to her, while still visibly pining for his company. She was obviously feeling the strain of her altruistic undertaking, and began for the first time to speak of going away to attend to some personal business. Her life at Sandaig during that darkest period of the year was undeniably hard, and I realized that she had begun to dread her nightly trips over the mile of rock and moorland to meet the mail van and collect her provisions and the post. Gavin had instilled into her a conviction that it was necessary to obtain the mail every night so that urgent letters might be read out to me on the telephone. I assured her that such punctiliousness was quite without point, since 99 per cent of all letters contained demands for money about which I could do nothing at all. But she was grimly determined to carry out his instructions, and the more morbid and bitter she became over considered slights the greater grew her determination. I could do little to ease her situation—by the end of January it was an event to have enough money to fill the petrol tank of the Land Rover, and my trips to Sandaig had to be limited to once a week, or less.

If Catherine had not been personally able to find someone to take her place at Sandaig she would have had a nervous breakdown, for she would never have asked for mercy. If Gavin had gone out of his way to give her extra warmth and thus deny her growing conviction that both he and I were making use of her (which was only partly true, as far as I was concerned, for had not she offered him the means of keeping his ottery intact?) she would have joyously coped with all the knotty problems that long, cold winter provided and come out of it smiling. But he had not done so, and she was miserable and confused. Fortunately Michael Cuddy had recently written to her and expressed great willingness to stand in for her at Sandaig at any time she wished to get away. It was the answer to her prayer, and in early February she drove south in her little car taking her daughter and a fair number of smaller and more precious dogs. She left two large ones, a Great Dane mother and her son, with us.

Shortly after Michael came to Sandaig a local general store —of a kind which is gloriously peculiar to the West Highlands —called a halt to our credit. They had given us a run for their money, and their account—which as far as I could see from my records had not been fully paid up for about four years— stood at just over £500. The manager summed it all up neatly with gentle Celtic irony: "Aye, Mister Maxwell is a fine gentleman as we all know, but 'tis just not possible for a wee store like us to support him in his expensive ways." Nevertheless, they had done pretty well for a long time and with never a word of complaint.

It did, of course, produce a situation of extreme crisis. There was no money left in the company account, and since it was now all too obvious that I must personally meet the day-to-day expenses of running Sandaig I decided I was entitled to a share in it. We shut down Drumbuie House and moved to the west.

Just before we went there was a tragedy. The young Great Dane ran amok and swiftly savaged half a dozen sheep before falling to an outraged shepherd's gun. His end was just, as the law stands, and the shepherd's summary act above reproach, but we mourned the great creature and we dreaded giving the news to Catherine. As it happened she was out of touch and there was nothing we could do but wait for her to telephone. Our apprehension at the thought of having to tell her what had befallen her pet was extreme; in her eyes the dog was a member of her family. It was ten days later that we spoke of it to her, and her reaction to the news was one of extreme shock, quickly repressed. She asked us never to refer to the dog again, that was all, but there was a new note of bitterness in her voice. Nothing more was heard from her for some time.

The move to Sandaig was a welcome change for me despite the drain on my small resources. There were many practical things to do there which provided a therapy after the unending frustration of offering promises which it sometimes seemed would never be fulfilled. And Sandaig was a euphoric place, no letters were forwarded from the office at my home and the name I gave to indignant people who reached me on the 'phone was a nonsensical invention designed purely to confuse them and extend my stolen peace of mind for a little longer. The weather was oddly calm, as it sometimes is before the furious onslaught of the equinoctial gales, and each morning the sea was flat and white. The small neap tides sauntered up the beach, paused and gently withdrew. The mountains ringing Loch Hourn hunched quietly together in the dark weather, their cardboard-clear outlines anticipating rain. After a few weeks I began to feel guilty, and thinking about the miserable situation I had a sudden brainwave about how it might be eased. I spent some time on the telephone with Raef Payne, Gavin's very old friend and a director of the company, and as a result of my proposals he was able to release a sum of money that would take care of Michael's expenses and the cost of otter feed for quite a long time. This money had been in Gavin's private account to which Raef had the power of attorney. I informed its owner that I had no option but to borrow it.

To remain any longer at Sandaig was insupportable escapism (and funk, considering what the accumulated mail must contain) so I gathered my family together and we left a contented Michael and went home.

As expected, there was a pile of bills of a conventional nature, and one shock. The hire-purchase company from whom we had been laboriously buying the Land Rover had become shirty about the return unpaid of three bank order instalments, and wished to have the vehicle back. I immediately rang their local office and told them bleakly that the vehicle was wrecked, written off and out of their reach forever, but that our insurance would be in touch to put the matter to rights. They said they were sorry to have troubled me, which was nice. Anything to gain time.

The bills provided me with some new "stickers". Since I had inherited this poverty-stricken company I had determined to take some pleasure out of adversity, and had formed on the wall above my desk a small gallery of those persuasive notices that are stuck to overdue accounts. I suppose I had upwards of a hundred: they covered an area of about three feet by six. Some of them were very euphemistic. "May we draw your attention to . . ."; "We think you may have overlooked . . ."; "Can it be that you have some reason to question this account?"; "Please . . ."; et cetera all in technicolour. One creditor disdained mass-produced inducements and wrote as follows:

> I am astonished at your failure to pay the above account. What do you expect me to do about it? I would hardly insult you by taking legal action, and short of sending you a continuous stream of conscience-pricking letters (in which it becomes increasingly difficult to sound original) I find I am at a loss.
>
> If you haven't the time to write a cheque, could you at least send me a few fresh ideas?

This buoyant approach in the midst of all those drab complaints so delighted me that I instantly waived the strict rule of priority—the older accounts to be paid first—and sent his small cheque by return.

Catherine telephoned us. We were happy to hear from her after a long silence. She sounded her old exuberant self, with a touch of something else that I couldn't quite explain: an air of new confidence, perhaps. She had some news for us which caused me to sit down and immediately write to Gavin. It appeared that a friend of Catherine's husband, a progressive Indian gentleman with a weakness for buying property, had shown an interest in the two lighthouse cottages, would come north to view them and if pleased would make an offer for one, or both, My urgent missive to my employer was to sound his reaction to the prospect of parting with Kyleakin as well as Ornsay if the bargain required them both to be included.

In the end it proved fruitless. It also caused an acceleration in the decaying relationship between ourselves and Catherine. The man of property came north in style, casually chartered a fishing boat to show him round the islands and we spent a comfortable weekend basking in the material warmth of his opulence. Like many men who have made themselves rich, he was narrow-eyed and cautious when asked to commit himself to prices and possibilities, but he said he liked what he had seen and would be in early touch with me. With that we had to be content, but it was very frustrating. Time was very much against us: more of our creditors had obtained judgements against us, and expenses were mounting up. The property man's interest blew hot and cold it seemed, and as the weeks wore on he became more elusive, and when not elusive positively evasive, so we began to think that nothing would ever happen. I questioned Catherine, now back at Sandaig, as to what we might expect from her friend, and she dodged off the subject so quickly and on to another that my suspicions were aroused.

The second subject concerned the fact that I was still putting pressure on her to pay us the balance of £1,000 for the deplorable Cremona, and she now announced with a certain truculence that she had been advised that it was not worth it. From whence that advice came was very clear to me, as was the fact that the worm had indisputably turned and that Catherine now held the strings. Gavin, always on the look-out for duplicity in women, stormed in distant Africa, and was not best pleased when the former grateful suppliant dashed off a score of abusive letters to him accusing him of ingratitude and indicting me as his minion. It was sad, but in the prevailing climate emotions were out of vogue, and the money situation left no time for lamenting lost friendships. Rights and wrongs became confused in the general acrimony, but pride was left and murdered the chance of any real reconciliation. A cold and guarded bitterness took the place of the once warm relationship, and mutual esteem turned to ashes. Gavin and I were both aware that we had been worsted by this guileless woman and he took it very badly indeed.

We dropped the property man—or he dropped us, no matter which—and we were back where we were, with more time lost; and time was running out. Our creditors had their heads together and were finding new ways to grind us in the dust, all at our expense.

Looking back on that time I can think of few events that either raised or lowered the general level of my mental distress,

as the business I had been hired to preserve continued to fall
apart at the seams. I became like a fox hunted by our creditors,
but having a foxy nature anyway it was not difficult to assume
and develop the characteristics that make possible the survival
of that Jew of the animal kingdom. As things had been going
before Gavin's departure for Tangier, we had been advised to
transfer a few assets to his name, for pressure was mainly on
the company; but people began to get wise to this ruse and
assets then became the temporary property of anyone, including
myself, who was not being chased for money at the time. Gavin
had left behind him many bills for which the company could
not possibly claim responsibility if it were to retain the separate
image of an independent body (e.g. tailors' accounts) and as
the company was called Gavin Maxwell Enterprises and
had an address at my home, people who had been deprived
of the fruits of their trading began to turn up at my door
hoping to have a brisk word with the culprit. Most people in
Inverness knew us both by sight and many confused us with
each other, and since a great mass of debt was owed in the
Highland capital the incidence of these calls began to rise.
Often I would go in answer to a knock at the door to find a
man there who would greet me with a question: "Mr Maxwell?"

"No."

"Does Mr Maxwell live here?"

"Not often."

"My name is McStoat. I have come about my account.
Are you sure that Mr Maxwell is not here, or that you are not
he?"

"Reasonably."

"May I ask when I can see Mr Maxwell? Perhaps you can
give me an address?"

"You cannot see Mr Maxwell at all. He is in Africa."

This usually had a nonplussing effect, but sometimes the
applicant would complain more or less bitterly that he thought
it unfair that the debtor should be travelling when the creditor
went without his money. This point of view was entirely
supportable and produced a stock answer: "He is not travelling.
We have sent him there so that he can pay your account";
which was both flattering and encouraging.

The likeness between us, unremarked by close friends, often

proved amusing. A woman of my slight acquaintance once walked past me with shyly averted eyes after an initial look of recognition. I wondered how I had offended her. Later I saw her again in the street and she came up to me with a smile: "I am sorry if I seemed rude. I thought you were the other one!"

One night, very late, the telephone rang. I was alone in the house with little Jane; Joan had started the evening with a political meeting and had gone on afterwards to continue the discussion. The wildly weeping voice was Catherine's. She asked me if I could come over to Sandaig at once; she had just heard that her husband was dead. Jack Baxter, thirty years his wife's senior, had followed the same profession as the disappointing Ashburton, but he was a different sort of chap. Not suave or fashionable, with none of the professional detachment one might have expected, Jack Baxter was a warm sociable person to whom I had taken a liking at once. He had a reputation for taking on lost causes and was known in some circles as the poor man's barrister. He had come north with the Indian fellow and had confided to me that he had a very bad heart and did not expect to live much longer. It surprised me that he and Catherine had elected to live apart, for he seemed extremely fond of her, doted on his pretty little daughter and their time together seemed to be filled with exchanges of cheerful humour. I gained the impression that neither of them discounted the possibility of a reconciliation: now it was too late.

It would have been a good time for me to make some amends to Catherine by giving some human comfort and support when it was most needed: this time when I failed her it was against my will. I could not leave Jane in the house alone, and I was unable to contact Joan. After expressing my sympathy for her I told Catherine this and she seemed to understand. I promised that Joan and I would come to her first thing in the morning and in the meantime I suggested a hot drink and bed. Oh, what facile advice.

Catherine was dazed and miserable. Suddenly it was all too much for her. Out of the warmth of her nature she had taken on an exacting task and the thanks she had received in return had been less than effusive. Gavin and I had been too much preoccupied with material things to spare much time for her feelings, and the fact that she had volunteered for this gratuitous and onerous duty did nothing to absolve us from responsibility. Now, in her emotionally weakened state she had received a heavy shock, a *coup de grâce* if ever there was one, which might have driven a lesser person out of her wits. As it was she was temporarily prostrate, and it was well that she had my wife, whom she liked and trusted—and who is supreme in cases of emergency—to bully the feeling and sense back into her, and set her and her daughter on the train to London and the sad business ahead.

We went back to Sandaig to hold the fort once again. Gavin, on hearing the news, sent Catherine a formal letter of sympathy. To me he addressed a request—to go birds' nesting! I had written to him for advice on the most economic way to feed Teko and Edal and he replied with full details of how to harvest and feed gulls' eggs to them. It was now May and the herring gulls were beginning to lay. Young Jane—to whom this was a great adventure—and I set out out in the patched-up *Black Dinghy* and spent a day collecting this revolting source of protein from two large colonies near by. Between us we pocketed over 500 eggs and thus made a small adjustment to the ecology of the area. The herring gull is a frightful scavenger and breeds to indecent excess; it elbows out other species such as the tern, eider and common gull, and it was a satisfaction to make a change in the balance of avian power at such an advantage to ourselves. In the last part of his letter Gavin said: "As otter food the eggs are crushed and beaten up with their shells, embryos and all, and with the addition of a certain amount of lard turned into a sort of mixture between scrambled egg and omelet. The resulting unappetizing but highly nutritious mess is packed in wax fridge containers, each large enough for one full otter feed, and deep-frozen."

It was well that we were obtaining additional otter food, for at about this time the resident otters were joined by visitors Mossy and Monday whose unexpected return is so delightfully described by Catherine in her letters to Gavin, which he published in *Raven*. I saw them once or twice—little darting faces or the momentary whisk of a disappearing tail—and their fleeting presence made Sandaig a happier place and offered a truce in their otherwise bitter correspondence. Catherine was nursing her sense of grievance with a neurotic fervour and her complaints to him were continuous. This particularly angered Gavin—who, after all, had gone to Tangier to write a book—and he became so apprehensive about her that he refused to return to Sandaig until after she had left with her entire menagerie. This was not all. He would engage a certain seventeen-year-old boy who had corresponded with us for some time to look after him for the remainder of the summer so that he could finish his book in semi-solitude. That was the real slap in the face. Catherine, freshly back from her husband's funeral, raged over it. And about leaving Sandaig, she would do so—but only when she was ready. Over this she was adamant, and her readiness depended on a wide range of happenings coming to pass and certain conditions being met. Her true reason for this awkward attitude was her belief that Gavin was casting her aside now that her usefulness was at an end, although her own over-expressed sense of grievance had given him some justification in his search for another companion. I had now shut my soul to the moral rights and wrongs of this sorry situation, for I do not like to vacillate, and I owed allegiance only to Gavin. Much of my sympathy lay with Catherine, but she did not employ me. It was as bleakly simple as that.

Gavin arrived in London on 18 June and took up indefinite residence in his Chelsea flat. Peter Janson-Smith had welcomed him back with the news that some literary income was becoming available, although what there was of it went straight to Gavin and the company remained out in the cold. We had no income but also very few expenses. Catherine kept herself at Sandaig, the otters had their omelets (poor brutes!), and I had kept enough money in hand to retain the supply of electricity there while she paid all her personal telephone calls. I went to Sandaig very seldom now, for there seemed no reason pressing enough to offset the cost of petrol, and Catherine had developed a rare knack of making me feel guilty and embarrassed—although we were still on perfectly affable speaking terms. Each time I saw her I returned to the question of her move to Cremona. Gavin and I had agreed that some modest renovation to that house—God knows, it needed it—might encourage her to go there. Its condition had become so bad that a few days' work spent on superficial decoration and essential repairs produced an impression of dramatic improvement. Catherine was pleased; it looked as if we were winning the battle for a vacant Sandaig, but it was Joan who finally persuaded her that it would be in her best interests and her child's to give in and go. Joan used the same arguments as I did but coming from her, who was answerable to no one, they had an honest ring, and Catherine knew that it was not just a further ruse to promote Gavin's interests, but a genuine concern for her well-being.

Gavin had recently decided that the two otters should go to Woburn Park, the Duke of Bedford's commercialized stately home, and his enthusiasm for this new scheme almost banished his frustration at the goings-on in the north. In fact for what he had in mind he was better where he was, he made frequent trips to Woburn to inspect the proposed "ottery" site and to talk about the scheme with various interested people, while in London he lived near to a man who had said he might back it financially. With something new to get his teeth into Gavin was happy; his active mind required stimulus and challenge, and although the concept itself might well be crazy he would apply his absolute attention and work towards its outcome fanatically. This was a characteristic we shared, but I lacked his vision.

The outcome of the present planning was the establishing at Woburn Park of the two otters by the autumn, in the care of the lad who was soon to be employed at Sandaig; then Gavin would move south and Sandaig would be closed down finally. I had heard it before, or something very like it; much as I admired Gavin's clear-cut conception I had some reason to doubt whether he had sufficient emotional strength to part with his two animals and break the strong links that bound him to the north. Somehow I could not see him living in Bedfordshire.

The day of Catherine's move became close, and Joan and I stayed at Sandaig to help her with it. Back and forth I went between the two houses with full loads, for Catherine was something of a hoarder and had concentrated many of her possessions, material and animal, in the house she was about to leave. At the end of one such trip I was just entering the front door when the telephone rang. I assumed it was for me. My employer was at the other end of the line and he sounded remarkably unwell, both in spirits and in health. He spoke in a low, grating voice—as though he had recently swallowed an abrasive—and cleared his throat at frequent intervals.

He opened with: "Richard, are you alone?"; and I said "Yes" and wondered what new confusion this secrecy heralded. "Are the other receivers on their hooks?" he persisted. (Sandaig was a snooper's paradise with no less than three extensions in its modest interior.) "I'll have a look," I said with mounting curiosity and some misgiving. A quick glance into the living-room showed Joan and Catherine placidly drinking coffee. I returned to the study: "Yes, we are in private. Whatever's happened?"

He began sententiously: "Whatever I tell you must be kept to yourself. I have some news that will affect our plans. You're sure you are alone?"

"Yes, yes, what is it?" My growing alarm charged my voice with irritation.

"I have lung cancer: it's pretty certain."

A shock wave went through me as though ice had been injected into my veins. Not quite irrationally my first feeling was one of outrage that the buoyant mood he had exhibited when I spoke to him last had been so brutally shattered. Then a tide of sympathy broke over me in which compassion for him was swamped by personal fear of the thing which he must face, the one truly private event in any man's life which is the end of him. It struck me that I had not realized how strong an affection I had for him, and the knowledge became ashes in my heart.

"*Are you still there?*" he asked urgently; and at last breaking the silence which is reserved for remembrance I said: "My dear chap!" and added with a candour forced out by the instant pathos of the moment, "What does one say at such a time?"

"Nothing emotional, at any rate. And don't write me off yet, for though all the indications are there it isn't certain. They tell me they will know when the X-rays are examined in a few days' time. Keep your fingers well crossed for me. Meantime my case is *sub judice*, so not a word to anyone: we'll not cancel any plans but we'll make no more in case the gods are angered by our contempt and strike us down all the sooner, and—" here he broke off to cough most raucously, "now I'm going to drink a bottle of whisky so that I can first come to terms with and then put the whole thing out of mind. We'll not speak any more now. I'll 'phone as soon as I have news. 'Bye, now." He rang off.

Gavin's death sentence was never quashed but it was suspended three days later. His X-ray photographs showed no sign of what had been feared. It says much for his control that the neutral voice in which he gave me his news offered no hint as to whether the verdict was life or death, and I had to wait for the words to find out. When I had done so I said: "You've no idea how pleased I am to hear this"; at which he chuckled and replied: "So am I."

And for us the darkest hour had certainly been that before the dawn, for following swiftly upon Gavin's deliverance came an event of a different sort which raised a great weight from shoulders now habitually bowed, and brought the almost forgotten sun back into the sky. After a chilling lack of interest in the place two people within a single week came north to view Isle Ornsay cottage: Sir Alec Guinness and a certain Mr J. S. Johnstone. Sir Alec liked the cottage and doted on its situation but felt sure that its difficult access would deter his wife. As I set him down at Inverness station a message was brought to the Land Rover (one of the advantages of having Britannia written in large Arabic letters on your car is that it makes it conspicuous!) that I was to 'phone Mr Maxwell in London. I did so. I was told not to mind Sir Alec's decision because somebody else was on his way and his interest was in no doubt. He, accompanied by an old friend of Gavin who had told him of the cottage, would arrive in Inverness by the morning train. I seriously wondered if it might prove less tiring for me just to sleep on the station, rather than go home at all. It was eight months and more since Ashburton had left the bargaining scene and in that time we had had two active enquiries—within 48 hours. Oh, the eternal unfitness of things.

It was worth it for the outcome, and would have been in any case, for Stuart Johnstone was a good man to bargain with, whether one won or lost. As it happened not much bargaining was needed. The day and the tides were right; as soon as he set his eyes on the place he decided to have it and if the price I quoted had been too high for him he'd have fought me tooth and nail. But it wasn't, nor was he in any way deterred by the rampant fungus that almost withered under his bold scrutiny or the great damp patch that sprawled all over a bedroom wall. One didn't dissemble with this big, bluff man and I remarked boldly, as though I was proud of them, that we had Merulius and poria and rising damp. "So I see," he said, "and no doubt dry rot as well. But we'll worry about that later. I want this place—and my wife will love it, she's a painter—and that's all there is to it. But I'm surprised you don't touch up the paintwork before people come to see the house."

I laughed: "Normally I always have done. But in this case there wasn't time. I only heard of you for the first time 24 hours ago. But it seems that even unintentional honesty is a good policy, that is, if you are going to buy the place?"

He gave a great laugh, and I knew the matter was settled.

There was a satisfaction in having waited so long and tried so hard, for if the cottage was what they wanted they were the authentic people for the cottage, and I could very clearly see that Mr and Mrs Johnstone were going to be in love with Eilean Sionnach for the rest of their lives. There was also a shade of sadness in realizing that I would no longer be able to come and go here as I wished, and I thought of the early days, Jimmy Watt's skeleton, finding my feet in the pram, being tested by big seas, many and varied crossings of the Sound, David and Marco Polo, dust and more dust. Little things amuse little minds, perhaps. Oh, well.

On 1 August—bang on time—Gavin eased himself from his Mercedes at our front door. We hadn't seen him for nearly a year and we had a lot to talk about.

12

UNEASY INTERMISSION

———————

ONE MIGHT HAVE thought that with this plethora of good news—the company coffers no longer empty and its chairman saved from the kind of death that everyone avoids (if they have any choice), while Catherine was about to take up her long intended residence—all would have been sweetness and light, but, alas, life and human nature can be singularly perverse, and it didn't work out like that at all. Personal relationships went from bad to worse. Gavin sheltered under our roof determined to avoid Sandaig until Catherine and her zoo were gone. He would not speak to her on the telephone, far less meet her, and all observations between them went through me; like an electric condenser I absorbed the sudden shock of their outrage with each other and metered it out at a more acceptable level. "You'd think I had the plague!" she remarked to me bitterly, and indeed the determined aversion he showed her suggested nothing less.

Looking back on it I see how unfortunate, how unnecessary, it all was. Catherine was very fond of Gavin. It was not in his nature to give all of his affection to any woman, but he had respected her and held her in some regard. A variety of small circumstances had sown seeds of distrust on either side, and Gavin's fear of becoming further involved in an acrimonious situation led to his determined avoidance of her. Thus communication was lost between them and in this silent vacuum anger grew apace. Catherine thought of me as Gavin's bad angel, and in possibly trying to discredit me incurred his added wrath. In the end the reconciliation I had hoped for when she was independently housed in Cremona—which Gavin had more than hinted he would seek—did not take place, and poor Catherine, bitter and disenchanted, gave up

Cremona and left Glenelg. If I have ever felt guilty or ashamed about anything, it is about my part in her disenchantment.

Gavin's weakness in acquiring unusual pathological states had helped him to bring back from North Africa a rare intestinal protozoa. Said to be self-limiting, this occupant could not be evicted and would only leave its host's body in its own good time. Medical opinion would not confirm a link between it and the sinister symptoms that had suggested lung cancer, but so little was known about the African emigrant's performance that it seemed impossible to dismiss a possible complicity. It plagued him unmercifully during the negotiations with Woburn Abbey, and when he came north he brought it with him, though by then it was failing. He accepted it with his usual rueful stoicism, remarking: "At least, it's out of the ordinary. That appeals to me." He did, indeed, like to be exclusive, and greatly favoured unusual things, His car, to be fully acceptable to him, had to be sufficiently special for it to be unnecessary to remember the registration number.

The good fresh air of Drumnadrochit coupled with an opportunity to drink in peace completed the cure, but no sooner was he free of the protozoa than he complained of a fierce pain in his right lung. Job was never so afflicted. This was most alarming in the context of what had already been feared, especially when he began to spit up some blood. A clot on the lung was diagnosed, and further examination and treatment strongly advised.

This condition coincided with Catherine's vacation of Sandaig, and he was now anxious to return there and join the new boy who was called Andrew Scot. He was determined to make this landfall first, then talk about hospitals again if necessary. On the way to Sandaig we called upon Mr and Mrs Stuart Johnstone, now resident at Isle Ornsay cottage, to discuss some matters arising out of the purchase. Here he looked most abominably ill, and seemed infirm of wit as well as body, and I felt that the Johnstones must have thought his days were numbered. I took a more cheerful view. He often got protectively drunk on meeting new people, and on this occasion as on others he was able to misrepresent the spirituous effects to be symptoms of his current illness.

At Sandaig I left him in Andrew Scot's care. Next morning I was summoned to take him back to hospital in Inverness.

He was bringing up a fair amount of blood and his state could not be disregarded. He stayed where I left him for no more than 24 hours, then rang me up begging to be rescued. He was not happy in hospital, the discipline irked him and he had been told—or had discovered—that the clot of blood might be expected to disperse. It was reluctantly admitted that out-patient facilities would serve to keep him under observation and he discharged himself at once and returned to Drumna-drochit. From there we commuted daily to the hospital.

Gavin had been still in the south when Andrew Scot reached Scotland, and he had told me how I should recognize the lad by various items of clothing and footwear; the telephone conversation in which these marks of identity were mentioned contained much other material of a complex character and brown shoes were the only items he emphasized sufficiently for me to remember. A short search of Inverness station at ground level revealed more than one pair of shoes of this colour but before long I came across an appropriate pair of legs and looked up to find a dark-haired boy regarding me with speculation:

"Mr Frere? Am I right?" he asked. "How do you do? Mr Maxwell told me how I should recognize you."

"And me, you," I laughed, shaking his hand. "As a matter of interest, what were my points of recognition?"

Andrew looked rather embarrassed: "He told me that your hair would be wild, you might be unshaven and in all pro-bability you would be going round in circles looking at peoples' feet."

"Mr Maxwell has a name for being devious. Come and join me in a cup of coffee, and then I'll take you to your new home."

We were good friends, Andrew and I, from that moment onwards. At seventeen years of age he had a sturdy nature, a strong body and an appreciative mind. A Kentishman by birth who had from an early age been fascinated by the wild Scottish highlands, he combined the traditional solidity of his native county with the mystic imagination of the Celt. He would speak openly of having tears in his eyes at the sight of a sunset; such explicit expression of emotion might have sounded affected in a person of lesser substance. As I grew to know him better I detected a hint of a certain darkness and introspection in his nature which made me a little uneasy; its interaction with Gavin's complex personality was too unpredictable to forecast, but I saw on their meeting at emotional level the stuff of which crises are made. It was some comfort to know that, with their solitary days at Sandaig limited to the time before its closure, such possible confrontation would only be short-lived.

By late August the plans for the otters' new life at Woburn were far advanced. Gavin was still living with us—although his condition had improved—and he spent his convalescence working with boyish interest on a scale model of one of the two creations of steel, glass and wood which were to house the otters in the Park. The model gave us both a lot of fun. Gavin had a fine sense of detail and colour and the small masterpiece grew in complexity. Soon the time came when we decided it was necessary to introduce the figure of a man (to represent an otter-keeper and to indicate the scale) and we scoured the Inverness toyshops in an effort to find a figure of the right size. Finally, almost in despair, we came across Bat Man—who has, I am told, some significance to the younger generation—an upstanding, plastic fellow attached to a board, and it must have done the shopkeeper's heart good to see two middle-aged, respectable and apparently sober gentlemen going into raptures over their find.

The model owed its existence to Gavin's proposal that I should build the full-scale counterparts at my house, and have them transported to Woburn in early December, where I should fit them into a colonnade around a certain folly named the Chinese Dairy Lake. I have never been able to follow plans so I asked him to provide me with a simple facsimile, and out of this request the model blossomed and became an end in itself. From it I saw clearly the details of the structure he expected me to build, but I was still unable to visualize how the units would be fitted into the colonnade so I proposed to Gavin that I should make the trip to Woburn Park to see for myself what was involved. Here I met Gavin's friend, Michael Alexander, a practitioner in the art of animal presentation who had recently acquired concessions at the Park, and he showed me the site chosen to be the otters' future home. I found it impossible to share Gavin's enthusiasm for the place: a muddy pond, encircled by a horseshoe-shaped ring of near derelict wooden columns and arches, lay quivering in a cold east wind. The Chinese style and its forsaken air ludicrously suggested a massive and unwanted present from a serving soldier in Hongkong to his mum and dad.

Michael Alexander, however, seemed satisfied: it was he who was putting up the money for the extensive alterations necessary to prepare the lake for the otters and the colonnade for a public viewing point. After stamping my feet and walking briskly round the lake I felt warmer and more prepared to appreciate possibilities: no doubt it would be all right. Yet it worried me that the Woburn hierarchy had not so far made any firm pronouncement upon the suitability of the design, and that liaison between them and the associates was only intermittent. More alarming still was that between the associates themselves there were major points of disagreement. Gavin's design was flamboyant—in the true sense of the word —and thus appropriate to the pseudo-oriental character of the place, but solid in its use of traditional materials, and it made (as one would expect) no concession to cost. Michael's conception was rather more trivial both as to decoration and construction, and nowhere was this conflict of intention more apparent than in the question of the central division of the lake. Gavin's two otters were never partial to one another; it was always accepted on good evidence that Edal would kill Teko if given half a chance, and it was an absolute necessity to keep them well apart. To do this Gavin demanded a submerged fence with central steel stakes and weld-mesh sides. It was indisputably the right thing, but it was to be very expensive, and Gavin was not paying for it. Michael had no first-hand experience of Edal's curious vendetta against Teko, and therefore proposed a flaccid offering of reinforced polythene with which both Gavin and I were notably unimpressed. We warned Michael that this slender barrier would not resist the onslaught of an angry otter and that the outcome of his parsimony would be muddy slaughter in the Chinese lake in full view of his animal-loving public.

However, general observations apart, I had obtained all the data I needed to carry out my part of the plan and soon returned north to inform Gavin of my findings.

By then he had left my house and was presiding over

Sandaig in great contentment, filled with praise for Andrew
Scot and re-establishing his relationship with the otters in
exactly the way he had planned for his new book. For once
he had no need to stimulate events. Andrew who had nurtured
his young mind on the Camusfearna books found the reality
exceeding his expectations.

And there were other things about to happen, good and
exciting things which began to make us think that the spirit
of malignancy that had dogged us for so long had turned
away its frowning countenance and left us, for a little season,
to make our own mistakes. Money now began to arrive from
various sources and I was able to budget comfortably up to
December and the move to Woburn.

One such source of income was a television company who
sent a team to Sandaig to interview Gavin as part of a feature
called *Smith on Solitude*, which was concerned with the life
patterns and philosophy of some of those who had opted out
of the madding crowd. The members of the team were jolly
people, amiably controlled by a trades unionist who smoked a
disapproving pipe at the signs of Gavin's rather triumphant
capitalism, and they turned the cottage upside down with
cameras, lights and gadgets. Being ignorant of the problems
I was amazed that so much time could be wasted. Gavin's
study remained inviolate and I sat across the door like the
angel with the flaming sword while he got peacefully drunk
within.

One of the film sequences (designed apparently to show how
solitude was having its effect upon a formerly balanced mind)
involved Gavin in a seaside trudge followed by the two deerhounds, Dirk and Hazel. In the middle of this walk he had to
stop, pick up a piece of driftwood and examine it with an
enigmatic expression as though it were the skull of old Yorick
himself. If he did this sequence once he did it twenty times,
and each time something went wrong. The successful recording
of this simple act seemed as elusive as the sun, which had shone
heartily in the early morning and had only now chosen to
dodge behind small clouds. While its inconsistency was the
main problem there was no shortage of others and Gavin
began to grow weary in the repetition of his walk and became
more peevish and irritated every minute. Only the deerhounds played their uncomplaining part. Impressed by the

gravity of the occasion they walked gravely behind him, never doubting the sanity of their human masters.

At last a time came when all seemed well. The first of the two cameras was set up where the walk was to start, while the other was arranged for intimate observation of the wood-lifting sequence. A board was held up in front of the camera and Gavin and his two companions in solitude began to stalk away across the beach. He was going at the right speed while the sun shone in friendly approval. Soon the recluse halted, bent down and lifted the predetermined piece of driftwood, at which he stared in anger and disgust as though it were a peculiarly obnoxious piece of litter which he had found in an otherwise immaculate park. The second camera now took over, zooming in to capture the profound effect of this supposedly significant moment upon his face, then focused back in disappointed haste as Gavin dropped the wood on the beach as if it had soiled his hands. At this very second Hazel, unable to contain herself any longer, took the opportunity provided by the halt to defecate blatantly in full camera view. A young French assistant, leaning against the Land Rover from which I obtained a grandstand view, murmured, "*Merde!*", which seemed to sum up every aspect of the situation to a nicety.

The film producer Joe Strick had held an option on the rights of *Ring of Bright Water* for some years. Now he decided to take it up. This news caused great excitement; it would mean a solid sum of money which would confirm Gavin's return to solvency, and if the current plan to make the film at Sandaig were to take place we could leave it in December wreathed in a fresh immortality. Or, in fact, we might not leave it at all, as a chance remark of Gavin's, volubly supported by Andrew who had no wish to return to England, seemed to hint. I was not as alarmed by this as I should have been. My employment, of which on the whole I was very fond, would obviously end when Gavin's Woburn period began, and after all the only valid objection against keeping Sandaig going was lack of money. The expectation of riches tends to warp sober judgement, and when it was suggested that the Sandaig location would result in such things as sponsored road improvements and other marginal benefits, it was clear that if some major snag hit the Woburn plan our next move could be deliberated in comfort. We eagerly awaited further news from Peter Janson-Smith who with his customary thoroughness was building up a climate for a successful deal; having done which he would send the director up to meet Gavin, discuss the script and decide upon the suitability of the location.

When the day of his arrival was known there was a scramble at Sandaig to produce a good impression. Labouring under the popular impression I imagined he would be fat, ruthless and semi-literate, impressed more by Gavin's lineage than by a million odd copies of *Ring of Bright Water*, cigar-chewing and tough-dealing, readily diverted but not easily foxed. Since no worthwhile business deal is ever concluded around a pauper's table and all the best financial empires are founded on port and cigars, we planned to stock up Sandaig in such a way as to really impress our man and gain our advantages in an atmosphere of well-fed euphoria. Gavin 'phoned Joan to implore her to spend a day in Inverness for him shopping in the grand manner; she went to work with a will. Neither she nor Gavin was ever able to accept the restrictions placed on good living by indigence, and in this dangerous unity I feared that all my cautious precepts would be overthrown—although I fully agreed that we must put on a show, I hoped that the show would not run too long. Sheepdogs brought up uncomplainingly on porridge show a marked disregard for it once they have tasted meat again, and I had a worried feeling that this necessary relaxation might lead to a crippling resumption of gracious living. It also struck me that Gavin—who took serious exception to any interference with his art—would not care for an American interpretation of his famous book and might fall out heavily with the director when the script came up for discussion. In that case we should probably be left with an epicurean larder and no money to pay the milk bill.

The day came. The director, whose name was Jack Couffer— a man of considerable note in his profession, closely associated with Walt Disney—was due to arrive at Tormor at ten thirty in the morning. I was there to meet him, for supposing our guest to be like Hamlet "fat and scant of breath" we had offered the Land Rover for the descent of the hill. Only a small non-American car was parked carelessly at the head of the track. I waited for a while, then assuming that Couffer must have walked, drove down to Sandaig.

The man who rose to greet me as I entered the house was the absolute reverse of what I had expected. A huge, rugged fellow with the undeniable stamp of outdoor living upon him, he grated my metacarpal bones with his earnest grip, and the ramshackle Sandaig chair muttered its protest beneath his athletic bulk. He rejected our whisky with courteous finality but under pressure accepted a light beer—it was only by chance that we had such anaemic stuff in the house, for we had not thought it necessary—and the next shock came when he refused a mighty cigar of quality from a box whose ruinous cost had made me wince. "I never use it," he said, with what, in a smaller man, would have been primness. His taste in food was simple and he showed delight in the venison which Gavin always cooked in a masterly fashion. The meal was a success and after a decent intermission we began to talk business.

It soon became apparent that Jack Couffer was as tough as nails. Money was not being discussed: that was Peter Janson-Smith's concern. The script was *pièce de résistance* and it was left until other less important matters had been resolved. Gavin was pleased with Couffer's wish that the film might be shot on authentic location and I saw many practical benefits emerging from this plan.

The script like a dubious guest had been kept waiting at the door; now it was brought out and laid before Gavin who read the first few pages rapidly, then more slowly, as though to convince himself of their reality. He said, in a voice of deep hurt: "But you can't *mean* it—this is just not possible. You have depicted me as a middle-class business man" (unconscious humour here at which, in happier circumstances, he would have been the first to laugh), "as a, as a——" He was unable to finish and as his voice trailed away he began to tremble with rage and grief. Jack Couffer looked on with adamantine composure thinly mixed with compassion, while Gavin called upon all his reserves of composure. While doing so he pushed the script across for me to read. I opened it at random so it was quite by chance that my eye fell on a phrase attributed to the author on wearying of the attentions of his greylag geese: "Scram, you guys!" I promptly turned the page in case Gavin should see it, and read on. It was certainly a travesty, and although the book obviously posed a substantial problem in being adapted to the screen, I felt that the dialogue need not have been quite so puerile or carry such a strong American flavour. My reflections were interrupted by Gavin who had renewed his strength by consultation with the whisky bottle and was now ready for battle.

He belaboured the script with rich invective. He said it was a shame, a prostitution, a crime. He ended with the bitter remark that unless it were entirely rewritten he would not allow his name as author or his identity as principal character to appear in the credits and would take anyone to law who plagiarized his story. Said Jack Couffer in his soft drawl: "Then I guess we don't have a deal." The situation was now getting out of hand and I suspected that things would soon be said that would take some swallowing. Gavin, head resting on hands in his most theatrical attitude, gave me a cunning look and said: "Richard, would you minding quoting Kipling's 'If' to Jack, beginning with the verse that starts: 'If you can bear to hear the Truth you've spoken . . .'?" Unthinkingly I recited those uncompromising words unaware, until I saw a look of satisfaction in my employer's eyes, that in doing so I had inferred that Jack was a twisty knave and the cinema-going public fools.

Something had to be done quickly. I asked the now sardonic director if he would mind my having a few words in private with Gavin, for as his business manager I had some proposals to make which might relax a rigid situation.

Jack guessed he would take a turn round the house while I bullied Gavin into a compromise. In the end there was a limited amount of give and take and "we had a deal". Gavin Maxwell, business-man extraordinary, vanished from the script to be replaced by Graham Merril, a discontented and computerized clerk who had for the purposes of dramatic licence formerly lived with Marsh Arabs. Parts of the script— but not much—were to be revised. My poor friend thought his art debased, which it was impossible to deny; but I was equally prepared to agree with Jack when Gavin was out of the room. This, I believe, is the misuse of diplomacy. The sum of money we could now expect was quite large: I remembered the lean months of the "rearguard action" when I had fought a lone battle against an army of creditors, and was quite prepared to bend, then as ever, my concept of truth in the interest of expedience.

*   *   *

At home I was busily building the two otter houses which were destined for Woburn. Each of these amorphous objects consisted of a large box, lined with sound- and temperature-proof materials, on four stout legs. The front of the box was a steel frame containing two opening windows, and there was a fixed window in the back. All these windows were to be double-glazed with one-way glass, so that while the public could observe the otters, the creatures would not be demented by the sight of goggling humanity. On each unit there were two wooden staircases joined to an exterior veranda, one leading down to the ground (up which the otter walked) and the other up to a platform above a big glass tank (into which the otter dived). In their final positions in the colonnade each unit would be separated from the other by an extension of the under-water fence dividing the lake. Because it has always been my hobby I thoroughly enjoyed building the units and employed every free moment of each day hammering, screwing and cutting. A week before the original date planned for the move the units were ready.

But though they were, it seemed that little else was. At Woburn a state of confusion existed: delays and shortcomings were the rule and no one appeared to know who was in charge of the construction upon the site, or who was answerable to whom. Michael Alexander had been out of the country for some time and his factotum was a disconsolate cynical man, available only by telephone in an office he seldom appeared to occupy. The great glass tanks, made in London, had arrived, but one had been dropped and was no longer watertight, and a variety of other misfortunes and ineptitudes seemed to dog the scheme.

It was no surprise to us when on his return to London a distraught Michael Alexander telephoned Gavin to bewail a state of unreadiness, and announced that there would be no provision for the otters at Woburn until some time in the New Year.

It was the beginning of an old story, in a new setting. But this time it was no belated change of heart of Gavin's that was threatening the scheme. He had decided that as far as he was concerned the otters should go to Woburn as planned and that Sandaig should be shut down then, or after the film company had finished their location work. On the other hand, if the Woburn owners suddenly decided against the idea then the otters could stay where they were: there was, at least, a choice. Gavin had asked for a house on the Woburn estates, confirmation that he intended to take the whole idea with the utmost seriousness. The old order was indeed changing, but what new thing it gave way to would be no concern of mine. My performance on this stage was drawing to a close and the thought made me unhappy.

Work was now resumed on the site. A compromise had been agreed upon for the central division of the lake, but Gavin was still chasing Michael to provide the maximum safety with a spectacular presentation to the public. It might have been remarked in mocking disapproval that Gavin was prepared to spend his associate's last penny in the Chinese Dairy, but the whole set-up was, or had been, flamboyant and grandiose and unless the otter display could match up with its gaudy splendour there was little chance of it pleasing the hierarchy. And, as far as I knew, no serious inspection of the work upon the lake had been made since the plans for its division, and the alterations on the colonnade had only been provisionally approved.

And when it was inspected in the middle of December, a cry of outrage was made and all further work on it was forbidden. Just what it was that had upset the aesthetic taste of the owners we were never allowed to know, and having seen the many abominations already violating the stately grounds we felt we had been discriminated against most unfairly. The terse note from the management denied us the use of the lake but offered a choice of two consolation sites: no decision could be reached without inspection. We decided to go to Woburn in January, meeting Michael in London en route, to see what chance remained of coming to terms with Woburn. Privately I knew there was none. Gavin wanted the Chinese Dairy Lake, or nothing. I did not blame him. He had steeled himself to sacrifice Camusfearna at last in exchange for what he conceived to be a nearly ideal alternative, which was now denied him. Compromise never suited him. He preferred to scrap an idea rather than modify it, and he could now do this without courting immediate disaster.

Joan and I spent the New Year at Sandaig. There was

contentment in the old house at last, yet, as I wrote in my
diary, it was an uninspired occasion, overshadowed by the
inconclusiveness of everything. On 8 January we travelled
south in bitter arctic weather, met Michael in London and
went to Woburn two days later. Our meeting with the Comptroller was more sterile than stormy, with the air of a foregone
conclusion. In frost and snow we took a cursory glance at two
small waterholes in a forgotten corner of the Park. My
immediate impression was that to modify the two units with
their pre-designed dimensions and lack of weatherproofing
would cost as much again and take twice as long, and I
whispered this opinion to Michael who was understandably
upset about his investment. He, poor man, was not much
encouraged by this negative information and favoured some
form of compromise, but Gavin shook his head in deadly
finality and stalked off through the snow.

There was nothing more to be said. We took our leave of
the Comptroller to discuss what had happened and what was
to be done. On our way back to our car we passed through the
colonnade of the Chinese Dairy. Derelict it now looked with
the supports of the unfinished fence marching across the lake,
and the bases of the great tanks half built among the wooden
pillars—but it needed no visionary to see it in its completed
form, as Gavin had, and I marvelled at the management's lack
of confidence and foresight.

Before we left London to come north we had several talks
with Michael Alexander. We agreed that with all the work and
scheming behind us it would be a great waste to terminate our
association and Gavin and I proposed that we should search
for a site in the north, somewhere, unlike Sandaig, which
would be in public reach. There we would establish a wild-life
park with the "ottery" forming the nucleus of a wider complex.
Unfortunately the burden of further sponsorship always seemed
to fall on Michael, who in view of his recent total loss over the
construction work on the colonnade, tanks, units, et cetera,
was inclined to be reticent over money. But he was interested
in a general sense, and when we parted company it was with
the firm intention of keeping closely in touch.

Back in the north it seemed sensible to look for sites in my
own area before Gavin returned to Sandaig. In the end the
one we favoured most was on my own ground—a narrow stretch

of rough woodland adjoining a stream. Gavin had great hopes
for it. We went to bed that night with continued rather than
renewed hope, the setback at Woburn having been too short
in duration to have led to a lapse into melancholy. In fact, so
far as I was concerned things had never looked better, a
continuation of the work that pleased me so much, in the
convenient setting of my own home.

I drove Gavin to Sandaig in the morning. Jimmy Watt had
joined Andrew for the few days of our absence. The two of
them listened with approval to our new plan. Jimmy, who had
spent much of his early youth in successfully grappling with
the many problems arising from Sandaig's isolation, saw no
flaws in it while Andrew applauded any undertaking so long
as it took place in his beloved Highlands. Gavin's passion for
planning had taken hold of him again so strongly that he had
all but forgotten the weeks of frustrated effort that he had
given to the Woburn scheme, and in his mind's eye the
Drumnadrochit Wild-life Park was taking shape hourly. It
delighted him to know that Sandaig would be still in reach,
and he proposed to leave the house semi-furnished for the
occasional use of any of our group. That afternoon I went
home to a few days of concentrated office work, writing
innumerable letters to people whose plans would be changed
by the rejection of Woburn's offer and to others who might
be expected to help with the current idea. On Saturday
morning I set out again for Sandaig to report my progress,
and, incidentally, to return Jimmy Watt to Inverness and his
train for the south.

It was a quiet house I came to that morning, and outside a
great thaw was taking the iron out of the rutted road and
stripping the hills of their modesty of snow to reveal the dun-
coloured nakedness beneath. A young girl cousin of Gavin was
playing chess with Andrew from the red hessian-topped fish box
seat below the provision shelf. Gavin and Jimmy, I was told,
were sleeping off a merry night, and I had no need of them in
what I had to do. I spent some time in Jimmy Watt's former
room—the wooden wing that had been added to house the
expanding household—taking some notes from the otter-house
model, and walked across to Edal's quarters and said, "Good
morning, otter!" but she was engaged in happily rolling about
on her back and gave me not a glance. In the loo I chuckled

for the hundredth time at Gavin's comprehensive collection of newspaper clippings and cartoonery: one which never failed to amuse me showed an apprehensive prisoner, head upon the block, about to be attended to by a grim-looking executioner carrying a large handsaw: "Damn it, old man. Sorry about this. I'm afraid I've mislaid the axe!"

The day which followed was slack and slow. Gavin, looking distinctly "hung-over", gradually emerged from his bed-study and with amiable taciturnity prepared us all what was known as a "Maxwell's Bean Feast", a sophisticated variation upon a theme of Heinz. His attractive cousin was brightly vivacious, but everyone else seemed a little deflated. At about three o'clock Jimmy and the girl—she was riding up the hill with us in the Land Rover—began to collect their belongings and a hesitant attempt was made to leave. Gavin chose this moment to request a private word with me: this took half an hour, or more.

Now we had to rush away, for Jimmy's train left Inverness at seven o'clock. In view of later events I have often tried to make a sketch in memory of that scene in the living-room because I feel that something must have been different. The curtains were drawn, the lights burned brightly, the carcase of a Maxwell's Bean Feast congealed on somebody's plate, a piece of massive driftwood smouldered stubbornly below the engraved Latin inscription about the Will of the Wisp, a photoflash unit charged itself from a wall-socket and the old, ruptured pair of bellows lay in the hearth in ironic attendance upon what was so soon to happen. Gavin and Andrew in the midst of all this friendly confusion had returned to the chess board. We said our good-byes and went out into the dark, windless, rainless night, closing the door of Sandaig behind us for the last time.

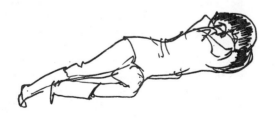

13

A FIRE AND ITS AFTERMATH

WE TOOK SOME time to climb the rough track from Sandaig to Tormor. Although no rain had fallen for several days, neither had there been sun or wind to dry the snow-sodden surface and somewhere on the moor all four wheels slipped into an old deep rut and it was not easy to extricate the Land Rover. It was now impossible to reach Inverness in time to catch Jimmy's train, and I suggested to him that we should go to Newtonmore where we should be sure to intercept it. He thanked me and since the Glenelg bar was open and close at hand insisted that he express his thanks in a practical manner. We met some friends and the time gained by our change of plan was soon drastically curtailed.

After what seemed an endless drive through the dark night we came to Newtonmore. Not knowing the scheduled time of the train's arrival there I had pushed the Land Rover to its limits: now we learned that we were twenty minutes ahead of it. We said a relaxed good-bye and I started on my way home.

My son Richard was at that time learning the essentials of hotel management at an hotel at Aviemore, and what more pleasant near the end of a long day than to call on him for a nightcap? We were pleased to see each other and spent some time at the bar, and it was not until eleven thirty that I reached home, to Joan's well-concealed delight. I was tired and a little unsober: asleep, as the saying goes, before my head touched the pillow.

The formal announcement of Sandaig's destruction came about six hours later. The telephone stands beside our bed. At just before 6 a.m. its metallic summons broke into my sub-conscious to provide the appropriate climax to some forgotten dream. Dry-mouthed and dizzy I picked it up and said stupidly: "What is it?"

"Mr Frere? This is Nairne, Glenelg police. I want you to come here as soon as you can. Sandaig house has been burned to the ground."

"Is this some poor joke? Nonsense, man. I was there about an hour ago!"

"Mr Frere, Sandaig House has been burned to the ground. It is no joke."

"Oh, my God, no!"

"Yes, but Major Maxwell and the boy Scot are safe—an otter's dead."

"Which otter?" I asked. It was hardly important, but one clear detail might add reality to the news.

"Edal, I believe." (Poor Edal, poor little female otter. She might have been safe in Aberdeen, with the doctor's wife, or at Woburn.)

"Right. I'll come as soon as I can."

I told Joan what had happened. Then I dressed quickly and put on the kettle for tea. While waiting for it to boil I went into my office and rummaged through some files. What I found there gave me no encouragement at all.

The journey to Sandaig usually takes rather more than an hour and now I had this time to consider what might have happened. Every so often the process of conjecture was swamped by a sense of incredulity. There hadn't been time for it to happen. And the constable had plainly stated: "burned to the ground". But how did he know? Perhaps it was a whisky-inspired tale told by a local idiot bent on causing confusion. I wanted to think so, but logic blotted out this ray of hope. Nairne would have most certainly confirmed a report before referring the matter to me; he had merely to telephone Sandaig to do so. The news must be true. How then had the fire started?

Such speculation was without point. Within a short time the facts would be all too clear. But this sombre guessing had become a therapeutic need, for in its absence returned the appalling belief that something that I should have done or confirmed I had neither confirmed nor done.

At Glenelg it was grey morning, dry and bland, a small breeze from the south-west rippled the sea gently and in the village not a mouse stirred. Only the police station showed a tired light and the policeman's car was gone. Oddly enough, nothing seemed changed, but at Tormor, sinister and dramatic, stood a fire engine, frustrated by the two miles of impossible track.

I had driven fast from Drumnadrochit, spurred on by fear and fascination, but with the final revelation now so close at hand nothing was left in my mind but dread of what I must see. Slowly the Rover crawled across the boggy flats until it stood poised on top of the final hill. A wreath of smoke billowed up from the valley and I looked down into a very fair imitation of hell.

All was gone. The house, splintered and roofless, glowed like a crucible and ugly black stains twisted from the lower windows up the face of the walls. Were the wooden extension buildings intact? The heavy smoke haze and the tears in my eyes made clear vision impossible. Then I saw only the ruined contents, like those of a dolls' house kicked flat beneath the feet of a petulant child. No need to wonder how Edal had died; her compartment, like the rest of the room, had ceased to exist in three dimensions. But Teko's house alone of all the independent structures had resisted the flames and still stood bravely against the stark north gable. All round the devastated buildings the grass was scorched yellow by the heat, and round this periphery walked a few firemen poking the embers in an apparent search for anything that might have survived in its original form.

I drove down the hill to comfort Gavin as best I could, filled with a certainty of my dreadful oversight, yet determined to prolong a cowardly silence by the thought that he would be in no state to learn that the total contents of the house were uninsured. I found him in the drawn-up *Polar Star* looking like a plant blasted by frost, black and drooping, and Judas-like I offered him my hand. He smiled bravely through the sedation the doctor—already on the scene—had given him, and said he was sorry to have dragged me out so soon after my last visit. To this I had no answer, being overcome with miserable guilt. He was without shoes, and almost without clothes. Fortunately I had a spare pair of boots in the Land Rover which I gave him. It was a very small exchange for what I had taken away. Constable Nairne was standing near the boat and he came over and spoke to me, drawing me aside.

"The doctor says not to disturb him too much—he's heavily

sedated, he may sleep. They had a hellish time. Andrew's gone with the doctor, he cut his hand badly—saving the guns."

"Did they get anything out?" I asked hopelessly, scanning the smoking ruins.

"They got the manuscript of the new book, the guns and Teko. Everything else is gone."

Tom Nairne began to fill in some details of the picture. He had been wakened in the early hours by Andrew and the tenant of Tormor who had driven the exhausted boy to Glenelg to bring belated help. By then it had been all over with the old house. Andrew had only left Gavin when it was plain that nothing more could be done. The telephone wires had been burnt away in the undetected stage of the fire, but had it not been so it would have made no difference to the outcome. No effective aid could have been brought anywhere near in time.

Gavin now asked for me so I returned to *Polar Star*. After a while he began to speak in a discursive fashion about the immediate problems: the shock had been so intense that his mind was disorientated and he made little sense. Suddenly he sharpened, mentally shaking himself—a trait I had observed in him more than once—and asked obliquely the dreaded question, phrased in such a way as to give me every opportunity for honesty: "Richard, I suppose there wasn't much insured, was there?" To which I answered, "Oh, yes. I think that everything is all right." It was not quite a lie, I was still not sure but I had the gravest doubts. With the moral coward's hatred of confrontation I saw no reason to precipitate what might just be an unnecessary crisis.

At my answer he nodded absently, almost without interest: when he spoke again it was in a voice so low that I had difficulty in hearing the words—"Richard, could you find it in your heart to bury Edal?"

"Of course," I replied. "Where do you want me to put her?"

A flicker of understandable pain and distress, coupled with an expression hard to identify, crossed his face; he pointed without hesitation to the solitary rowan tree that stands between the ruin and the river. "Below that, and mark her with a stone, if you will. Later we shall do her some justice." He muttered something beneath his breath and then, seeing my awkward pause, added with firmness: "She's over there. You see, she couldn't get out."

In the general chaos on the ground it was not easy to find her body. Only the outline of her compartment was there. I had not expected that her body would be so shrunken, for the tiny, crusty object I found was easily contained within the cups of both my hands. I picked it up and took it to the bottom of the tree. Here I scraped out a shallow hole with the heat-softened blade of a ruined spade, and buried the thing beneath the garish, unscorched berries of the tree which is the witch's enemy, and placed a stone on top.

Only then did I remember that this was the tree upon which he had been cursed. I knew it well from him, but he was yet to tell the tale in *Raven Seek thy Brother*. It was a curious story of a poetess with whom he had had a deep and almost mystical relationship. She had been his close companion in the early days of Camusfearna, where they had spent much time together in the company of the otter Mij, forming a kind of trinity. Here he had quarrelled violently with her, and in her extreme grief she had rushed from the house. Placing her hands upon the tree, she had cried out: "Let him suffer here as I am suffering."

Behind me I could feel the heat from the glowing heart of the fire while overhead the cracked and blackened gables stood stark against the dull grey sky. As I went back to Gavin I glanced into the smoking crater. The destruction was all but absolute, nothing that had been of wood remained. Bedrooms, staircase, living-room, study and kitchen had vanished as though they had never been. Within the naked walls, heavily stained by the oily tar of the pitch-pine lining, lay a ragged mass of metallic débris, slate and stone, much of it still red hot: here and there protruded the twisted, paint-stripped shapes of larger household appliances. At the north end of the shell the smoke was thickest; it rose in slow and surly protest from the ashes of Gavin's priceless library. I stood there in the gap where the door had been and pondered the many things that had been in that house, some of high material cost, others of much greater value which had been the rewards of a lifetime of travel and experience, and I shuddered at the totality of the loss. Faced with it and the near certainty of my calamitous contribution to the tragedy, I almost forgot to give thanks for the unexplained miracle that had saved my employer and his assistant from being reduced to a condition like that of the charred, crusty fragment under the rowan tree.

I walked slowly back to Gavin. Now that Edal had been buried he appeared to accept an end to Camusfearna, a chapter burnt and dead as that in any of his ruined books: shocked and miserable he yet managed to summon up his capacity for detailed planning which never deserted him, even in his most profound defeats. We went into the Land Rover. Gavin had begun to shiver and shake; I ran the engine to provide some heat in the cab. As we sat talking a small motor boat rounded the point, and a few minutes later Andrew Scot stepped ashore. He looked very tired and his right hand was bandaged, all his personal possessions were lost but all his concern was for Gavin and the otter in Raef's cottage. From what I had learned he had behaved with great courage, particularly in the transfer of Teko to the cottage and the last-minute salvage of the guns. He asked me at once to confirm that Teko's shed was safe so that we could return him there, and thus make the cottage available to shelter Gavin and to prepare some food and drink. The shed was miraculously undamaged, we pushed a few overhanging slates away from the gable and Andrew went back for the otter. Teko gave the ruined house a frankly disapproving glance as he was carried past—as if to say, how badly these humans manage their affairs!—but otherwise seemed remarkably composed.

Gavin was anxious that a simple statement should be given to the press, who throughout the morning had been appearing on the scene. We composed a short paragraph which told of the house's destruction, the safety of the two humans and Teko, and the death of Edal. We added that, at this stage, Mr Maxwell had no further plans. Predictably one newspaper given to outstanding inaccuracy and melodrama in its reporting spoke the next morning of a "roaring inferno" on Mr Maxwell's remote Scottish "island" out of which Mr Maxwell and his assistant had walked "unscathed". It added strangely: "Belco, a companion, perished in the flames." Whether the third member of the family was otter or human was not revealed but later when the passage of time made such jokes permissible Gavin and I would describe anything which had no substance in fact as Belco's ghost.

But the press had been kind to us, declining to jostle or

scratch for any information beyond our simple statement. Not so the police. Constable Nairne had been gentleness itself but another, of higher rank, who came after him seemed anxious to reduce Gavin to emotional rubble. The final question, "Mr Maxwell, did you set fire to the house yourself?" was too much altogether, and I determined to make use of my guilty conjecture to some advantage. I drew the detective aside and said: "Cannot you see he is quite broken up by your questions? He has had a terrible night. If you imply—which is pretty clear—that this is an insurance swindle let me tell you that I think nothing in this house was insured. The building was not his property. Your offensive question does not even apply therefore." This seemed to satisfy him, for shortly afterwards he went away.

As the brief dark winter day merged into night reporters, firemen and police made their weary way up the track and the three of us were left in Raef's cottage. Raef had carried out a robust conversion upon the former byre, and the accommodation consisted of one long room with bunks along the east wall and two windows opening on to the rocky foreshore. It is much closer to the sea than Sandaig and within range of the spray of a south-westerly storm. It had electricity for light and cooking and an open grate at one end which smoked abominably in certain winds, but the question of sanitation had always been referred to Sandaig. When Raef came north in college vacations he had been accustomed to "commute" from his cottage to its more sophisticated neighbour, and accordingly life might be just as spartan as he wished. But suddenly the cottage was isolated and a stay there which might have been invigorating in May or June would be cold, uncomfortable and grossly inconvenient in the dark months ahead. From what I had sensed from him Gavin had no intention of leaving the immediate area until provision had been made for Teko, and this would take time, for the otter was no longer a household pet.

We ate a small meal—no one was hungry—and drank whisky. Slowly their miserable story emerged. Gavin, habituated to the use of sleeping pills, had been deeply asleep until woken by a choking sensation. His first thought was that he had been struck by a recurrence of his recent lung trouble, but as soon as he opened his eyes they smarted violently and the stench of smoke was strong in his room. The switch of his bedside lamp produced nothing more reassuring than a click. He knew he must warn Andrew, who slept in the bedroom overhead: "Andrew, Andrew, this house is on fire," and he stamped his feet and beat the walls with his fist in order to attract the boy. There was no immediate response. Fearing that the boy had been overcome he began to climb the stairs, only to collide with the falling, half-blinded Andrew who had missed his footing in the darkness. He was gasping painfully; Gavin thrust him through the front door to recover.

From the living-room came a subdued deep-throated crackle. Determined to find the origin of the fire Gavin took a deep breath and snatched an extinguisher from the wall; kicking open the living-room door he went a few feet inside. He was met by a wave of heat and a great cloud of acrid smoke. Through it he could just see that the far wall around the fireplace was bubbling with burning varnish and just below the ceiling a fringe of flames was greedily attacking the open beams and planking of the upper floor. He discharged the extinguisher at the hottest area; the flames winked and briefly died, then returned in force. No longer able to hold his breath he rushed from the room.

Andrew had recovered. He was in Gavin's study and had already removed the manuscript of *Raven Seek thy Brother* to safety. It was then that they thought about Teko, who in the shed which was integral with the main building, was in greater danger than Edal in her compartment in the annex extension. Or so it reasonably seemed. Once they had Teko out and safe in Raef's cottage they would return to see what they could salvage from the house while time still remained. But as they moved away from the house they saw that time had all but run out. The whole roof was on fire from end to end: its dark outline was punctuated by tongues of flame that darted out between slates already cracking in the intense heat. As they watched in astonishment at the speed of the fire a mass of burning débris crashed down the stairs, all but sealing the entrance. Entrance by the side door from the extensions had been denied them from the first, for it seemed that there, or in the adjacent fireplace, the conflagration had originated.

Andrew dashed into the lean-to shed and having flung the astonished otter over his shoulder, ran through the gloom over a hundred yards of rut and bog to Raef's cottage. He unlocked the door and bundled Teko inside.

Meanwhile Gavin had gone to confirm that Edal was safe. She did not appear to be in her compartment but it was impossible to be sure, because the only light came from the burning house, and its flickering caused odd shadows to dance in the room. But her hatch, tied up by a piece of rope, was open and there seemed no cause for alarm.

The only further items that might be salvaged were Gavin's guns. Their case stood at the bottom of the stairs opposite the entrance. To this Andrew turned heroic attention and pulled and shook in an effort to tear it from the wall, but it was well secured and would not budge. With his elbow Andrew smashed the glass and passed the guns out to Gavin one by one. Before he had them all the latter shouted: "Andrew, for God's sake come out of there *now*. Look, the ammunition——" But Andrew had seen it too, several hundred rounds which had fallen out of the case and into the burning débris at the foot of the stairs. Andrew shot out of the door like a rabbit, leaving behind a pair of spare barrels, a Colt pistol and a Winchester rifle. Almost at once came the harsh cough of exploding ammunition. Gavin got out of the way while Andrew went to reaffirm that Edal was in no danger.

The roof had collapsed in several places and flames were roaring out of upstairs windows. Only the floor of the north bedroom and part of the staircase remained as recognizable shapes. The living-room was a furnace, a single protracted sheet of flame: air howled in to feed the firestorm through the front door and the shattered window.

Andrew came back, ashen-faced he cried out: "The long room is on fire!"

Gavin said: "And Edal?"

"I don't know," replied the boy, "I just don't *know*. It's all black in there, thick and tarry smoke. You can't see a thing. I just got in through the nearest window but I couldn't open my eyes. I tried the window on the other side, next to her compartment, but it's too hot to touch. The grass is all burnt up——"

Gavin interrupted: "But it's not on fire?"

"Yes it is, just above the lavatory—look, this end—"

Gavin must have seen it from where he was without registering the fact. Flames had swept through the side door and set the annex ablaze. Now it was filled with the heavy gas from melting tar of the felt covering which dripped down the sides of the wooden shed and came in through cracks and gutters. The tar ran like hot treacle, smoking thickly; the atmosphere inside was unbreathable. If Edal was inside she was certainly dead, but there was no way of finding out.

Suddenly flash-point was reached. The long room blew up as the gas ignited, the walls fell over sideways, the roof fell in and that was that. Unfortunately, unpredictably, unbelievably Edal was beneath it when it fell, though probably already dead from suffocation. Why she was there at all must always remain a mystery.

The night's macabre entertainment was not quite over. The fire having glutted itself on the long room turned right and swept through the workshop. Within minutes it touched off tins of paint, Calor-gas cylinders and two jerrycans full of petrol while almost simultaneously the remaining floor and the rest of the roof fell into the furnace of the old house. A brief glare lit the circle of the wooded bank and cast sharp shadows behind the watching trees, while two muffled explosions like the salute of guns proclaimed the end of the house at Camusfearna.

That was the story which I pieced together from them, and when it was told it was very late. I refused to stay the night, for I would have felt like an intruder on the private griefs of those who had gone through so much together, and I had a selfish wish to escape from the unavoidable atmosphere of gloom which must prevail. Nor, if the truth be told, could I look Gavin in the face as I feared that by my monstrous carelessness not a penny of his great loss might be recovered.

Promising to return in two days' time I left them in their misery and took mine with me. I started the Land Rover and drove to the bottom of the hill, hesitated indecisively, stopped, got out and walked over to the ruins. In the still strong glow from the heart-fire the walls and gables stood like the face of a mountain ridge in the red light of a harvest moon. Nothing was there, between the walls, where men and women had loved and hated, triumphed and despaired, died and been born. Nothing of their essence was left, nor the echoes of their cries. Fire had sterilized their ghosts and wiped the vibrations of emotion clean from the slate.

Somewhere away to the north there was a cry like an otter's. Was it Mossy or Monday, perhaps, crying from some holt of their choosing in the dark river's bank? I could see the rowan tree in the glow and I walked over to it, found the stone and rested both my hands upon it, staying there a while until the cold and a sense of desolating loneliness sent me back to the Land Rover and the long road home.

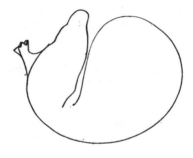

14

THE PHOENIX

DURING THE COURSE of the next week I made several trips to Raef's cottage with all manner of articles for the survivors. It is impossible to imagine (unless it has actually happened to you) the effects upon everyday life of the loss of everything you possess. Because Sandaig had been so much his favourite place, Gavin had gradually taken everything he loved there as well as much that he just liked to have around him. There were a few things in his Chelsea flat, some more at Kyleakin, but the great bulk of his inherited possessions and those he had accumulated on his travels were hoarded in the half-dozen rooms of that house. The inventory which we compiled listed over 300 noteworthy items of substance which totalled a value of nearly £10,000, and would have cost double that to replace; other things could never be assessed or restored as their value was contained in the circumstances of their acquisition.

And nothing was insured.

From the moment of my brief glance at the files on the morning of the fire I had little real doubt that this was the case, and a closer examination served to confirm it. The insurance situation had been confused when I had taken responsibility for such things eighteen months earlier, and it had been my obvious duty to clarify it; but instead with a kind of indolence I had credited a vague belief with much more substance than it was worth, and had assumed that a newly-appointed firm of brokers had taken over *all* the insurances from the old. Acting inconsistently I had given full attention to exploring the market for the best terms for boats and cars, but as far as the houses were concerned it seemed that I had rejected the possibility of any harm ever befalling them. I fell into a trap which exists for the unwary and imprudent by accepting the fact of a past immunity as a future guarantee against harm. Fate had called my bluff, which was hard luck for the man whose interests I was supposed to have at heart.

I wrote to the former brokers setting out the details of the loss in the normal way but saying nothing of what I knew about the unpaid premiums. It occurred to me that the concerned insurance company might be prepared to make an *ex gratia* payment since my oversight had resulted from confusion, and I myself had nothing to gain by the outcome. Until I had their reply there seemed little need to confess the truth to Gavin, and the presentation of a letter would be the easiest way to introduce this most painful subject. In the end I was spared the need to do even this, for Gavin heard the facts from lips other than mine. An insurance agent from the estate (owners of the house) called upon him and requested information about the scope of our insurances and Gavin, rather than trouble me for the information, 'phoned the brokers direct. He was told by them that in their reply to my letter they had expressed the opinion that the concerned company had no liability towards us since the premiums had been unpaid for nearly two years.

At this time, about ten days after the fire, my whole family were suffering from a feverish infection. Gavin was nervous that he or Andrew might contract this infection in their primitive situation where they could do little to help themselves or the otter and it was agreed that I should not visit them until I was free of it. Therefore the news came to me by telephone.

He started by asking how I was. "Very low," I said.

"I am sorry, for I have some bad news. Can you stand it?"

"I shall have to."

"Well, there was no insurance on anything in the house. I have just had to 'phone the brokers. They have answered your letter. The premiums don't appear to have been paid."

Though taken initially unawares I had prepared a seedy voice to suggest an illness greater than I felt, in order to gain some sympathy. I said: "This is my fault, certainly."

"Your responsibility!" he replied, and I was amazed at the absence of anger in his voice.

"There is no difference in the outcome. I have all but ruined you through carelessness. If I were rich it would be easy for me, for then I might reimburse you from my own means, but

I am a man of small substance and this would be impossible. I cannot even work for you for nothing."

"Neither of these would I permit. Look, Richard, let us get this matter in proportion. We have been associated for some time. I asked you to manage my company—which means, as you know, my affairs also—because I liked and trusted you. Since you took charge I have felt a different person —the very first time in my life that I've felt it safe to leave things to someone else, and try to get on with my work un-hampered by neurotic worries about practical problems. Up until this moment your performance has seemed immaculate. Now you are found to have made one mistake: it is undeniably unfortunate that its results are so disastrous. But since we are both rational people we surely realize that the degree of blame is not proportional to the outcome of what at most is a sin of omission."

At first I could speak no word in answer. Guilt which stemmed from my carelessness was added to shame that I had not understood him to be so big a man; and to these was added self-abasement that in my ignorance of his tolerance I had felt it necessary to employ devious means to protect myself from his censure. Often I had doubted his integrity: it seemed that he had not doubted mine. His capacity for forgiveness extended beyond anything I had thought possible, and since that quality stands high in the credits of the Christian faith (and other faiths of good standing) never again did I doubt his presence among the immortals.

At last I said: "Thank you."

He went on: "The milk is spilt and this is an end of it. Please keep your mistaken guilt feelings to yourself or, better still, forget them. When we have the brokers' letter we may find that there is still something useful to be done."

That letter offered no hope of a happy outcome but slightly eased my conscience. With it was a copy of a note sent to Sandaig in late June of 1966. This contained a stern reminder of money owed on premiums, and an ultimatum that unless a cheque was promptly received the papers would be returned to the companies for cancellation. By some mischance this letter had never reached me; had it done so even I would not have turned my back on its urgent message.

Now came books from friends, clothes from relatives and

goodwill from all over the world. Raef's cottage lost its spartan emptiness and began to fill up with the widest possible range of offerings which included such things as a Scout knife from a Manchester boys' club and a tin of sardines from a little boy of five years old who lived in Cornwall. This pointed gift suggested a prevalent belief among his junior following that Gavin was even more destitute than he actually was and Gavin—who always ensured that his fan mail was answered—sat down to write to the kindly child to thank him for the gift which "had arrived in the nick of time". Fortunately one of us noticed that a message was glued to the tin. This said: "Thes is for TEKO case hees hungry." It was pleasing to see Gavin, who had seldom laughed since the fire, chuckling delightedly. "I must do this one again," he said, tearing up the freshly written letter, "or I'll lose a fan. Can't have the little blighter think I'm taking sardines out of the otter's mouth, even though I'm starving."

And numerous other things more serious—though no more sincere—than the little boy's sardines poured in to fill the vacuum which the fire had left. A well-known zoologist sent a typewriter, and many were the gifts of substance and value which a grateful public offered to the writer in his hour of need.

Three weeks after the fire the winter began in earnest with a succession of heavy snowfalls and hard frosts. Life at Raef's cottage became much harder, although neither complained very much about it. One of the most distressing aspects of the situation was the impossibility of having hot water and to overcome this I would drive them in turn to Glenelg where such luxuries were available in the houses of some of Gavin's friends.

By the end of February, all of us having recovered in some degree, we gradually began to plan where to go. Kyleakin was the obvious, even the only, choice, and apart from the recurrence of an isolated situation with its threat of costly services the move there had much to recommend it. Gavin wrote in his still unpublished book, "I loved Kyleakin and everything about it, and I planned to live in it later". Prophetic words, though now the implied choice was lacking. Not only did the character and situation of the island appeal to him, he had a deep interest in the development of the eider duck colony with which he had started to experiment in 1965. Due to divers happenings he had been unable to give this project his personal attention; now it would be on his doorstep, so to speak. He began to speak of it in terms as the nucleus of his next book, and I knew that he had never given up the idea of the wild-life park which sprang from the Woburn débâcle, and had been halted in the confused situation that had followed the fire.

It made me happy to see such a strong resurgence of interest. He was now at an age when accumulated blows from unpropitious Fate might have been expected to floor him, but Gavin was nothing if not resilient and his elastic powers were in no danger of being numbed.

As for Andrew, the prospect of going to Kyleakin fascinated him. He loved the sea, and boats, and was never happier than when an opportunity occurred to take the dinghy out among the Sandaig islands in the short days of that clear, sharp and flamboyantly beautiful winter. At Kyleakin he would be going to sea every day. So they both looked foward to their new home in their different ways, and they could have gone there without more ado had it not been for the requirements of Teko the otter. About his demands Gavin spoke to me in detail; they involved quite a lot of work.

The walled garden would offer him space for his terrestrial activities only, but he could do without swimming for a while. The garden was far above the level of the sea and it would require a powerful pump to send water up to it. There was going to be enough work in preparing the garden to contain him in safety, for he was a bold and wily otter whose unmatched ability to escape made him the Houdini of his species. As it was, it was far too ramshackle to contain anything: in many places the walls, massive and six feet high, had crumbled into the heather and brambles and across the south-west corner a broken gate hung from its rotting posts. We discussed Teko's sleeping quarters and it was decided to use an old hen-house for the purpose; lying outside the garden it would require enlarging and reroofing before it would be fit to contain him, and then a stout corridor of weld-mesh would be needed to give him access to the garden.

We had to decide who was going to do the work. To me this was a simple decision—the best person was myself. But Gavin objected violently. He was not going to ask his managing director—I had been promoted recently, certainly not on merit—to do manual work. My days for that were over. Such a thing would be most unseemly. We argued for hours about it. I knew that Gavin who assumed a very democratic attitude for practical purposes held in reality no such ideas, and readily reverted to the views more appropriate to his background. He had recently found out that one of my ancestors had been honoured by a Spanish king and he assured me that the right to the title lay in perpetuity through the male head of my family. Not content with this information which seemed to give him some satisfaction, he demanded that I give him permission to promulgate it in *Raven Seek thy Brother*. He now declared loudly that he was not going to have Marquis de la Union, Visconde de la Alianza, digging up walls, and that it was time that I gave up my preoccupation with manual skills and got down to some serious thinking.

It took me some time to show him the flaws in his argument, but in the end it was settled. I went back to Kyleakin.

So, on 29 February of the leap year 1968 I was back on the rocky beach struggling with the old *Assunta*, inert as ever despite the fact that she was as dry as a cork. Once in the water she leaked fearfully through dried and shrunken planks, and it is a mercy that the crossing is such a short one; otherwise she would have sunk, for though I baled her with a big bucket the water steadily gained on me. Once at the jetty I took away the movables, filled her with stones and let her go down—it was the only way to make her partly watertight, but I fancied she was by now quite past her best.

The island had not changed, the house was musty and cold but not as damp as I had feared it would be. As always it took me the whole evening to get used to it again. There was the well-remembered eerie feeling as the short day faded into the long northern night. The new moon had called up a monstrous tide which rose so high that I wondered if it would ever stop rising, and soon it began to freeze. I spent a cold, damp night just out of reach of my immortal companions, and in the morning came the reassuring thud-thud of the generator and the cooing of early eiders.

March was mostly damp and windy; in the middle of the month there were gusts of up to 90 mph along the western seaboard. I had left for a weekend at home and thus missed the full fury of the gale, and it was fortunate that by chance I had drawn the *Assunta* much further up the beach than usual. At Sandaig the ill-omened *Black Dinghy* had received punishment that would have destroyed a normal boat. Lying on top of the dunes it had been caught by the wind and hurled about 40 yards, and not a plank was split, although more of the caulking fell out. If such a thing had happened to the poor, faithful *Assunta* not one plank would have been left joined to another. Gavin called upon me to witness this miracle when I stayed at Raef's cottage two days later, on my way back to the island.

The occupants had been exhilarated by the hurricane and were certainly none the worse for it. At its height the waves were almost breaking on their doorstep and the crash of cascading water and the scream of the wind made speech impossible. They had rolled into their sleeping bags and listened in comfort to the elemental turmoil so close at hand. By the time I arrived it was dead calm, the only evidence of the storm (apart from the *Black Dinghy*'s spectacular flight) was huge piles of seawrack thrown high up upon the shore. Gavin and Andrew were pretty cheerful and I was invited to stay the night.

Despite the discomforts of cold water, very hard beds, a diet limited by the means of cooking it, a cold and draughty dwelling, an army of mice and Owl, the two humans were faring much better than I had expected. They both had an infinite capacity for making-do, a quality which I had underestimated in Gavin, although its presence in Andrew was obvious enough. To pass the time they wrote letters, took photographs of Teko on his daily walks (Andrew was now on full terms with the big otter), played chess, fed Owl and planned what they would do when they reached Kyleakin. They were pleased with each other's company: Gavin thought the world of Andrew, while the boy looked upon the man with a mixture of fondness and respect.

I find that I have not introduced Owl. He came, if I remember rightly, from the estate of Sir Robert McEwen, one of Gavin's oldest friends and my fellow director in the company. Owl was a delightful little chap, full of innocent fun, although it did seem to me that his sense of humour bordered on the Rabelaisian. Gavin and Andrew were his friends; they were there to minister to his needs and tempt him with choice morsels of rabbit fur and flesh. I was the intruder, coming infrequently and doing nothing to amuse him when I came. To cut a long story short, my bunk was at the south end of the cottage and wherever Owl started the night he always ended up perched on the rafter directly above me. I do not care to sleep with the blankets over my head, but only by doing so could I avoid the distressing possibility of a direct hit if the diabolical little bird chose to defecate. Gavin, whose sense of humour could be as Rabelaisian as the bird's, roared with laughter at this, as he did when I deplored the constant passage of mice over my bed at night. Fortunately the evenings I spent with them were pretty alcoholic ones, but even when drunk I like to select my bed partners; also it occurred to me unhappily that Owl would soon be old enough to swoop upon his prey.

But apart from these minor deterrents, most of the evenings I spent in Raef's cottage were fun. We had bought a record player; Hancock and Sellers entertained us into the small hours. But I was aware that Gavin and Andrew were still haunted by the memory of that January night. Often as I lay awake in the cottage I would hear one or other of them utter an anxious word or warning cry, as they acted out again in sleep the experience which had scored their minds so deeply.

On the island my programme was coming along rather well. Of great importance was the weather: extreme cold or con- tinuous rain would have brought my work to a standstill, as it was all outside. But the elements were very kind to me; though predominantly damp, and often windy, the month of March was a moderate one. In fact, after the storm which had tossed the *Black Dinghy*, the weather became unusually calm and mild, and I delighted in the pleasant creative work outside, and my solitary evenings in the house reading or watching the recently introduced television. So bland indeed was the climate and so comfortable the house that I suggested that Jane and Joan should join me for the last week in March. I always preferred to have them with me if they would otherwise have been alone at home; there was no telephone in Kyleakin cottage, and I always felt some misgivings at being out of touch for so much of the time.

Jane was in heaven. It was her favourite place, as she lost no opportunity of reminding us; she always found something of interest to do there, whether it was "her rock"—a small outcrop near the jetty which she had been climbing since she was six—a trip to Kyle or Kyleakin in the *Assunta*, preferably in brisk weather, or simply exploring the foreshore for shells, sea-urchins or anything exciting which the sea might have thrown up. The week went by happily, the weather was dry and mild, and my various projects advanced by leaps and bounds. By 31 March, as I recorded in my diary, I had completed the re-walling of the garden and almost all the reconstruction of the henhouse.

"April Fool, Daddy!" shouted Jane, the next morning, at the end of a straight-faced account of how she had watched the unmoored *Assunta* drifting out to sea. And what an extraordinary morning it was for the time of year. The sun shone palely from a sky of the purest eggshell blue, not a breath of wind rippled the surface of the channel, while in the air was that subtle smell of spring which is compounded of all the sweetest breath of earth and trees and water. "Let's stay here for weeks and weeks," said Jane longingly. "Don't let's go home with all this lovely weather."

I spent a routine day fitting a roof to the henhouse. It was now a home fit for any otter. Towards evening I decided to make a quick trip across to Kyleakin to telephone Gavin and to buy some stores. As I walked down the jetty Joan said: "Must you bother to go? It's going to rain. Look how dark the sky has become"; and indeed within the past hour a change had taken place overhead. I remarked that I would only be away for half an hour, and climbed aboard the *Assunta*.

Simon MacLean who had been painting the lighthouse store had just started his motor as I pushed off. As his boat swung away from the jetty he shouted: "Going across?" I nodded, and he went on—"I wouldn't be too long if I were you. That wind's coming down from the north," and he pointed up over the back of the island. To be sure there was a very peculiar dun-coloured cloud racing down from the Crowlins and along the coastline of northern Skye. It looked like a squall of rain and I didn't suppose it would last long. Within minutes the light faded, the wind hit us with a great slap and it began to snow. In seconds it had become a blizzard. Ahead of me Simon vanished into a white curtain of snow, and spume whipped from the crests of the rising waves. It happened so quickly that I hadn't time to adjust my mind to the sensible idea of going back to the island. Still assuming it to be no more than an unusually violent shower, I resolved to do my shopping and 'phone Gavin and wait, if necessary, until the weather improved.

I soon became very cold, for I was not dressed for the occasion. The jeans, shirt and ragged sweater had been comfortable wear half an hour earlier, but now exposed me to a full heat loss in the icy wind. Anxious as I was to get off the sea as soon as possible I forced myself to make the detour round into Kyleakin's harbour (entirely sheltered from a north wind), for I knew that to beach the *Assunta* on a south shore would be folly.

Drawn up against the harbour wall I tied the *Assunta* and went to do my shopping. Local people, unused to such arctic punishment in their mild littoral environment, wore blanched expressions and cringed inside the shops. I was no happier than they and had no stomach for the return on that alien sea; the storm, instead of abating, was steadily increasing in violence, drifts of snow were building up behind banks, and objects standing proud of the ground were plastered. I spoke briefly to Gavin, then ran back to the boat along the deserted road. A vicious gust of wind sent me spinning to the ground and I rolled miserably in the snow.

Mercifully the engine started with the first pull of the rope and I nosed the *Assunta* out of the harbour. With the driving snow and spume bridging the tops of the waves, it was not possible to see how rough the sea was in the channel, but I soon found out. It was unlike anything I had previously experienced, and had the extreme cold left me with the power of active emotion I would have been terrified. My body was now one long continuous shiver, and loss of sensation was creeping up my arms. Dressed as I was for a mild spring day I realized that I was taking a considerable risk in continuing in such weather, but never had it taken me more than ten minutes to reach the island, and in that short time no damage would occur that could not be remedied by a hot bath.

The wind was screaming down from the Crowlins, almost due north of me, and it was unimpeded by any land until it struck Eilean Ban and the Eider Island, whose low shapes only briefly deflected it from the surface of the sea. The waves were short, steep and vicious, separated by narrow troughs, and random in individual direction: the whole ocean, moving with the inevitability of an escalator, seemed to be pouring on to Kyleakin beach. I could hardly see, breathe only with difficulty, and the cold was producing a violent palpitation of my heart. I bent my head, aimed at the Eider Island and, in the absence of more immediate comfort, prayed heartily to God to preserve me.

The boat was taking a terrible punishment. Had she been young, or newly planked, she would have laughed at this treatment, for she had been a trawler's lifeboat and was built on sturdy, practical lines; but now she was an old, tired lady and each time she crashed into a trough, spurts of water came in from between her timbers. Once I saw a distinct ripple run through her length, at another moment she visibly bulged. As she slowly filled with water she grew more and more sluggish and rode deeper, but even so the propeller was frequently spinning in air, so great was the violence of her pitching. These facts, coupled with the huge press of the wind, reduced us to a snail's pace; in fact for about a quarter of an hour the forward motion was cancelled by the drift and we stood out a few hundred yards from the ferry pier, for all the world like an anxious runner marking time. The ferry boats had stopped running, which gave the occasion the stamp of an awesome authenticity, were any needed.

Having started out with the intention of returning to my wife and child there now seemed every reason to continue. I desperately wanted dry clothes and a hot bath; I knew no one in Kyleakin village well enough to call upon to this end without explanation and apology. Then I was worried about my family: had there been a telephone in the lighthouse cottage I would not have set out in the first place. It was now growing dark and in that welter of snow and spray it was unlikely that I could be seen from the cottage. If I did not arrive they would be bound to assume some accident and spend a miserable night of worry on my account. Even assuming I could signal my survival they would be due for much discomfort: there was insufficient fuel in the generator for more than a few hours' running.

With only this miserable conjecture for company I crept along, gradually easing the boat into the lee of the Eider Island. If I could only acquire this relative shelter it would be a simple matter to keep so close below it as to cheat the wind, and nose my way westward into the south bay of Eilean Ban. What must not happen, though, was any premature turn beam-on to the wind, for once the waterlogged boat wallowed in a trough or presented her flank to the turbulent north, no power I had available would ever return her bow to the line I so desperately wanted to take, and we would end up either on Kyleakin beach or on the bottom of the channel.

I judged the struggle had gone on for nearly an hour. I was distinctly light-headed and all the heat left in my body seemed to be contained in a narrow segment between my genitals and my navel: nor was there much of it even there. My right hand gripped the short tiller entirely without sensation: a blow on arm or steel would have produced an equal lack of response. My feet were deep in the sloshing bilge and even in the near freezing sea water were less frigid than my thighs.

Slowly, agonizingly, we advanced upon the dark shape of the Eider Island. When no more than twenty yards remained it slowly occurred to me that here *was* salvation. I had only to find a suitable cove in which to tie up the *Assunta*, land on Eider Island, wade, probably no more than waist deep, across the short gap, and I would be within a few minutes' walk of Joan and Jane, hot bath, steaming cups of tea, everything that at the moment my heart desired. Hubris destroyed me, as it has many others. I had come so far, haltingly, fearfully, yet with determination, and I resolved to push my small luck to the limit and take *Assunta* into Eilean Ban's south bay. It was only a couple of hundred yards away; no hazard remained to dispute a successful outcome except the wind funnel between Eilean Ban and its neighbour. My miserable state was all but forgotten in the growing triumph of the moment. Cautiously I edged along the small, black coastline, with the welcoming lights of the cottage growing larger every minute, turned gently to avoid a large tidal rock that guards the division between the islands, swung back in panic as the wind rushed to meet me, steered straight at the cottage, lost momentum, lost my bow to the wind, my pride to the storm, and was borne away like a leaf towards the thundering surf on Kyleakin beach.

We nearly sank in that five minute journey, the engine was swamped and stopped, I rowed to keep the boat's bow to the wind and baled to save my life. *Assunta* landed half sideways and well up the beach, flung there from the very crest of one of the biggest waves of the day. I thought by the sound of it, the grating shingle and the crunching boat, that every plank in her body was broken.

My first thought was to get into the Land Rover and start the engine so that I might get warmth from the heater. As an addition to my indescribable discomfort I received a powerful electric shock when I touched any steel in the vehicle; in some odd way I had become "live". While waiting for the cab to warm up I positioned the Land Rover in such a way that its headlights were pointing towards the lighthouse, then slowly turned them on and off several times. I felt sure that Joan and Jane would be on the look-out and would understand who signalled.

A fisherman offered me rather grudging hospitality by allowing me the use of his parlour floor for the night. I slept in my clothes, drier than formerly but still damply uncomfortable. I slept badly, worried for Joan and Jane, and from time to time glanced across at the dim lights on the island, not always visible through the flurrying snow. At last I fell into an uneasy sleep and when I woke it was grey dawn without a whisper of wind. It was uncanny in its sudden end, as had been its beginning.

It was a white world outside, the channel rolled dark-blue in the frosty air. Unbelievably *Assunta*, tied to a fence-post, was undamaged, and since the whole foreshore was glittering under a skin of ice her launching posed no problem. She skidded down into the sea and I rowed briskly across, rejoicing in the rejuvenating exercise and in the reassuring sound of the generator. Wife and child rose sleepily to greet me from a pile of bedclothes in the sitting-room. They had understood my signal but seemed nevertheless to be glad to see me.

Despite its uproarious start the rest of April was traditional showers and sunshine. My experience in the storm had set off a disabling pain and stiffness in my back—legacy of a boyhood injury—and I did not return to the west for over a week. When I did it was a painful waste of time. I staggered about with my upper body thirty degrees from the vertical, looking like an arthritic ape and feeling like death. I could concentrate for only short periods of time on any one thing, for movement which was excruciating was the only remedy for a paralysing stiffness. Even in bed I groaned. Fortunately there was plenty of time to complete my programme at Kyleakin, for another factor outside my control was determining Gavin's date of entry. This was the provision of a telephone. After the fire the GPO had installed an instrument in Raef's cottage in next to no time, but at Kyleakin it was a different picture. The situation, to be fair, was in no way comparable; we were informed that the only economic service would be by way of a radio link and this equipment was in short supply. We would have to wait our turn. While doing so I explored costs and my findings showed that the word "economic" was purely relative.

Gavin was very determined to have a telephone. His artistic temperament was not impressed by "cheap rates" or the comparative cost of a postage stamp. Ideas, even the more ephemeral, were seldom allowed to mature on paper, but were offered up to the instrument for instant and costly transmission. None the less, its absence at this time would have been a grave inconvenience, with *Raven Seek thy Brother* at the publishers and all manner of questions and decisions having to be answered or made. He was determined not to leave Raef's cottage until there was a telephone at Kyleakin, and in this I could not blame him. There was accordingly little pressure upon me to complete the building work, and I stayed at home for nearly a fortnight nursing my condition. Towards the end of that time the onset of summer offered the medicine which will always effect a cure (or has done for nearly thirty years)—a strong May sun, shining from dawn to dusk upon my naked back. Gradually the muscles relaxed and the pain vanished as if by magic. Life had suddenly returned in full; I set off for the island once again.

All day long the cuckoo sang in the dark grove of trees that topped the tall rock on the other side of the channel, and the morning eiders cooed their welcome. Around me summer was painting in the colours in what during the short days had been little more than a black and white sketch. It was idyllic and I made the most of it in my quiet, appreciative way, for I knew that while in the future I should certainly spend much time on the island, it was unlikely that I should ever be alone there again.

This thought saddened me as it had on Isle Ornsay when the same thing was about to happen, for I am cast in a solitary mould and derive little comfort or stimulus from mankind, nor they from me. During the month all the plans were completed. Teko's future home was surrounded by an impregnable wall, a stout corridor of steel mesh led to his sleeping place, stout double doors into the garden made entrance possible without a corresponding exit on the part of the wily otter. Gavin had continually emphasized the absolute need of eliminating irregularities on the garden wall or the sides of the corridor, for Teko had always excelled at climbing. Time and again I walked round the areas, trowelling concrete into every crack until it seemed that no living thing could scale the smooth surface unaided.

Now the bulk of the film-rights' money came along, several thousand pounds, which allowed me to pay the last of our old debts. Gavin had been for some time without a reliable car, his sporty 300 SL Mercedes having the flickering brilliance of a menopausal prima donna; anxious and able to travel to friends in the south before the new life began at Kyleakin, he hired another member of the same family from the garage where his flashy lady was having the mechanical equivalent of hormone treatment. He fell in love again, this time with a 220 SE saloon—he was always a sound connoisseur of cars, though less fortunate with women (through no fault of theirs, I hasten to add)—and remarked that as his business manager I ought to think of buying this fast, stylish machine which would be the "most sensible car he had ever owned".

"In any case," he said, "we do not need to return her for a day or two. I shall take her back to the west; come over with me, and you shall drive her to Inverness. Then you can telephone me and let me know if you approve."

Of course I did, just as he knew I would. Neither of us could resist a good car. When I 'phoned him that night I said Yes and promised to negotiate. Reason had been partly dethroned by enthusiasm, but there was more to it than that. He had recently had much to make him miserable; here was something that would make him happy. Life is not forever. And we could just afford it.

When in June there was still no firm date for the installation of the telephone Gavin abandoned his intention to stay any longer at Raef's cottage, and a day was fixed for the move. On the morning we met in a Kyleakin hotel, and had a few drams to celebrate the occasion and then crossed to the island. Andrew, Teko, Owl and most of the belongings they had accumulated at the cottage were coming in a local fishing boat. As he stepped ashore I shook him by the hand and said: "Welcome home. I hope you'll be very happy here," and he thanked me soberly but with a look of blank disbelief, for I think that at last he was losing his faith in the possibility of sustained good luck. As it turned out his doubts were fully justified.

Soon the fisherman's boat appeared as a growing dot in the wide expanse of Lochalsh. Well, we'd made it (as they say nowadays) one way or another. He was here; soon he would be joined by the boy who had become very close to him; by his famous otter; by his little owl. The problem of money no longer gnawed our vitals and had become discreetly inapparent in just the way it should. Money from the film, money from the new book, money from this and that, all our debts paid— the situation was better now than I had known it.

A cloud shaped like a doughnut sailed across the sun. A long beam, searching through its centre, turned the crinkled sea into an inverted firmament of sparkling stars. It drifted on, bringing colour and detail to the rocky, broken shores, and a warm, rare beauty to the summer-green hills gay with their patches of yellow, aromatic broom. Within minutes the doughnut had split apart and the sun-blessed world at our feet became one great uncomplicated smile.

It was so nice that I was now quite sure that everyone was going to live happily ever after.

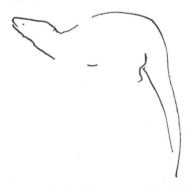

15

THE GARDEN OF TEKO

"This is a glorious place," wrote Gavin to Peter Janson-Smith in early August, "and you must come and pay me a visit. Next year, when I have some animals on the island and the eider colony is in full swing, I am going to open the house and island to the public—but the interior of the house is so beautiful that one could almost open it now."

His life on the island had begun well, only slightly marred by the adventurous Teko, who showed his contempt for my efforts to imprison him by promptly finding half a dozen ways out of his enclosure. His first escapade was the most daring and might have been his last. As soon as the fishing boat had arrived at the jetty Teko had been taken to the garden, where Andrew and Gavin studied his reaction to his new environment for nearly an hour. The otter seemed content, and though his curiosity led him into every corner of his little kingdom he made no attempt to leave it. The two humans returned to the cottage to unpack their belongings, and Teko was left to his own devices until the time came for Andrew to take him his evening meal of fish. He was absent from us for some time and when he came back he brought the news that Teko was gone.

"He's in the long grass, Andrew," I said sceptically. "There isn't any way out of there, except by the door. The brute can't fly."

"I've looked everywhere," said Andrew firmly, "and he always comes when he's called for his fish. I tell you, he's gone."

Gavin, who had shown immediate alarm on hearing Andrew's news, suddenly seemed to have lost interest and was looking through the window apparently preoccupied with the sight of a small rowing boat which was making straight for the island. "Pass me the binoculars, Richard. Yes, yes, I thought so. Have a look at *that*!" he said; and I took the glasses from him and saw an astonishing sight. A man was rowing the dinghy; in the stern were four delighted children; between them, rolling about in ecstatic joy, was an object which was undeniably the missing otter.

The man told us all he knew and we filled in the rest. Teko had been found in his house. To get there he had left the garden, swum the channel, crossed a busy road, entered somebody's house and got into their empty bath. There a child had found him and they had promptly made friends. It was fortunate that by then all Kyleakin knew that Gavin had arrived, so the man realized at once where Teko must have come from, and his returning him so promptly was the act of a good neighbour. The otter was fascinated by his young friends, as they were with him; it took quite a lot of persuasion to convince him that his home was on the island and not in the village opposite.

There was a problem of what to do with him that night, for it was too late to try to detect his way of escape. The best thing was to exclude him from the garden (there was a hatch for this purpose) and allow him the freedom of his corridor. Gavin didn't want to put him under house arrest, as though he was being punished for his initiative. The corridor was escape-proof. On that I staked my reputation.

Our first evening in the lighthouse cottage was merry. Gavin was basking in the warmth of present satisfaction, some of my lingering guilt had been dispelled by his obvious satisfaction in my recent work, and Andrew was delighted with the prospect of unlimited seafaring. We spoke of the many new plans for the eider project which now seemed at last to be within our grasp. Even the generator, usually prone to failure if overworked (the night of the storm being a felicitous exception) hummed happily away and all, as Gavin aptly remarked, "was sweetness and light". Suddenly there was a confused noise at the door as one would expect from the bashfully drunk, a kind of scraping thud. "God!" whispered my employer inapplicably, his recluse-like nature coming to the fore, "I do hope that it's not a load of peasants with welcoming bottles; at any rate, not so soon." Aloud he said hospitably: "Richard, I think we have visitors. Would you be so kind as to welcome them?"

I opened the door. Apart from the twinkling lights of Kyleakin I could see nothing. Then something wet brushed against me and I felt some whiskers at waist-height. "It's Teko again," I said conversationally, "and he wants to come in. Gavin, do you mind if I stand on the back of your settee? After all these years I've never actually met him. There might just be an incident." From the top of the settee I felt more Roman than Christian. At arena level, Teko pointedly urinated in a wide circle over the expensive carpet. Gavin was delighted. "You can come down now, Richard," he said, unkindly, "he'll be perfectly content now that he's established his territory." Much against my will I came down. Immediately the big otter climbed on to my lap, put his paws against my face and made how-do-you-do noises. I replied faintly and to the best of my ability. Teko then got down and lay at my feet. Gavin and Andrew were in fits of laughter.

They wouldn't trust him in his quarters again that night. The only place where he would be secure was the bedroom which I had occupied on and off for the past four years. "I know you won't mind," said Gavin, "if I offer you a sleeping bag on the sofa." It was the first and only time that I have given up my room to an otter.

The next morning we examined the garden walls. What Teko had seen at a glance remained invisible to us. We decided to allow Teko to demonstrate and took up strategic positions round the perimeter of the garden. Gavin had a good idea where the attempt would be made, and concealed himself behind the angle of two walls just outside the otter's house. On being set down in the garden Teko looked smug, secretive and unconcerned: ten minutes went by without a positive move. Then he raised his head and turned it in a slow, full circle as though examining the whole extent of the wall through his myopic eyes. Then with a swift lissom movement he bounded away through the long grass into the corridor and along it to his house. But he did not enter it; instead, without hesitation he sprang against the right-angle formed by the two walls and swarmed up it. As he reached the crest Gavin rose up behind it—"Well, Teko, and where do you think you're going?"

By cementing a sheet of steel across the angle we made it escape-proof, but Teko's ingenuity was not exhausted and he led them a merry dance. But he never left the island again. Indeed it seemed to me that he might be left to roam around the house at will, as in the old days at Sandaig before the otters' aggression made their continued freedom impossible. To me he seemed a mellowed fellow, well disposed towards everyone. But Gavin explained that, quite apart from the safety of others which could not be guaranteed, Teko's compulsive curiosity would draw him to every corner of the island and beyond, even into the rushing tides that girdled it; that one day he would not come back.

In retrospect, I think that the months before Christmas 1968 were happy ones for Gavin, and in them he achieved at last a sense of tranquillity which was not to be repeated. During August and September he proudly showed off the house and island to a succession of friends and business associates, while as *Raven Seek thy Brother*'s publication day drew near, he was in constant communication with Peter Janson-Smith and his publisher. But the absence of a telephone was a great inconvenience. Gavin made few trips to Kyleakin, and in any case he was not the kind of man to use a public telephone in comfort. While the restriction on distant communication was total—either Andrew or I would relay his messages from the Skye mainland—the island's proximity to the Kyleakin road produced its own frustrations. Guests who would have 'phoned from the village had either to come to the beach at a pre-stated time or wave, shout, blow their horns, or flash their lights in the faint hope of being heard or seen. Sir Robert McEwen, arriving once unexpectedly, lost patience with the invisible pair in the cottage opposite, threw his clothes and caution to the winds and plunged into the channel, and did not give up until, more than half-way across, the inexorable flood tide began to carry him away into the Minch.

   The radio telephone came in early October; to start with it proved worse than useless. Three out of four calls were inaudible; the loudest shout was transmitted, or received, as a whisper, and if normal volume chanced to be present it was drowned by a gravelly high-pitched grating noise. In the rare event of neither of these nuisances there was the "epileptic condition", which took the form of random breaks in power of very short duration—sometimes a word would be lost, sometimes only a syllable, but it made sorry nonsense of the average message. Gavin became very angry indeed—the more so because he had waited so long, and he rang the exchange at Kyle twice a day to shout his complaint down an instrument which was filled with the sound more appropriate to a stone crusher. The engineers came regularly and did what they could, but it began to look as if we were the target for some cosmic shooting-range and that the fault could never be cured. Yet sometimes it seemed to respond to people it knew, and one might listen in repressed anger to soft-spoken engineers communicating with each other down what seemed to be an uninterrupted line. No sooner had they stepped into the boat which was to take them away, than the whole gamut came back in strength.

"I don't understand it," I said breathlessly to Gavin, after my fifth attempt to make myself heard in Kyle, "these chaps *were* speaking to each other, weren't they?"

"They weren't bloody speaking to each other," he answered disgustedly, "not as you or I understand it. They just know how to interpret the screech!"

It took a month to obtain a clear reception, and it certainly made life easier for those on the island when it came. A noteworthy, but officially unapproved, addition to the telephone service arose from Gavin's addiction to his spyglass. He had recently obtained a low-priced telescope with a zoom lens from a firm advertising in his favourite *Exchange and Mart*, and this turned out to be an excellent bargain. Gavin mounted it on his desk at Kyleakin, and given uninterrupted vision no private act on the straggling ribbon-strip of the village might escape his notice. Nor could any character be suspicious without being noted, and lurkers and lingerers were subjected to severe and magnified scrutiny. His political involvement in Sicily and North Africa had made him enemies in both these countries, and he occasionally spoke rather vaguely of a possible attempt on his life; how seriously this was to be taken I never knew, but one wonders if his preoccupation with activity on the foreshore and his small arsenal of rifles and shotguns stemmed from at least a subconscious fear of being surprised. Be this as it may, the spyglass was usually used for more lighthearted purposes.

This would be a typical example. A visitor, perhaps a friend whom he had not seen for years, would arrive at the village and telephone for the boat to come across. Quite unknown to him Gavin would have plotted his progress as far as the telephone kiosk, which was obliquely opposite on the village green. This was only possible if the visitor had given prior warning by letter of his approach. Then his estimated time of arrival could be judged from the movement of an island-bound ferry. The powerful lens of the telescope brought every detail of the kiosk to the eye of the spy in the lighthouse cottage. The ensuing conversation might go like this:

"Hallo, is that you, Gavin?"

"Yes, Frank."

"You recognize my voice after all these years?"

"Yes, Frank, and I see that the years have been unkind to you. You are younger than I, but your hair is quite grey, and," chuckling, "you stoop disgustingly."

"What d'you mean—see, you can't see—you haven't set eyes on me for twenty years or more!"

"I can, Frank. No, don't bother to open the kiosk door—I'm not on the green, nor in the shop. Now you've dropped something—clumsy fellow—matches? cigarettes? No, I see it is the telephone directory. Now you're looking furtive; it's not closed-circuit television, if that's what you think. Now, Frank, just pick up your case from where you left it outside the shop and go to the boathouse—about 200 yards down the Portree road. Andrew is about to set off to collect you in the dinghy. I am looking forward to seeing even more of you soon——"

One feels that Arab assassins or Mafia agents would have had an uncomfortable crossing. The .350 big game rifle was powerful enough to sink a dinghy.

Dirk and Hazel had been sent away from Sandaig just before the fire to temporary homes. This had been part of the closure plan. Now Gavin had news that neither dog had settled happily, and their foster parents were quite content to return them. Neither animal had much personality or wit—indeed dear old Dirk was quite the most stupid dog I have ever met— and in the early autumn of their lives most of their time was spent in passing wind rather unpleasantly. Yet their great grey shapes, sprawled indolently in front of the big fireplaces, gave the place a baronial air.

Then Malla arrived—a three-month old female otter, born near Thurso. Deserted by her mother, she had been found on a river bank, and her finder knew about Gavin, and wrote to him suggesting that he might like the little creature. Gavin rejoiced in the idea; it was as though Fate had offered a replacement for poor, dead Edal, not to mention splendid material for a future book.

But it worked out happily only at first, for Malla proved to be an ailing serpent in a temporary Eden: a lasting bone of contention even after she was dead, post-mortemed and buried. She was weakly from the start and her fragility was time-consuming; love's labour became strained by the mounting exhaustion of sleepless nights, the pervading stink of her excrement, and the distress of watching a pathetic little object slowly abdicate from life. She was fed with as much care as any human baby, and the process required the full attention of them both. As she became older she became more difficult, and in late November her tiny grip on life relaxed completely and she died away. It was plainly unavoidable; no two people could have lavished more care on any animal than they had done. But nerves were strained, tempers worn and Gavin, for the first time with Andrew, became irrational, and blamed him for the otter's death. It was from this point that their relationship began to deteriorate: the only thing that spoilt the happier months before Christmas, it was a seed that was soon to grow into a tree of discord.

Raven Seek thy Brother was published on 2 December, my young Jane's birthday. Gavin was quick to take notice of this coincidence and sent to "his second favourite child" a copy of the book inscribed thus: "To Jane Frere, on the ninth anniversary of her publication and on the book's publication day, with love from Gavin"; which gave the little girl an enormous sense of importance at a time when it was most needed—her first term at boarding school.

Almost immediately after publication Gavin and I set out for London for a preview of the film *Ring of Bright Water*, and during the time we spent there he had several meetings with his publishers. They were pleased with *Raven* whose sales they hoped would be further boosted by the general release of the film, which was timed to take place in early April. Gavin's first viewing of that film was on a purely emotional level, for the extreme naïveté of the script appeared to leave him undisturbed; in fact he was nearly moved to tears by the scene in which Mij is killed, exclaiming that it was "far too near the bone" for him. My own feeling was that while a great deal of the dialogue was fatuous and the attempt to expand a slender theme laboured, the magnificent camera-work made the film a piece of visual art.

We were back in the north in time for Christmas. He was anxious to discuss with me his plans for the future of the island, and since he always complained that my one-day visits gave us no time to talk of anything but immediate business, I had arranged to spend a few days on Eilean Ban. His publishers wanted some idea of the scope of the next book. *Raven* had ended with the fire at Sandaig; its sequel—by reason of the period with which it would deal—must be very short of interesting material. Gavin was fully conscious of the need to stimulate events, and now demanded my approval for a start on the wild-life park which had been so much in his mind before the destruction of his former home.

Eilean Ban was not an ideal situation—that much was agreed—but in practical terms it was the only one available. Its obvious drawback was its insularity. On the other hand we were not far—as the crow flies—from a busy road, and the offer of "a visit to Gavin Maxwell's island" could be a great attraction to those thousands who knew his name and books, even if the only inhabitant of the park was the famous Teko. But Gavin was determined that they should have more than an otter to look at, and that Teko should soon become the only foreigner in an otherwise native gathering. Broadly speaking, the object of the park was to exhibit to the touring public, at point-blank range, a number of birds and animals of which they would otherwise be lucky to obtain a fleeting glance, or not see at all. The eider experiment, while remaining a serious scientific study which might, or might not, lead to some material reward, would be of further interest to the public, who could examine it through telescopes from the larger island.

The overall object was to provide material for the new book —as Gavin was at some pains to point out: "I am not a business man but a writer. Even if this idea loses money it can go against tax and we'll make it up with the book"—which seemed to me a singularly woolly way of looking at things until I realized that he was in fact saying: "I want to create this park, and damn the expense." We talked about it for two days and nights, and at the end of that time I had osmosed much of his enthusiasm.

I was finding that now I had no reservations in my friendship for him, and a strong increase in what I can only call telepathic empathy—a weird gift of being able to pick up a signal consisting of crude emotion from another person. My mother —who was oddly like Gavin in many ways and had a very possessive personality—used to transmit feelings of depression in my direction up to a proven range of 50 miles. She had an infuriating habit in the early days of my marriage of using the telegram as a means of emotional blackmail, and such messages as "Feeling desperately ill. Can you come at once?" were frequent intruders in our letter-box. I usually went, to the detriment of my marriage and status as a husband, for not only was I fond of her but she held quite a measure of financial control. Oddly enough, the telegram soon became redundant: she could throw out such a cloud of misery in my direction that I would find myself preparing to catch a train some time before the arrival of the formal summons. She gave me clear notice of her terminal illness, and I wondered in a rather sickly fashion what kind of mental jerk would accompany the moment of her death, but in the event I experienced nothing—a fact I ascribed to her prior unconsciousness. I mourned her as a dutiful son, remembering her many qualities, but glad to be rid of her unusual power of communication which had been almost exclusively used to transmit the misery of a frustrated possessiveness. I found, not in any way to my satisfaction, that Gavin had exactly the same power, and that the set of circumstances surrounding our relationship was, on analysis, not so very different from that which I have just described.

"From here," said Gavin on the morning of the last day of my stay, "you can see the whole layout of the park. Not large, but because it's on an island surely unique?" We were sitting by the water tank on the crest of the ridge on a dull brown and drab December day, with a wrinkled expanse of sea stretching out to the smudgy Crowlins and the cloud-capped pinnacles of northern Skye. All around us the lofty summits sang together

in the high east wind, prophesying snow. "Here we shall have
the aviary," he went on, pointing to the line of low rocks,
beneath which the spectral army was wont to whisper,
"between the ridge and the back wall of the house: divided
for buzzards, eagles and kestrels. Over there will be the
heronry, and on the north slope we'll make enclosures for
St Kilda sheep, deer and wild goats. Teko will have a situation
that fits his age and fame."

I smiled in agreement, my reservations as usual quite set
aside by his infectious enthusiasm; already I could see in my
mind's eye something of what he planned.

16

ANOTHER NEW YEAR

BEING AT LARGE throughout the festivities that drowned the old year in a flood of alcohol and gave the new one a hangover, I was able to observe—between the usual indiscretions for which this profligate period is infamous—the gentle arrival of the first day of 1969, calm, clear and cold upon a sepia world which was surprisingly unmoved by the drunken riot of its inhabitants. Inspired by the spirit I drew a parallel between propitious-seeming day and Gavin's future course, which seemed at that unself-critical moment a clever comparison. Later, all I had was a headache and the usual pangs of conscience, but for me the year had started well and I had the greatest possible hope for the rest of it.

For the most part January came up to expectations: in one event it exceeded them. Andrew had recently come across a man at Kyleakin who was looking for work, and Gavin suggested that we should employ him on a part-time basis to help Andrew with the construction work on the park. I had not met him but it seemed a good idea as long as we could afford it: in the event he proved to be a good investment. A man of protracted middle-age, tough as nails, cunning as a serpent, devious only in appearance, ingenious and possessed of an infinite capacity for improvisation, Kenneth McInnes could only be understood by those who bothered to study the severe defect in his speech. I never bothered. You did not tell this man *how* to do things, you just pointed out what had to be done; that was enough. McInnes had his methods which would not be found in any textbook; born of single-handed necessity, perfected through repetition, they seldom failed to achieve results. He was a comforting person to have about, and I used to look forward to his greeting which I had learned to

believe meant "Good morning, sir," and the smile, conspira-
torial yet obsequious, that would crease a face tanned to a
dirty beige by peat smoke, and leathered by the lash of salty
island rain.

At the end of January I spent a few days at Kyleakin. All
our conversation now concerned the wild-life project, and most
of my daily office work consisted in correspondence with
various bodies whose approval we were anxious to win. So
far we had achieved a small measure of support and an
enormous amount of goodwill—a not unusual proportion
where money is about to be mentioned—for our venture.
Gavin's name, in natural-history circles, never failed to evoke
an interested, though not always amiable, response, for as a
man with positive and sometimes provocative views he was not
without his critics. The people who were of greatest importance
to us, if we were to maintain a permanent establishment upon
the island, were the Commissioners of the Northern Lighthouse
Board who owned the bulk of it. Only a strip of land encircling
the house and the garden of less than half an acre belonged to
Gavin, and while it was unlikely that the Board, who had
always been friendly, would ever deny us the use of the extra
area it would have been patently unbusinesslike not to seek
some greater security of tenure. We decided that we should
offer to buy the entire island except the corner on which was
built the lighthouse and its installations. Gavin cherished a
private dream about owning even a modest chunk of land.
Coming from a family of great landowners he had never, as
far as I am aware, owned a complete acre, and he coveted
every inch of Eilean Ban's heather-shaggy surface.

Andrew and McInnes had already begun work on the
enclosures, for we had taken a calculated risk on the Board's
willingness to meet our offer. If they would not sell or even
lease us what we wanted, we were pretty sure that an informal
arrangement could be made, and Gavin was impatient to get
things under way so that the park might just be ready by the
next summer. The quiet frosty January days echoed to the
thud of melds on fence posts as Andrew and his versatile
helper began to loop a stock fence over a small heathery ridge
above the south bay.

Below this purposeful and progressive action an ebb tide of
emotion was drawing away the once idyllic relationship between

Gavin and Andrew. For some time Gavin's song of praise for his young assistant had been growing somewhat disharmonious; increasingly I had been charged to listen to a formidable catalogue of complaints about the former paragon. I was assured that he had altered from the happy, willing boy he had been at Sandaig and later at Raef's cottage, and was fast becoming casual, careless and untidy; that he was a persistent arguer; and that he was disenchanted with the lonely life on the island, escaping to Kyle or Kyleakin for long periods whenever he could. I strongly doubted the validity of these complaints, finding only some justification in one of them; that, like many boys addicted to outdoor activities, Andrew was domestically incompetent. But casual I never found him, and he was much less careless than most boys, at an age when new ideas and fresh enthusiasms tend to override more mundane tasks. As far as argument was concerned, Gavin had never "pulled rank" before, and I could only assume that his attitude to having his instructions debated had suddenly hardened. To be sure, it was true that Andrew had not learned that the best way to avoid confrontation when a discussion becomes an argument is to shut up, but Gavin himself would not always welcome so tame a termination, and would often grind a trivial bone into very small fragments.

He—whose public image suggested the inveterate hermit—only liked to be alone when it suited him, and this I think was not often. In fact prolonged solitude tended to depress him, an exactly opposite effect to that which it has on me. My introversion leads to a tendency to shun people, even those closest to me, when I am in certain moods, so that I can charge the batteries of my personality on an internal circuit. On the other hand my friend was not at peace inside, so he needed conversation, though not crowds, to divert him. When guests came—as they did increasingly—he preferred them to come singly and to keep their stays short. A lingering family could drive him to distraction: "Guests are like fish," he often quoted, "stinking after a few days"; and he was glad to see the back of them. He was intolerant of interference in his private habits. Being drunk in new company made him feel vulnerable, as do some animals when they copulate; he preferred to go alone (though *positively* he was no alcoholic) or with a trusted friend, down the road that leads to inspired confusion.

Andrew did not drink. Things might have stayed better if he had. To a degree he would adjust himself to his master's changing state as the bottle shrank, but even the least self-righteous of us find it hard to repress a sneer in such circumstances, or bother to veil a growing impatience with the drinker. Also, Andrew knew from experience that unless Gavin started his bottle amiably he would in all probability end it in anger and this, although he was not so far the butt of Gavin's acid wit, began to embarrass the boy. He needed no excuse to be away from the island during the day, for the growing programme of organization fell increasingly upon his shoulders. Gavin chose to misinterpret the delays inseparable from this and from shopping from a boat, and goaded himself painfully with the suspicion that his protégé was meeting people and making new friends of whom he had no knowledge. Whatever his relationship with the boy had been, it was now on the wane, but Gavin retained a fierce jealousy. He once remarked despotically that he reserved the right to vet Andrew's friends, at the same time making it pretty clear that no camp followers would be allowed on the island. Certain influences in Kyleakin were represented as being sinister, and Gavin constantly warned Andrew of entering into their sphere; what they were, or what dire results might accrue from contact with them, was never more than postulated. I assumed he referred to homosexual entanglement, but when I remarked that Andrew always spoke to me of a complete preference for girls, he shook his head in disapproval and warned that this would lead to even greater danger. I could not imagine what a lusty, emerging boy of eighteen was supposed to do.

Often, returning late from some ordered mission, Andrew would find his master with a neglected look, wreathed in the smoke of innumerable cigarettes and gloomily working his way through his whisky. He would exude almost visibly an aura of outrage. I was all too familiar with this affectation, for my mother had been gifted in the art of invoking sympathy. I have already remarked the extraordinary similarity between certain aspects of these two people; it was so strong as to lead me to the conclusion that here was—as far as I was concerned —a proven case of reincarnation, a whimsical belief only fatally marred by their co-existence over many years.

Sometimes, and increasingly often, Andrew would take

advantage of my presence there to escape to the kitchen or to his room if it appeared likely that Gavin's random wrath was about to erupt upon him, and this would provoke the acid comment that the boy was becoming unsociable beyond the point of rudeness. In fact, as they say today, he could not win. Everything he did was wrong. It was a sad change from the happy, spartan days in Raef's cottage, where I had almost envied these two people their ease and pleasure in each other's company.

At any time it is sad to watch the decay of a strong friendship, but when you hold the parties to it in high regard it also becomes an emotional strain. If, in addition, it is a matter of policy to keep the peace so that a plan can go forward, both one's loyalties and one's sense of priority become confused. I became convinced as the weeks wore on, and silent anger turned to hysterical violence, that no remedy existed except that of Andrew's departure. By its nature the breach could not be healed, and it was inhumane to contrive an extension of this nagging, uneasy companionship to a point at which communication between them at any level became impossible, simply because Andrew had become practically indispensable. His knowledge of the Kyleakin set-up, his sympathetic understanding of Teko, his prowess in handling boats and, even paradoxically, his knowledge of Gavin, would all make him virtually impossible to replace. Also his employment contained a very unusual benefit, and this had to be taken into account before I could, with a clear conscience, advise him to leave.

Gavin in his childless middle age, at a time when his sudden opulence had given such an idea the necessary substance, had decided to leave his money to some youth who had found favour in his eyes and who had served him well. For some years Jimmy Watt had been his accepted heir, but when Jimmy had decided to leave his employment the offer had been withdrawn. Gavin was the archetypal Lear in this, that he believed no man (far less a woman) would do anything exclusively for love—as insulting a piece of cynicism as one can imagine—and apart from a natural desire to perpetuate his name and to secure the future of someone of whom he was fond he was convinced that such an inducement would ensure present loyalty and single-minded attention. In order to hold him and instruct his course, I imagine he waved the terms of his will like a carrot in front of the young man's face, but Jimmy was no donkey and the affection he felt for his "adopted father" rose from more noble origins than hope of gain. Gravely he determined to go his way; in dismissing a bribed subservience he gained the present prize of a confirmed respect, and the continuation of a very deep and dignified friendship.

In December of 1967, just before the fire at Sandaig, a similar offer was made to Andrew who had inherited the crown of Gavin's approval. He accepted it with gratitude, and the prospect with a grain or two of salt. He had come into the picture just after a stroke of good fortune had warded off Gavin's insolvency, and he could not have been unaware of my inept handling of the insurance matter. Being a rational lad and aware of a somewhat improvident attitude in his elders, he could not be expected to discount further crises or trends that might well make his inheritance worthless. At that time—and indeed thereafter—he was happy to carry out his duties without any other inducement than the privilege of leading the kind of life for which he had always yearned.

That had been the state of things a year earlier, but now there was no longer any peace between them, and it was my plain duty—both as adviser to one and friend to both—to ask Gavin for the authority to send Andrew away. Gavin, who had been on the brink of drawing up a new will in favour of the boy, had tacitly dropped the idea and no more mention was ever made of it. It seemed then that the moment had come for a clean cut, and at the end of January I set out for Kyleakin to persuade Gavin to let me make it.

I was too late. Acting with uncharacteristic lack of planning my employer had decided to go on a visiting spree, and that within the next few days. He intended to be away for over a month. By doing so he was offering their situation a last chance of survival; the interruption in their stifling proximity to each other might reverse the downhill trend. Perhaps it would, but I doubted whether it would bring more than temporary relief, yet I was relieved that circumstances had intercepted my intention of making an irrevocable move.

On the first day of February I drove through the Great Glen to Spean Bridge, where I was to meet Gavin as he drove south. In his rather fussy fashion he wanted to restate to me all we had agreed to do in his absence. I arrived at his hotel at opening time, he greeted me warmly and we settled down to a comfortable drinking session.

I soon found out that despite his continual complaints about Andrew his main reason for wanting to meet me was to extract a promise that I would look after the boy in his absence, and spend as much time at Kyleakin as I could. I remarked sourly that I had no doubts that Andrew would survive the experience, especially with McInnes in everyday attendance, and if anything went wrong at night he could always use the telephone; adding that I had lived through many a period of solitude there without any of the amenities now enjoyed by Andrew. He detected the slight note of acerbity in my voice and said smilingly, but with an undertone of apology: "Don't think I haven't worried about you—but I've convinced myself that you are immortal. It is one of your qualities!" Much mollified I accepted another whisky, and before long we began to discuss poetry. He was in holiday mood, and to introduce a practical note into the conversation—such as how we might set him up with a suitable companion at Kyleakin—would have been inappropriate. We sat and talked for hours—long after the bar was closed, and he was most entertaining; even I, deeply inhibited and slow of thought, made a better showing than usual. While his conversation shone, mine glowed, and I was vastly pleased with myself when he asked me: "Do you know a poem that begins 'They are not long, the weeping and the laughter'?"; and I was able to say that I did, and quoted it. "Not in the front rank," said my friend, referring not to my powers of quotation, "but oddly moving. It has been going through my head all day." He paused, then added: "I have enjoyed this meeting. Please do not think that I only wanted to instruct you in your duties as a nursemaid."

I began to make half-hearted attempts to leave, but the distance to the parked Land Rover seemed to be an onerous journey, although I knew that once I was in the driving seat the trusty vehicle would take me safely home, no matter what gross errors of judgement I might make in the process.

Finally Gavin said: "Be my guest here for the night. I've learned not to doubt your capability at such times as these, but you must be tired." I thanked him but refused. It was late to advise Joan of a change of plan, and in the morning I was pretty sure I would feel less like driving.

"Let me hear Dowson's poem before you go, then."
I did my best, although my best was about two hours spent.

> They are not long, the weeping and the laughter
> Love and desire and hate:
> I think they have no part in us
> After we pass the gate
>
> They are not long, the days of wine and roses
> Out of a misty dream our path emerges
> And closes
> Within a dream.

At this we said good-bye, he to go to his room, I to the waiting Land Rover. Five minutes later it had taken entire control of the situation and was bowling along the road, homeward bound with the panache it always reserved for journeys after late-night bacchanalian occasions. I, more glorious than Tam, sang loudly between further flights of poetic fancy, and thanked my stars for the friendship of a famous and intelligent man, and the glorious chance that had provided me with such a sinecure.

17

OF GOATS AND GALLOWAY

HE WAS AWAY for all of February, and did not return to the north until the first week in March. The length of his absence surprised me; he usually cut short his travels rather than prolonged them. During this time there was a steady flow of 'phone calls both to Andrew and to me, and since we had nothing alarming to tell him he had no reason to hurry back.

Early in the month came the great snowfall of that winter. The new wide road down Glenshiel became a slippery lane over which the Land Rover advanced at a crawl. Conditions on the coast had all the elements of anti-climax, and it was hard to convince McInnes and Andrew of what was happening so close at hand when all around Kyle the ground was black and soft. Those two were getting along well together and had done wonders with the fencing. They were now planning to surprise Gavin on his return by obtaining a wild goat from Glenshiel and getting it inside the stock fence—a plan which required my help. They made me promise to take them to Glenshiel in a week's time, where on the west end of the ridge known as the Five Sisters we should certainly be able to catch a goat.

A slow thaw was creeping up the glen and the lower slopes were soggy with melting snow, but above our heads the high ridge glittered icily in the early spring sunshine. We climbed towards a broad, sloping shelf and at a height of about 500 feet began to cross the hillside to the east. From what we had heard the goats had recently been seen below this level. Our policy was to keep some distance apart; as soon as the goats were in sight we would approach stealthily from above, then rush fleet-foot to the capture, selecting individual prizes as we went. McInnes, the cunning old shepherd, advancing behind his nose like a dog, got wind of them and pointed down a wide gully. A hundred yards beneath us were five adults and two kids. No stalkers' hearts beat any louder than did ours at the sight of these shaggy goblins. Two of the grown-ups were venerable gentry with aristocratic horns and Spanish beards. I saw Andrew's eyes flicker with anticipation; already he could see them safely behind posts.

All three of us lay flat and advanced squelchingly through the wet peat. The wind came up the slope so they could not get our scent, and they grazed busily away, oblivious to everything except the demands of their stomachs. When we had reduced the distance by half, McInnes uttered a somewhat emasculated war-cry and we slithered to our feet and charged. I selected one of the big chaps who closely resembled a childhood pet named General Buller. His back was to me as I sped down the hill, but as the sound of my approach reached him he spun round and dodging me narrowly, rushed up the slope behind me. I gave chase but it was futile. No man can chase a goat uphill and General Buller outpaced me easily. Andrew had also been outmanœuvred and was impotently pounding after his retreating prize. McInnes had vanished. It took a moment to realize that his shepherd's cunning had been equal to the goats' and that he was lying in wait for them as they ran up the hill.

Suddenly General Buller swerved violently to the left as the gnarled figure of our companion rose in front of him: we watched in admiration as his strategy caused the General to retreat to a cul-de-sac, a wide ledge which girdled a steep crag to the west of us and which faded out on a smooth, vertical rock-face. From where we stood we could see neither confrontation nor surrender, and we climbed towards the terrace to help bring down the defeated General. As we neared it we were alarmed to see a body fall from the end of the ledge, accompanied by heather tufts and a shower of small stones. "Oh, God!" said Andrew, in disbelief. "Surely he hasn't driven him over? That goat won't be any good now even if it's alive. Why couldn't he be more careful?"

Leaving McInnes—now in disgrace—to follow us down we hastened to the bottom of the cliff where a deep indentation in the heather suggested the goat's landing place. I reached it first. The body that began to raise itself painfully was not that of any ruminant I have ever seen, nor have I ever heard one swear in the Gaelic tongue. Andrew came up to me, still furious. "Is it dead?" he asked; he could not bear to look at it. I patted him on the shoulder. "Not to worry, Andrew, it isn't dead, nor I hope mortally injured, and it's not a goat!"

A week or so later they took the *Amara*—a twenty-foot launch we had recently bought with half an eye on the wild-life park—to Sandaig to pick up some odds and ends still at Raef's cottage, and to tow home the *Black Dinghy*. Hurrah! That ill-fortuned boat had entered upon the last day of its life.

On their way back to Eilean Ban a tremendous wind blew up from the east, and the towed dinghy was literally dragged apart. Her bow post was torn out and she was split asunder; disintegrating near Kyle, what was left was washed up opposite the lighthouse cottage, held loosely together by capillary attraction. Her bits lying there had the pointed venom of an enemy who has hanged himself on your favourite tree to spoil its shade for you. Our insurers, who knew all about her, could not get it into their heads that she was a total loss—the manner of her passing was a trifle unusual—so I suggested a survey, but by the time they finally came we had chopped her up into little bundles of kindling, and that was all there was to be seen.

The time of Gavin's return was drawing near. I looked forward to seeing him and hoped that his absence had cured the possessive jealousy that had been a potent factor in his rows with Andrew. I had fully intended having a word with the boy in the convenient privacy of Gavin's absence, though exactly how I should broach the subject I did not know. His youth and exuberance seemed to have made him forget even the roughest moments of their association, and I do not believe in waking sleeping dogs. Thus my usual indolence swamped my useful intention.

In early March, Gavin and I met in Kyleakin village. I didn't think he looked very well. There was an odd hesitation in his movements and he set his feet down as though his shoes hurt him. As he climbed the path to the cottage he breathed heavily, quite out of proportion to the effort involved. But his spirits were good. He was bristling with ideas. On his travels he had received much encouragement for the wild-life park, and now he urged me to press the Lighthouse Board more urgently for a formal title, so that we could carry out our activities openly. But in the meantime the chief priority was the eider scheme, and the further preparation of that islet for the season's laying, along the lines he had so carefully studied in Iceland three years earlier. There was plainly plenty to do before the mother ducks got down to the business of nesting in May.

The next morning I started shopping in Inverness. I went to Woolworth's and asked for 200 children's windmills, remarking to a cretinous young assistant with a leer that they were to attract the birds. Another shop wonderingly sold me clusters of tiny bells. The Forestry Commission helpfully directed me to a plantation close to Kyle where they were cutting long thin poles. Peter Janson-Smith sent us yards of gaily-coloured bunting from London. I had already brought quantities of "brash"—the branches of young conifers—and several hundred canes. All these items had important parts to play in promoting the eider colony on the neighbouring islet, which already had a few indigenous eider and should soon have many more. The work which must now begin was not entirely from scratch: "Noddy" Drysdale and another boy had dug deep catchments for rain water, and these remained intact as a valuable contribution, for fresh water is the one thing that the fasting, nesting mother duck cannot do without.

But one mistake had been made and its outcome proved serious. The previous autumn Andrew and McInnes had set fire to the island with the intention of clearing the narrow gullies of dense thorn and brambles that led to the sea: thus allowing access to flat beaches for the ducklings. The fire almost at once got out of hand and burned fiercely for two days, to leave a blackened desert. We hoped that spring would bring a strong growth of young heather; by March a depressing sterility was still in evidence, so it was decided to provide artificial covers in the form of wigwams of "brash" above the last year's nests. Gavin concluded later—when it was obvious that the first year's breeding programme was a failure—that despite local cover there was a too general bareness which made the eiders feel over-conspicuous and insecure.

Despite this error the island soon became a visual reproduction of an Icelandic colony. The skyline bristled with poles, the air was filled with the tinkle of bells and the whirr of tiny windmills, and little green tents appeared all over the charred ground. When the coloured bunting arrived from London, it was strung between the poles where it flapped gently in the wind, looking for all the world like the washing of a marooned gypsy tribe. Two great notices with letters in bright paint told visitors of the nature of the experiment, and asked them to keep clear of the island.

Gavin and I spent a spring day there together, searching for old nests, marking them and putting in windmills at appropriate points. It was an amusing day and a fine one; Gavin was in high spirits and a dry wind blew from the east. As we worked he imparted to me all manner of relevant facts, and as always I was amazed at his aptitude and memory. Now he told me of the importance of the coloured, flapping bunting both as a deterrent for predators and an attraction for the eider; how the ducks were known to be fascinated by the sound of bells and whirring windmills; how such inducements as the maggots falling from the suspended carcases of crows or gulls discouraged the vulnerable ducklings from ranging too far afield; and many other rather odd facts such as are turned up by people who like to look deeply into the workings of Nature. Gavin liked nothing better, and consequently knew all about it as he did with any subject to which he gave his earnest attention.

On the human side there had been peace at Kyleakin, and I began to allow myself the cautious hope that all might now be well; but the fires of their contention were not out, still darkly smouldering, and about three weeks after Gavin's return something or other blew them into flame. The row which followed a chance remark was substantial and comprehensive; by the end there was little left unsaid. Andrew had rather bleakly admitted to an omission by answering an unqualified "No" when asked if he had fed the deerhounds; questioned why, he said he had forgotten, and that was enough space for Gavin to push in the thin edge of a wedge of mounting aggravation. Speaking in a spiteful, bitter voice he upbraided the boy for his untidy room, his casual attention to his job, his frequent absences, his evil friends on Skye, and from the cemetery of memories disinterred the old bones of that ancient theme—the death of Malla. He then began to introduce ideas which were plainly and utterly absurd, embroidering un-charitable conjecture with the lace of lunacy. For the first time since I had come to know him it struck me that here were the seeds of madness, for this was not the red-faced bawling of hysteria but a white-hot, rigid anger which stemmed from no external circumstance but from a violent conflict within. At frequent intervals he would turn to me to demand my agreement upon his interpretation of Andrew's behaviour, but I sat silently staring ahead, only wishing that the solid floor which I had built would open and let me through. It went on for hours. Andrew began by taking it all with a sullen stoicism which gradually changed into a desperate hysteria. He looked at me wildly. "Andrew," I shouted, giving way to the general mood, "please go to your room and clean it up." It was at once the only honest concession I could make to Gavin's complaints and the one way I could think of to stop the mounting crescendo of the moment.

Andrew obediently left the room, relieved that a spell had been broken. Alone with his tormentor I said: "You drive him too far. He is few of the things you say he is."

"Richard, sometimes you are a fool. Can you not understand? That boy will destroy me."

I was suddenly angry. I do not mind being called a fool—in fact I do not mind being called anything—and our relationship was substantial enough to sustain a few heated insults without any hurt, but he had no right to think I would believe his nonsense. Often in his wilder moments there had been talk of plots and of menace from persons unknown, but now he was speaking of Andrew, whose contribution to his comfort and the viability of his house had been enormous, and whose loyalty in the widest sense was beyond dispute. Gavin had slumped over his desk in an attitude of theatrical despair; by half closing my eyes so that only his outline was visible I saw a blurred picture of my mother.

"Why do you say that?" I asked, after a period of silence so long as almost to take the question out of context. He stared at me stonily, then asked: "Isn't it obvious?" to which I replied smartly: "No, it isn't obvious to me at all. How can he destroy you, and why would he try to?"

His answer—which might have been more concealing than revealing—was never given. There was a knock on the door and Andrew, looking emotionally spent, came into the room. He walked over to me without a glance at my companion and came straight to the point: "Mr Frere, I would like to give you my notice. I will stay as long as is necessary to find someone to replace me, at Major Maxwell's convenience and your own."

"Very well, Andrew," I said with equal formality.

The boy retreated from our presence without further remark. I turned to Gavin. Genuine regret at losing Andrew was coupled with a feeling of hopelessness at the prospect of looking for a replacement of anything like his calibre. I said somewhat spitefully: "Well, there you are. That's what you wanted, isn't it?"; knowing all the time that it wasn't, and feeling dimly within my mind the chaos and struggle in his. It did not surprise me to see that he was crying openly.

In the morning there was the usual aftermath of stress, a cold courtesy. Andrew's resignation was confirmed, but helpfully he was prepared to stay for a fortnight after his successor's arrival to show him the ropes. Neither Gavin nor I made any attempt to alter his decision. I went home at about midday. Just before I left Gavin asked me if I was ever troubled with headaches.

"Very infrequently, except as hangovers. But you don't have them even then, do you?"

"I never used to, but I've had a hell of a headache for about three weeks. Since I came back from my travels, more or less. Bit of a nuisance, because it makes concentration difficult. You've some medical knowledge. Any ideas?" he finished lightly, but wanting an answer.

Unfortunately I hadn't, but I don't suppose if I had it would have made much difference.

While riots and ructions were bedevilling Eilean Ban the film version of the Camusfearna idyll was about to burst out like June all over cinema audiences, and show how Gavin Maxwell might have behaved if he had been a fatuous insurance clerk turned introvert named Graham Merril. The former, distressed in mind and now certainly unwell, was not at all anxious, he confided to me, to attend the première of *Ring of Bright Water* in London on 2 April, but did not see how he could gracefully avoid this very social affair. I had a strong feeiing he would find a way out of his problem and he did, and although he was not shameless enough to reveal the means he employed to attain this negative end I knew him well enough to read the signs. With Machiavellian craftiness he skilfully provoked a situation in which he was shown as having been slighted, and thus ostensibly aggrieved; the only course of honour left to him was a firm refusal to attend the occasion.

Anxious to be quite out of reach upon the day, he arranged that we should motor over to the town of Keith where a certain person bred capercaillie and blackcock, both of which we wanted for the wild-life park. He stayed with Joan and me the night before, quiet, relaxed and apparently contented, much relieved to be out of range of his telephone, which he knew would be used by friends and acquaintances alike to find out why, on the evening before his day of days, he was not in his London flat.

I have a newspaper cutting which says: "The première of *Ring of Bright Water* was a glittering occasion, marred only by the absence of Gavin Maxwell himself who, we understand, found it impossible to escape business commitments in Scotland".

We set out for Keith in the green Mercedes. He drove as far as Inverness, where he had some business, and then made a remark which greatly increased the anxiety I was already feeling about his health. He complained that his headache had become so severe that he would not be responsible for driving and asked me to take the wheel. When he said it his brow was tightly clenched and there was a grey pallor about his skin which I did not like to see. By now I was extremely worried about him, for his continual headache, bursts of irrational behaviour, and occasional trembling of the limbs made me wonder unhappily if he was suffering from an incipient brain tumour or something of the kind. I knew that he intended to have a medical examination—a course of action I strongly urged—and I only hoped that the delay of over three weeks since the onset of his headaches would not prejudice his chances of recovery, or even of survival.

I now started the search for Andrew Scot's successor. Several young men answered my advertisements, a few journeyed north to see me; I gave them my ear, said my piece and sent them home with an increasing conviction that it was not going to be simple to replace Andrew Scot. Some of them had most of the qualities I needed; not one of them had the understanding to live with Gavin. He in the meantime had gone into hospital and was there for a week, during which time the most searching probes and tests failed to provide a clue to his continual head-ache and general malaise. For the first time since I had known him he was not a refractory patient, which suggested that he was worried by his symptoms, and each day I noticed an improvement in his spirits as test after test restored him to a full expectation of life. Oddly enough his headache suddenly became less severe, giving rise to a notion—shared by the patient—that it was psychosomatic in nature, and arose from the stresses to which he had been subjected. Privately I thought that this was putting the cart before the horse, but I said nothing.

On his way home from hospital he stayed with us, and delighted Joan the next morning by telling her that the warmth of her welcome and pleasant hospitality had finally banished his headache, and that she had thus done what the doctors had failed to do. In truth he seemed greatly restored, in spirits as well as in health; he was even looking forward to getting back to Eilean Ban and spoke of Andrew without rancour or complaint. On my last visit there the latter had made no enquiry about his replacement, and had clearly identified himself once again with the future of the project. With the facile optimism that has always misled me I concluded that all would probably be well, and withdrew my advertisement.

Alas! despite the fair promise of concord, violent explosions still took place between them. Gavin began to ring me up at all hours of the night and morning demanding that I should speak to Andrew; time and again I told him that I was not even *au fait* with the *casus belli* and accordingly had nothing useful to say. After nights of interrupted sleep I began to leave the receiver off its hook—for Joan's sake as much as my own —knowing that no words of mine would still the raging, or bring sanity back to that tortured companionship. Yet the pattern was not exclusively acrimonious, for alternating with their worst days and nights were periods of comparative calm. One day in May I wrote in my diary: "Good news from GM who is jubilant over a happy, settled arrangement with AS." But only a few days later my entry read: "What a depressing time. GM and Andrew at desperate loggerheads. There is nothing to be done with them!"

Towards the end of May I drove to Wigtownshire where Gavin and I were to stay with some of his friends. The journey —planned some weeks earlier—had, according to Gavin, three distinct objects which would justify the cost of taking two vehicles several hundred miles. He had agreed to address a cinema audience at the first night showing of *Ring* at Newton Stewart, which he regarded as his home village. Secondly he had recently conceived an idea—as far-reaching as it was far-fetched—to purchase the decaying mansion of Monreith from his eldest brother, Sir Aylmer Maxwell, who was resident abroad, and re-establish himself in his native county. He had urged me to give him my opinion on the wisdom and possibility of this unexpected scheme, and while by no effort of imagination could I see it ever reaching fruition the idea in principle had my full support. My own father left the colonial service in the '20s, on inheriting a small Norfolk estate from his uncle and retained it on a falling income until the disastrous farming situation of the early '30s impoverished his tenants and brought the shadow of hard times to the Hall. He sold up in 1932, and came north to spend the closing years of his life in the mountainous country for which he had always yearned; as a boy he had spent a few years in Inverness where my grandfather had an army command. At the time of separation from the soil of East Anglia, in which my family had wielded some authority for half a millenium, I was but eleven years old and had formed no traditional attachment, but in indigent adulthood I sadly missed the status and relative riches which my immediate predecessors had enjoyed in their own county and amongst their own people. Had it not been for my idolatrous love of mountains, and life-long addiction to climbing them, I might have made a bid at reinstatement in Norfolk to our former style, although unimaginative investment and rape by death duties had so reduced our fortunes as to make the chance of success a slim one.

Gavin's family was of greater substance than mine although their estates had gone the same way, and he was the youngest of three sons, albeit the most outstanding through the genius of his writing. The pattern of our early struggles had been the same, but his had a sophisticated and heroic quality which mine were lacking. Now he wanted me to see him against the background of his homeland, so that together we could lament the passing of the former glories and make a plan or two aimed at their recovery.

Thirdly, on a realistic and immediate note, we had to have the Land Rover because his friends in Wigtownshire had promised a pair of foxes; and Gavin from his boyhood knew just where to obtain young crows and ravens, and maybe a few jackdaws for the park on distant Eilean Ban.

The few days we spent together in the fine May weather in lovely Galloway were the happiest I ever spent in his company. Everything about that time was pleasing. We went to the House of Elrig where he was born and lived as a boy. Of a local man he enquired if a certain road across the moors could still be used by cars; the chap said "No" and added: "Do you know that road, sir?" Gavin smiled in the grey shadow of his birthplace and remarked: "Once I used to live around here." Back in the car we both chuckled; only a few years earlier I had anonymously paid a visit to my own village and had prompted yokel minds with good, strong Norfolk beer to raise the thirty-year-old ghost of a spoilt, shy, lonely little boy.

We found the wildfowler with whom as a youth he had spent many a dark morning amid the seawrack in Wigtown Bay, and he spoke to his people in the Newton Stewart cinema before the film of his famous book. Now he had finished his duties and we went on a nostalgic joyride. Our hostess had sent us out with a large, well-filled picnic basket containing smoked salmon sandwiches, Scotch eggs and several bottles of ale. "Today, at least, we shall eat like gentlemen," remarked my friend, who normally showed a deplorable propensity for a travelling diet of cold meatpies and Maltesers.

We wandered through beautiful wooded country in search of fledgelings. Every now and then Gavin would remember a tree where the birds we were after used to nest. It was a remarkable feat of memory over many years and the incidence of success was high. At one point I was well up a small oak reaching for a raven, Gavin was some feet below me with our prepared basket; we were close to the road. Suddenly a car stopped and the driver, apparently fascinated by the sight of two middle-aged bird's-nesters, took a photograph. "Sod that," remarked Gavin cheerfully; "what do you think he wants?" "Oh, famous son of Galloway," I intoned, quoting words with which he had been introduced at the cinema, "that is a reporter. Tomorrow the local papers will print that picture, saying underneath: 'Gavin Maxwell is here seen up a tree above his native heath, where in the company of his managing director he is pulling down birds!'" At which Gavin laughed so loudly that he all but fell to the ground.

We ate our sumptuous lunch on high ground above Wigtown Bay. It had become so hot that a thin haze hung over the sea through which the misty outline of the Isle of Man was just visible. The flowery hedgerows were filled with innumerable insect voices and a tiny, casual breeze just managed to sway the long meadow grass. The thin strip of our road looped out of sight over a long hill, its surface dancing in the heat. Gavin, who had been in a laughing, merry mood fell rather silent, and I knew that the blue, gold, scented day had carried to his mind a living picture of all the sun-bleached days of boyhood.

In the evening a quiet epilogue. Gavin wished to visit his old doctor who was frail and in failing health and to do so alone owing to the other's infirmity, and he asked me to wait for him at Monreith to which I had been introduced earlier in the day. I sat in the library of the tall Georgian house. It saddened me to see the damp stains on the walls, the foul necrosis that becomes an empty house: tears shed in protest against neglect, pain and sorrow at the passing of a gracious way of life. I loved it but I knew as surely as the sun would rise next morning, that there was no hope or substance in Gavin's last dream.

We set out next day for the north. In the Land Rover there were two foxes, five ravens and four jackdaws. By the time I reached Kyleakin later that same night I knew them all by name—and habits. It had been in every imaginable way an unforgettable trip.

We came back to fresh problems and sporadic discord. Early in June I brought to Eilean Ban a load of scaffolding poles for the aviary and a letter from the Lighthouse Board which contained an offer to sell the island to us for an impossibly large sum of money. This monstrously depressed Gavin who spoke of giving up altogether, something he had never done before: later I convinced him that all was not lost, and that if we could not buy I knew that the Board would give us a reasonable lease. I wrote to them; due to their former helpful attitude I deemed it safe to continue with the work while waiting for their further decision. The network of scaffolding rose behind the cottage until the phantom army was enfolded in a web of iron. McInnes' performance on the tops of the long, steel poles would have been the envy of any Indian fakir.

And as our accommodation grew so did our stock increase. Now we had herons—great, gawping youngsters whose eating habits in youth presupposed chronic indigestion in old age—which Gavin and his other brother Eustace had filched from their nests on Gillian Island; goats and a damaged fox from Kinlochewe; St Kilda sheep; ravens, jackdaws and foxes from Galloway; Owl, and a contented Teko. And yet another fox arrived, and with it came its donor, a blonde girl from somewhere south whose complex impact upon the occupants of Eilean Ban innocently set the final seal of dissolution upon that small assembly. Of infinite attraction, she seemed to embody the strong sunshine of those June days, and her mind was quiet and wondering and thoughtful. She was one of those women who have something for everybody; for Andrew, and for Gavin too, but as things were with them then, her entrance with her silly fox was untimely, whipping up a new flurry of emotions and leaving an aftermath of desolation. My story is too near its end for me to dwell on what was said and done, but three weeks later Andrew left us to follow the Woman out into the world beyond Eilean Ban. The last few days between him and Gavin were peaceful and they parted as friends.

Jimmy Watt came to the island to train the two boys I had hurriedly engaged. One was a small schoolboy with a cheerful disposition who would work in the house during his holidays; the other, an older boy, was intended to take Andrew's place. With these we had to be content. In addition Gavin had persuaded a young naturalist named John Lister-Kaye to join the wild-life project as curator: he had met him at Sandaig four years before and had taken a great liking to him which had resulted in further meetings and a regular correspondence. Essentially a countryman, John had been masochistically destroying himself in industry, and he counted that world well lost in exchange for the doubtful survival we offered him. His intended participation in the life of Eilean Ban pleased—and relieved me—greatly. Since the iron curtain of distrust and

jealousy had divided him from Andrew, Gavin had possessed
no resident confidant. Neither of the young boys could be
expected to entertain him intellectually; fond as I was of him,
his power to afflict me with his gloomy moods through telepathic empathy as a prelude to a detailed follow-through on
the more conventional telephone put me on a 24-hour alert,
and I was growing emotionally tired. Gavin, I knew, would
find much in common to talk about with John and would be
able to abandon the reserve which separated him—try as he
might, and deny it as he would—from those of different background from himself. Therefore I looked forward to John's
arrival, if only because it would allow me to draw some
emotional breath.

Gavin's health was still giving trouble—which was another
reason for my relief that a sensible and capable adult would
soon join him. His headache had gradually returned, a plateau
of discomfort interrupted by peaks of more severe pain, but he
seldom mentioned it: when more than usually oppressive I
could detect it by the tight line drawn across his brows and
what appeared as a mood of deep preoccupation. One July
morning, whatever enemy was inside him made a fresh attack.
He was speaking to me on the telephone at some length when
he suddenly halted in the midst of a sentence and cried "Oh,
my God!" with a sharp intake of breath. Knowing that he
would be looking out at his favourite view of the channel and
Kyleakin I at once thought that a dinghy had capsized and I
said urgently: "What is it, Gavin?" He could not answer,
being speechless with pain, but Jimmy (beside him and not
drowning in mid-stream as I had feared) spoke for him and
told me what had happened. Gavin had suddenly turned
deathly white, and half-turning in his chair had clutched his
left thigh with both hands. They gathered that without warning
he had experienced a pain of terrifying sharpness deep in the
leg—"as though a six-inch nail had been hammered into the
bone," he said later—which only gradually subsided, and even
the next morning he could still not walk properly.

The end was now beginning, and it was one unpleasant thing
after another. The headache had become a hated though
accepted lodger, the thigh bone ached, he began to cough at
nights, deeply and dryly, and one would have thought that a

whole family of mischievous beavers were at work damming his venous system just for the fun of letting their dams burst, so many and so frequent were the thromboses he experienced. Off he went to hospital, this time in Skye, for yet another range of tests and further photography, and once again the report came back, its conclusion no longer of comfort to those who saw his suffering, that there *was* nothing to report. "Oh well," said the unrecognized victim, "I suppose I'll have to consider myself a fit man, but I do feel bloody ill."

With great fortitude he carried on. He supervised the work on the park, wrote one or two book reviews, he entertained at the cottage—friends and those whom we hoped might help us with the project—and he fulfilled two more public engagements. He went to the Stuart Johnstones' house in Essex to implement a promise to open their own wild-life park at Mole Hall, and at the end of July dragged himself to Clydebank to introduce the *Ring of Bright Water* film at a new cinema there.

The first trip reduced him sadly, I looked forward with horror to the effects of the second and they came right up to expectations. I was there to meet him in Kyleakin when he came back on an evening in early August. He brought the big car to a halt and sat at the wheel breathing heavily. I helped him out. He could hardly stand, and although I had not expected better things his appearance was entirely shocking to me. Within a few days a rapid deterioration had taken place; he was grey of face and his eyes were clouded by pain, the effort of leaving the car had made him cough and tremble and despite the cold east wind his brow was sopping with sweat. "Come on," he said hoarsely, "for God's sake, let's have a drink. I'm just about done in." We went into the King's Arms Hotel. "Would you care to bring them over here?" he said, when he was seated in an inconspicuous corner of the bar. I did so. "I don't want them to see me like this," he added, referring to a few local men at the counter.

He then told me that he knew he had cancer. He insisted that I breathe no word of his suspicions to anyone before they were confirmed. I answered faintly with as much assurance as his pathetic appearance would allow that we could not assume this with so much medical evidence to the contrary; also I added, with the irritation that passes for callousness but is in reality no such thing, that it was not the first time he had suspected malignancy. He said: "This is *very* different," and as I saw that my selfish attempts at reassurance were merely niggling him I gave in and listened to what he had to say. As our conversation continued the sight of his ravaged condition brought me to full acceptance of his belief, and at length I could say nothing of comfort or cheer, merely nodding gravely as the blackest empathy swept over me. He asked me to assume that he was a dying man, so that we might make decisions here and now about the disposal of his property and the future of the island and the project. His intentions revealed what had always been in his heart and when he asked for my blessing upon them I gave it freely, and although I am human enough to have felt a slight sense of disappointment, even a little jealousy, those weaknesses were, I can only hope, so firmly repressed as to be inapparent to him.

Upon the subject of the conversation, as well as his condition, he demanded my present silence, telling me that we could work out all the details in public later. This sudden return to his brave, resurgent habit of planning when all he could now logically look forward to was the crematorium or the coffin was too much for me, and I fled to the urinal where I wiped my eyes on inferior lavatory paper. On coming back to him I said: "Look, perhaps all this won't be necessary. After all we are not *sure*." He knew that I was pleading with him to agree with me, but he was no man for dissembling, even to oblige a friend.

"Don't be stupid, Richard," said he with a look of affection, "that remark does your undoubted intelligence less than justice. We are *both* perfectly sure."

18

THE TUNNEL

THE SUPPOSED NATURE of Gavin's illness was kept a close
secret between us until the truth was confirmed just over a
fortnight later. He put off his admission to the Inverness
hospital for a few days because he had invited a young woman
—a secretary who had typed his later books and who dealt
with much of his "fan" mail—to visit him on Eilean Ban for a
short stay, and he had no intention of asking her to cancel her
visit. She did much to advance the domestic education of the
two new boys (Jimmy Watt had gone and John Lister-Kaye
had not yet arrived) and her sensible company comforted
Gavin on what he thought would be his last few days on the
island. Shortly after she left I drove him slowly and carefully
into Inverness.

Although some time had gone by since we made our pact of
silence I thought he seemed no worse—perhaps even a little
improved—than he had been on that day, and I allowed
myself the small hope that he might still be mistaken in his
self-diagnosis. The matter-of-fact and non-committal atmosphere of the hospital further fostered my optimism, and when a
variety of much more searching tests than hitherto seemed to
result in no clear-cut medical decision, the glimmer of hope
became a glow. I called upon him every day and we discussed
everything but the implications of his *sub judice* case. He gave
no hint as to whether his own conviction had altered, but I
believe that the delay in confirmation was beginning to suggest
that things could not be as bad as he had thought. When,
therefore, on the seventh day a clear diagnosis spelt out the
unpleasant word "carcinoma" it still had something of the
impact of novelty.

A very hoarse voice spoke on the telephone: "You'd better

come along as soon as you can. The last blood test has confirmed my belief," and without more ado I jumped into the
Mercedes and rushed into Inverness. By a strange coincidence
the first person I met at the entrance of the hospital was Jimmy
Watt. Unexpectedly arriving to enquire after Gavin, he had
run straight into the full blast of the news. He was white and
shaken and quite broken up by what he had been told.

Gavin, found breathing heavily in a corridor after 'phoning
me, had been firmly returned to his room. Considering his
very bad luck he looked little different and remarkably
unconcerned. Indeed there was an "I told you so" expression
on his face which told me that this, after all, had come as no
surprise. He got down to formalities at once—"You heard the
news? No condolences, *please*. They tell me they don't expect
me to recover. I've just asked Jimmy if he'll carry out my
plans for the island—with your help—and he's agreed to do so.
He'll also be my heir." At this I nodded with small emphasis
to suggest that the idea was new to me. There were, or seemed
to be, a lot of people about, and I found it difficult to concentrate. I wanted to go somewhere else quickly where I could
come to terms with the situation—it now being painfully
obvious that I had not done so before, or so a quite new feeling
of shock and sadness told me—and since it was plain that
Gavin wanted to talk privately to Jimmy (who had an urgent
obligation to continue his journey south) I suggested that I
should do some shopping for the invalid and, if he wished it,
return later. This met with his approval.

When I came back he was sitting up in bed, looking drawn
and pale, but his expression was impassive; it was impossible
to know what he was thinking but one might hazard a guess.
He greeted me warmly, asked me to help us both to a drink
and then said without preamble:

"Richard, you are looking uneasy. Please don't let my
situation embarrass you. I am selfish enough to wish that you
will spend as much of your time as you can with me, and in
return I promise not to afflict you with unnecessary sentiment.
We don't cry easily or make a fuss over the inevitable. Displayed
emotion has always been considered bad taste in my family as
I expect it has in yours. The fact of my fairly imminent death
—between six months and a year at most—will have to be taken
into account as a factor in our planning and as something

about which certain arrangements must be made. Consider it in that light, and no more."

He regarded me in silence and when I could not immediately reply continued with a small gesture of distaste: "Yes, they say in about six months I'll be living on borrowed time! There's hole in my femur—hence that bloody awful pain I had—but the primary is in the lung. They can't do anything about that; and the general condition has gone too far, it seems——"

"But why didn't these things show up in the X-rays you had in Broadford?" I interrupted.

"Don't know," he replied. "I suppose I must be specially opaque, or something. At any rate it's no use crying over spilt milk, as I'm always telling you. Actually the femur pain did give me an inkling as have one or two other little things I've noticed. This is the way several of my friends have gone; it's popular nowadays and I keep my eyes open. It all probably started when I had that first scare on coming home from Tangier, but God only knows why the headache and the thromboses. That's probably another death sentence—to run concurrently with the first."

Again he fell silent, staring ahead, and now there was a tiny look of fear in his eyes. Comprehension would be coming in waves and all the banter in the world would not help until it subsided. I hated to think what his thoughts would be on waking.

He blinked his eyes rapidly. "God," he said, "this won't do. Pass me a cigarette—at least I can now smoke as many as I like with no risk at all—and let's have another brandy, there's a good chap, and don't worry. It could easily happen to you, so reserve your sympathy until after I've gone."

I soon latched on to his mood and to his ironic attitude, which in the circumstances I may perhaps be forgiven for having at first believed to be bravado. As the days went by I came to know better. For the rest of my life I shall remember the two qualities which were the highlights of a peerless performance: the bravery with which he approached the most private and solitary moment of un-being; and the courtesy he showed in making light of it, in so convincing a way that one did not feel that one had to follow to the very edge of the abyss down which he must so soon fall.

I spent the next two days in advising those of his friends whom
he could trust to be silent at the turn events had taken. While
Gavin languished in bed I made for the hospital telephone and
spread ill-tidings to selected homes. With his doctor's help
Gavin was planning his brief future and he had decided that
he would like to return to Kyleakin for about a week to tidy up
his affairs. This tied in with medical requirements. The only
part of his body which could safely respond to radiation without
the fear of general destruction was the thigh bone, and it was
getting its share. Other measures might start when he returned
from his leave of absence on his island. During this conversation
Gavin asked the doctor to give him some idea of how the
disease would progress, and the latter, having been acidly
instructed not to dissemble, offered a bleak and honest picture
of the cancer's rapid spread to other parts of the body, increasing
weakness and death from sheer exhaustion and/or internal
bleeding. My friend looked even more impassive than usual
and remarked "Charming!"

Lying in bed was one thing, and painful and uncomfortable
enough, but Gavin found the round trip to Eilean Ban an
agonizing odyssey. Almost as soon as he entered the car the
upright position produced pains in his neck and chest, and it
occurred to me that a brief break at Drumnadrochit might
have some therapeutic value. He had told me, however, that
he wished to avoid as many of his old friends as possible having
sight of him until he was back in hospital, when he could
settle down to dying with as good a grace as possible and be
tidied up for their visits. My suggestion was turned down as I
suspected it would be with: "What! Let your wife see me like
this? Never. When I'm back in hospital they can make me
look a little less like a cadaver, and then I'd dearly love to see
Joan. But not now. One has one's pride."

We drove along Loch Ness, through Glenmoriston—where
early autumn was tipping the branches of the trees with rust
—and on across the bare hill country of Cluanie into the
green, boulder-scattered cleft of Glenshiel. As we reached that
long hill I noticed that my passenger was fidgeting most
uncomfortably, and asked him how he felt. "Bloody awful,"
he said briefly, and after a pause added: "I think I might
benefit from a spell of light activity. Perhaps I could drive

for a few miles? The idea doesn't make you nervous?"

"No more than usual," I remarked, remembering more than once when I had sat beside him, low in the passenger seat with closed eyes and clenched hands, hoping for the best. Neither of us had the temperament to dawdle in a car, but he had been a very fast and skilful driver.

Grunting and groaning he moved into the driving seat, and off we went. Illness had not impaired his ability. A few touring cars, rambling down Glenshiel, cringed into the side as the big green Mercedes swept past them on squealing tyres. At the bottom of the glen he told me he had had enough driving for one day and we reversed our positions. The effort had taken more out of him than he liked to admit; he was paler and more shaky and his breath was short and rasping. We stayed with very old friends of his at Glenelg overnight, then continued to the island. Here I set him down, and as soon as good manners would permit left gratefully for home. Jimmy Watt was there with the two new boys; he was in good hands. I was now feeling a strong physical identification with his condition as well as considerable mental confusion, and although mere distance would not alter this state it seemed necessary to be out of his immediate company for at least a short time if I were to stay the course.

Less than a week later I brought him back to hospital. His failing condition was all too apparent and the former indomitable truculence was broken now and again by peevish outbursts, firmly and apologetically repressed. He was content to ride in the back of the car, supported by cushions, and through his reflection in the driving mirror I could see how much pain he was experiencing. I gave no credence to the idea that he would last for anything like as much as six months; and I realized that he knew beyond any doubt that this was his last sight of the wild country which he had loved and understood so well.

Back in the hospital bed, under professional care, he was in less discomfort and was allowed less pain. Friends who had been summoned or who had become anxious came to see him. Peter Janson-Smith—that honest and humane person who had always been Cordelia to his Lear—left his London office and took the train to Inverness. John Lister-Kaye rushed north in his battered car, driving through the night in his usual boisterous fashion. He was about to begin his sojourn on Eilean Ban; when he left three months later he had gathered material for his book, *The White Island*. Raef Payne, Gavin's old and beloved friend, flew up. Jimmy Watt, his long intended and now established heir, was there, and his brother Eustace Maxwell (who Gavin told me had a reputation for being late) had arrived just in time. They all came and went in the days of his dying and gave that process a traditional dignity.

"Richard, do we still owe money to John McAbre? And what about that lawyer's bill? I think we must pay them as soon as possible."

Gavin had become very punctilious about settling with remaining creditors. Formerly he had often assumed an aristocratic indifference to the inconvenience of tradesmen, but he always intended payment in his own time; he would not be pushed. Now it was logical to settle up debts as quickly as possible since time is always the last thing one runs out of, and he knew he had only a very little left.

"What about the work Frasers did for us? Do we still owe for it?"

"Yes, and we owe a cock to Aesculapius, but it, like the others, shall be paid and not neglected."

A short pause and a rather tired smile: "Richard, you put me in worthy company."

"No more than you deserve, Gavin," I said, breaking the rule that said emotion was bad form and looking hard out of the window to conceal it.

He was worried about Jimmy's future and the wild-life park. I knew that as soon as his name and knowledge were withdrawn the scheme would come to nothing. One last attempt to obtain a massive injection of money failed; this blow could not be kept from Gavin, but I managed to make light of it and implied that I still had something up my sleeve. Since we no longer put gold trinkets in people's coffins to provide them with credit in the world to come, it is permissible to lie to them about their bank accounts. This I did. Gavin died under the impression that he was better off than he was; that gave him comfort as far as Jimmy's future was concerned.

Peter Janson-Smith spoke with Gavin and devised a plan that he should—if granted the time—begin to write a final book which was to be entitled, *The Tunnel*. If he died before it was completed I was to carry on and finish it as I thought fit. That book was never started, but this is the chapter I should have written if it had been. Later that evening, after Peter had caught his train back to London, I asked Gavin why he wanted to call his book *The Tunnel*, and he explained that in recent days and nights a recurring fancy kept coming to him that he was walking against his will down a long, dark tunnel. In its sides were openings through which he was permitted to take a few steps towards shadowy people whom he thought he recognized, in a world not unlike his own. But the further he travelled the more vague and unreal the scene outside became, only the tunnel being solid and oddly comforting until he passed the openings without even a wistful glance at shapes that had no further meaning for him. Soon he kept his eyes straight ahead towards the far distance where the tunnel ended in a patch of velvet gloom.

Because none of us who knew him would let him go without a struggle, we sought another opinion from an eminent specialist who was called upon by John Lister-Kaye: the second prognosis was as bleak as the first. My friend was now a wreck, the rabid cancer was tearing at him and what life he had left was utterly burdensome. Now he knew that no one would attempt a pneumosectomy he wished to die as quickly as possible, and based his hopes of a quick and painless release on a cerebral or coronary thrombosis, a reasonable supposition as his whole circulatory system seemed to be in ruins. In an attempt to release the fluids from the pleura and thus relieve his breathing it was proposed to drain the area through the chest wall. I spent much of the day before the operation with him, for with that morning's post had come news which would once have been significant to us both—an offer from the Northern Lighthouse Board to lease us the ground we wanted for a peppercorn rent. Gavin was delighted for Jimmy's sake; he believed that it would simplify the management of his inheritance.

"Richard, what do you think of this?" he said in a voice which was becoming hoarser day by day. As I was about to leave he beckoned me to his bedside, and with the look of an impish child who is about to do something he knows will shock or dismay he drew down his pyjama trousers so that I could see his groin. Despite myself I winced. In the shrunken groove between pelvis and abdomen was a thick, raised ridge, visibly pulsating with violent heartbeats. Beyond the fact that it was a grossly distended blood vessel I could not put a name to the condition, nor say what it might mean, but I had seen a similar thing in my own father's groin 24 hours before his death from a cerebral blood clot; so I thought, from Gavin's point of view, it looked promising. He looked at me enquiringly: "This might finish me, mightn't it?" he asked.

"I am not a doctor and know no more than you do, but I've seen this before in someone else and—well, it finished him," I said, giving him the answer he wanted even though I had no earthly professional sanction for doing so. He gave an audible sigh of relief.

I only saw him once again. When I arrived at the hospital the next day he was recovering from the effects of the draining operation, which as I gathered from the nurse had not been easy and had given him much pain. When I was allowed to his room I found him sitting upright in bed, obliged to hold that position for the operation of a simple plumbing device that consisted of a tube inserted into his chest wall which emptied in a bucket half filled with a blood-stained fluid. In his face was the authentic look of death. He detected my revulsion and muttered in a gurgling voice: "Isn't this awful? I could have done without this." I found that I had nothing to say, so I sat and stared at the wall above his bed while he, almost unable to rotate his head, looked straight forward. Our glances bisected but it was too late for any significant human contact. He was near the end of the tunnel.

After ten minutes of silence he whispered: "This is wasting your time, Richard. Come back tomorrow; they say I shall feel better then." He gave me a distorted smile, adding: "That's what they say: see you tomorrow then." But I don't think he believed it for a moment, any more than I did, and when I shook his cold limp hand I was pretty sure it was for the last time. And it was. He died early the next morning of a massive coronary thrombosis.

When I heard within the hour by telephone, I thought: I should have stayed with him, and gone so far; it might have been a comfort; but later I realized that he had all the strength he needed and I would have only drawn on that reserve.

He was a much braver man than I, all said and done.

To establish the cause of death in the interests of medical science they asked me—who in the confusion had been named his next-of-kin—and his brother Eustace if they could open him up and study what they found inside. We said "Yes", for we both knew that Gavin's enquiring mind would have jumped at the idea. The findings were unpleasant: the cancer was everywhere and explained everything, even his headache—for the top of his skull was deeply pitted—and there was little left of his cervical vertebrae. The primary tumour was still small but very active and the cancer was on the rampage; had he waited for it to kill him untold misery and pain would have been his lot.

Having made a further and final contribution to medical knowledge we sent his body to Aberdeen to be cremated, as he had instructed, and all that was left of him—at least in this sphere of activity—came back in a little casket.

He intended that his ashes should be buried at Sandaig in a grave below the place where his study had been. During the last weeks of his life there was a strange coincidence. He had made the burial arrangement knowing that the estate intended to raze the ruins to the ground and conceal the débris in a pit dug deeply in the dunes. Terry Nutkins (unaware of the gravity of Gavin's illness) was camping nearby with the young woman who became his wife, and they watched the bulldozers pulling and pushing from dawn to dusk as though in a desperate effort to clear a place for him. By the time that the last of the blackened stones had vanished below the sand the man who had given the house a kind of immortality was dead.

The interment was on a Tuesday. The evening before, I had brought his ashes from Inverness and suggested to Joan that they rested in some suitable place within the house. To this she objected. It offended her sense of fitness that we had no sanctified place to put him down, but I remembered the irreverent fun he poked at religious institutions and consigned him to the boot of the green Mercedes which he had loved and gifted to us in his will. While I had been ready to defer to Joan in the matter of its night's lodgings I was not going to yield on the question of who was to take the casket to Sandaig, for I had a strong suspicion that Gavin's managing angel still had a trick or two untried, and if the safeguarding of his ashes were not personally attended to the ceremony would in all likelihood go on without the guest of honour. As I drove into the green, boulder-scattered cleft of Glenshiel on our way to Sandaig a wry thought came to me—confirming human mortality, if that were necessary—that three weeks earlier almost to the day the handful of ash in the boot had taken the wheel from me and driven this car ferociously down this very hill.

At Sandaig the morning was dawning cool and bright with all the fresh poignancy of early September. She had put on her finery for him who had so delicately window-dressed her beauty for the less discerning. The heather among the birch in the wooded circle was a blatant purple and the gold blazed on many a tree which had outrun its neighbour into autumn. An east wind sang above the hillside and danced away with the waves on a sparkling sea towards the low green hills of Skye. Where the house had been, the ground was disturbed, bare and sandy but it would soon mend and blend, and the place was wholesome once again now that the broken remnants were gone.

Some who came to see his ashes go to earth had been with him in his dying; others who had not known were here now. Among them were those who had been foils to his unquiet genius as he had been a foil to their humanity. I saw the woman of the rowan tree standing on a ridge of the dunes against the sky, and I wondered if her impassioned words had been of no more moment or account than the cry of seabirds on the wind.

Jimmy Watt with tearful eyes walked hesitantly to the open grave and a minister of Christ said pleasant words of comfort. The assembly murmured and whispered in the soft afternoon beneath a sky of eggshell blue, while the waterfall which he had called the soul of Camusfearna roared its throaty praise of the departed and welcomed his spirit to its dark caverns as he had hoped it would. I was quite overcome by all the beauty and grief of it and moved closer to my wife and little daughter, sure anchors against a perverse desire to shout for joy in this place of graves.

The day ended as the Guest of Honour would have wished, in a spirituous gathering in Raef's cottage which went on until the setting sun laid a golden girdle across the Sound. Then people slowly began to walk away, companionably in twos and threes, or to drive up the rocky track. The sky had turned apricot at the edges and royal blue overhead, and the twilight fell like dew upon Camusfearna and its ghosts. I gave but one backward glance at the darkening field ringed by the flat white sea and thought still of my dear and worthy friend as my feet stumbled on the rough track which led back to the uncaring world. And I mused that Gavin Maxwell, like another magic spinner in the web of words, had become:

> A portion of the loveliness
> Which once he made more lovely

and it would take a better man than I a long time to find a more fitting epitaph.